Comments About

Let's Get Results, Not Excuses!

By James M. Bleech and David G. Mutchler

"This is the most exciting concept in management I have ever seen. The authors have done a remarkable job of taking a very difficult concept and simplifying it in such a way that it can be swiftly implemented. I know if I get rid of excuses in my company, my results will greatly improve."

> Barry Grahek
> CEO
> Shred All, Inc.

"What a remarkable approach! If everyone paid attention to this message, millions would be added to our corporate bottom lines."

> George Bennett
> President
> BBS, Inc.

"Customers will always decide when they have had one excuse too many. The authors have pointed out how leadership can provide the guidance necessary to minimize those excuses, get the business, and provide superior customer service."

> Patrick C. Kelly
> Chairman, CEO
> PSS

Let's Get Results, Not Excuses! brilliantly combines principles of business and psychology into a simple action plan to get things done right—on time, the first time. It is must reading for anyone who manages human behavior, including their own, in the business world or anywhere else!"

Kenneth Sass
District Manager
Waddell & Reed Financial Services

"So often I have looked at corrective actions directed towards my people. Neither I nor our executive team ever saw the relationship between our organizational structure and our processes as they related to improving the acceptance of responsibility by our people. This is truly one of the most exciting concepts I have ever read."

Mike Johnson
OmniAmerica

"We have put up with mediocrity in this country for too long. We must get back on track. Excuses in the workplace create lack of focus and much shirking of responsibility. People need to be held accountable. This book is a strong, positive answer to many long-standing organizational problems."

Marilyn Plank
Vice-President
SYLVAN LEARNING CENTERS of West Michigan

"This book is long overdue! It has opened my eyes. And I believe it is destined to be the force that awakens a sleeping corporate America."

David Pugh
Bell South Communications

"An incredibly exciting book! It gets to the heart of the issue in the workplace today. People continually give excuses which interfere with performance. By eliminating excuses in the workplace, there is only one place to go with quality and productivity: UP! The excuse-free concept promises to be the beginning of a revolutionary cultural change in corporate America."

Doug Hunter
St. Lawrence Steel

Let's Get Results, Not Excuses!

Let's Get Results, Not Excuses!

How to Become Number One Again

by

James M. Bleech and David G. Mutchler

MBP PRESS
Grand Rapids, MI

LET'S GET RESULTS, NOT EXCUSES!

James M. Bleech, 12-15-48
David G. Mutchler, 6-9-42

FIRST EDITION

Library of Congress Catalog Card Number: 94-77372

ISBN 0-9642474-0-2

1. Corporate culture. 2. Leadership training. 3. Management training. I. Title.

Printed in the United States of America
10 9 8 7 6 5 4 3 2 1

Dedication

To all the leaders in corporate America—past, present, and future—committed to the cause of becoming and remaining number one in the marketplace.

Contents

Contents

Acknowledgements

It would be impossible to single out all the people who contributed so generously to this project with their comments, suggestions, and ideas. We owe a deep debt of gratitude to all.

Many readers will know of an international organization called The Executive Committee, which is dedicated to the accelerated development of CEO's. Jim, as chairman of one of the 400 TEC groups, has met many unique resource speakers who have contributed greatly to our thinking. While something has been gained from each, two individuals in particular have added to the breadth of our knowledge. Peter Schutz, former CEO of Porsche AG, not only gave us insight, but also the courage to tackle the project. Peter introduced the concept of *organization, process, and people,* which has become a central part of our book. Del Poling, independent consultant extraordinaire, first introduced us to the importance of recognizing excuses, as well as how dangerous they can become to a company. We owe the concept of *four-year-old behavior* to him.

Without doubt, our biggest source of material has been the clients we've served over the years who have talked openly about their problems and concerns. It was the many late-hour discussions and painful board meetings with them that furnished our first glimmer of awareness that we were conceiving a very different approach to effective management. In effect, our clients have been our laboratory for the gradual testing and development of excuse-free behavior for use in corporate America.

We are grateful for the wisdom of Stephen Covey and W. Edwards Deming. Their thinking helped form the cornerstone for many of our ideas. Also, as season ticket holders we appreciate the example set by Don Shula of the Miami Dolphins for creating an extraordinary organization with extraordinary processes—a model that we have built much of the book around.

A special thanks to our editor, Gwyn Bersie, whose tireless effort helped keep us focused and on course. Her insight, guidance, and editorial talents are dearly appreciated.

Finally, to our wives, many thanks. They have generously worn several hats throughout this project: proofreaders, sounding boards, single parents when necessary, and sources of love, strength, and support. Without them, this book would never have happened.

Preface

Writing this book became an unexpected adventure. When we first began the project, we anticipated the possibility that we might be exploring a *few* uncharted territories together. At most we thought that what we had to offer would serve as an addendum to an existing body of knowledge. It was difficult to imagine that a concept that seemed so obvious to us—**that excuse-making is a sizeable problem in the American workplace with respect to getting desired results**—wouldn't be given considerable attention elsewhere.

Preface

To our surprise, however, we found ourselves blazing new trails in a previously untravelled wilderness! For when we went to the literature to research the subject of how excuses influence the achievement of results, we found that very, very little had ever been written on the topic at all. Yes, there were a few titles here and there that had the word "excuses" in them. Many of these were humorous in nature, suggesting excuses to use for this or that occasion. Only two related specifically to business, and they were more prescriptions for how to manage employees than studies of the ramifications of excuse-making in organizations. Surprisingly, the more we looked, the less we found. The obvious question we began asking ourselves was, how could this be?

One possibility, of course, was that our premise was mistaken. Maybe excuses *don't* really interfere with getting results. Yet we knew this was not true. Our experience working with companies on this very issue has proven time and again that excuses are in the middle of problems of immense proportions in corporate America. Staff conflicts, absenteeism, and poor teamwork, to name only three, are often about employees denying personal responsibility, projecting blame, and making excuses.

Next we speculated that excuses are viewed more as a symptom of other problems, and that the attention was directed more to the underlying cause of excuses than to excuse-making itself. This seemed plausible, yet we were unable to find any significant evidence to support this idea. Similarly, we wondered whether excuses were addressed under a different name, such as irresponsibility or blame. Once again, we found little such evidence.

Then it dawned on us. Bingo! It is not that excuses aren't a problem. Far from it. But it can be extremely difficult to recognize the problematic nature of excuses, including the correlation that exists between excuses and unacceptable results. Unless one is looking from the proper perspective, it may be almost impossible to see the problem. It's a bit like looking at a sheet of paper. If the only view one had were from the end, the surface area of the paper would look very small.

Figure 1

But if we could change our perspective by looking at the paper from the top,

Figure 2

the total area would look considerably larger than it did from the first perspective.

Preface

So it is with getting results. Excuses are only little problems so long as our perspective is from the edge. As soon as we take a view from the top, we find that the problem is far more pervasive and serious than we had previously thought it to be.

After years of steady decline in the world marketplace, we have made a rather remarkable turnaround. But few people would deny that American business still has its share of problems. Over the past 25 years or so we have looked to countless "solutions" that blossomed and bore fruit. Examples include Quality Circles, Management By Objectives, Cost Justification Analysis, and more recently, Total Quality Management, Corporate Re-engineering, and Self-Directed Work Teams. But in spite of their effectiveness, they have not kept us in front of the pack in the world race, and therefore—one by one—they have faded. Something is still missing.

That is exactly what this book is about—the *something that is still missing*. It is an investigation into what happens when we change our perspective on how to look at problems in the workplace. We will explore in some depth what a powerful tool this new perspective is for solving many of the long-standing, nagging problems that have perplexed the corporate world for years. We will demonstrate how the elimination of excuse-making from the workplace will actually yield the outcomes you want, and how it can save (and therefore, *make*) our companies literally billions of dollars every year. And we will show you how to get started on the pathway that leads to the goal of getting results, not excuses.

As you view it from this new perspective, you will quickly see that excuse-making is such an astronomical problem that it cannot possibly be handled in its entirety in a single work. This book is therefore only an introduction. Other books on the subject that are already on the drawing board will follow.

Three other points are noteworthy. First, examples cited throughout the text are based on real corporate situations. In all cases, names and locations have been changed to protect client confidentiality. Second, in the majority of cases we will be using the masculine pronoun for the sake of simplicity and easy readability. Under no circumstances do we mean to imply sexism. Last, we apologize for the small number of references we make to other resources on the subject of excuses. Again, we simply couldn't find them. Nevertheless, we will show that the conspicuous absence of information on excuses in the workplace testifies to the critical importance of beginning to recognize this very real problem. *Sometimes the simplest and most profound things in life are the most difficult to see.*

James M. Bleech   *Jacksonville, Florida*
David G. Mutchler   *August, 1994*

Notes and Quotes

Ninety-nine percent of the failures come from people who have the habit of making excuses.

George Washington Carver

Part
I

The Nature of the Problem

The Relationship Between Results and Excuses

1

The Winning Formula

"I don't want excuses—I just want results!" We can still hear our football coaches barking these words at us whenever we failed to execute some assignment in practice. The point was always instantly clear. *Don't tell us why you didn't or couldn't or wouldn't do it; just get the job done!* And as a coaching strategy, we have to admit, it was very effective.

Could the Same Principle Apply to Our Companies?

Wouldn't it be great if those in positions of leadership and management in the corporations of our country today could make this same demand of their people? But why can't they? What prevents our "corporate coaches" from doing exactly the same thing?

There is probably not a simple answer to this question, since corporations in many ways are quite different from football teams. The sheer number of people involved, for example, differs significantly. And the ratio of managers to employees is often a much different number from that of coaches to players. Victory isn't as easily measured, nor is the season so precisely defined. There are multiple layers of management in a corporation, where there are only a few layers of management on a football team. There are no "game days" in corporations as such, and no cheering crowds to inspire performance. And so on.

One Element in Common

But there *is* one thing that is comparable between the athletic playing field and the corporate playing field, and that's the truth of the excuse/results formula as it relates to winning. *Winning is getting results; and if you want results, you must get rid of excuses!*

****

We submit to you that there is a valuable lesson to be learned here, one that can be taken right from the play-books of winning coaches. *They get results because they will not allow excuses.* Excuses are simply unacceptable in the winning athletic environment. **No excuses allowed!**

This same rule for victory must become true in the corporate environment if we are going to achieve and maintain high levels of success in the global marketplace. The reason it hasn't yet been accomplished is because the application of this winning principle takes more subtle twists and turns when transplanted into the corporate world, and it is more easily lost in the organizational maze. But that doesn't make it an impossible task—only a more difficult one. Which brings to mind the common saying: "The difficult we do immediately; the impossible takes a little longer."

The challenge is clear. If you want to achieve the same winning edge in corporate America today that successful athletic coaches have enjoyed for years, you must get rid of excuses if you want to get results. Those companies that make rising to this challenge their first priority will be the clear winners. They are the ones that will surge ahead and enjoy the thrill of victory in each of their respective industries.

The Point

Positive results are the natural outcome of the *absence* of excuses. To get results, excuses must go. They cannot be allowed, encouraged, tolerated, or modeled in the corporate environment in any way. They must be wiped off the face of the corporate map. When, and only when, this is accomplished, the results will be there—the very results that you have long hoped for, that you have long planned on, and that you certainly have long deserved.

Just as the absence of disease is health, so the absence of excuses is results. This book is a prescription for how to get over the virus of corporate excuse-making so that results can happen. The treatment described here can save an ailing company, setting it on the road to full recovery and enduring health. As in athletics, it is a formula for winning—for becoming number one—and it works!

2

What's the Big Deal about Excuses?

Many CEO's, business owners, company presidents, and managers at all levels have told us over the years how much they wish they could get their people to stop making excuses. They've all known—just as you've known—that excuse-making is in itself a problem. Excuses are annoying, and they often interfere with getting the outcomes that we want. This is not news.

Yet it is difficult to think of excuses as *big* problems, partly because they are familiar. They are *so* familiar, in fact, that the word "excuse" is often used in place of the terms "reason" and "explanation"—both respectable concepts, by the way. "Oh, you have to leave for a doctor's appointment in a little while," says one employee to his associate. "That'll give you a good excuse to be gone from work for the afternoon."

Now does he mean "good excuse," or does he mean "good explanation" or "good reason"? There is a difference between excuses and explanations or reasons, and we will address those differences in the next chapter. The point here is that since the terms *excuse, explanation,* and *reason* can often be used interchangeably, the concept of excuse-making is apparently somewhat respectable, and is therefore **not** typically seen as a big problem.

We Are Going to Challenge This Point of View

The basic premise of this book is that *in the corporate environment, excuse-making is more than just an annoyance. It is a huge problem. In fact, it may be the biggest single problem that exists in corporate America.*

We've known that excuses happen in the workplace. And we've known that they can be a problem. What we haven't known is what an enormous problem excuses are, nor have we been aware of how damaging excuses are to the bottom line in the corporate setting.

Excuses Do Not Exist in a Vacuum

For every excuse that is made and allowed, there are always multiple negative forces at work behind that single excuse. These negative forces are the lifeblood of excuses. Without them, no excuse could exist for long by itself.

8

What are these negative forces? One way to approach this question is to look at why people make excuses:

- **Excuses are given to keep from accepting responsibility.** "I didn't have any input in making the decision, so this shouldn't be my job."

- **Excuses are made to project blame for one's own mistakes.** "We're late with the report because accounting was late getting it to us."

- **Excuses are used to procrastinate.** "I've been very busy this past month; I'll get to it as soon as possible."

- **Excuses are used to deceive ourselves so as not to face the criticism of failure.** "I lost the account because the competition undercut our prices" (rather than "I lost the account because I haven't been servicing it well").

- **Excuses are made to cover incompetence.** "I was never trained adequately to do this job."

- **Excuses are used to keep from stretching, taking risks, and being creative.** "We've never done it that way before," or "That's not the way we do things around here."

• **Excuses are made to voice entitlement.** "It's not my fault that the order was messed up. I still deserve my bonus."

• **Excuses express pessimism.** "We're never going to catch up to all the competition. Everybody's just too far ahead of us in so many ways."

Excuses Indicate Other Problems

The point is that excuses are not just pesky little problems in themselves. *While excuses may appear that way on the surface, they never exist apart from more severe problems at work in an organization. That makes excuses* **gigantic** *problems because they always point to one or more of a multitude of other crippling corporate problems*: not only denial of responsibility, projection of blame, and so on, but also reactive thinking, can't-do-attitudes, victimization, helplessness, poor teamwork, avoidance of issues, and fear of failure.

Every one of these, and more, are indicated to one degree or another whenever and wherever there are excuses in your company. They tend to stop the planning process, drive good employees away, and create bureaucracies. They foster behaviors that can bring companies to their knees: staff conflict, absenteeism, failure to meet important deadlines, loss of pride in workmanship, incompleted work assignments, avoidance of tasks, and so on. *Excuses are 100 percent poisonous to the success of an organization—they do nothing but interfere with achieving results.*

How Excuses Happen

Excuse-making is a natural, self-protective mechanism designed to keep people from feeling the pain of criticism, blame, or failure. To accomplish this, excuses necessarily distort the truth in order to hide it from self and others. Since corporations provide uncountable opportunities for the expression of excuses, the truth can be disguised in large ways. As a result, problems—the resolution of which are critical to the success of the company—can be easily overlooked or ignored.

In addition, companies often operate in ways that arbitrarily put people in a position where they are faced with the possible pain of criticism, blame, or failure. So organizations commonly create the context in which people are almost forced to make excuses. (This will be explored in detail in Part II.) The result: excuse-making in the workplace becomes very commonplace and very familiar—even to the point that it seems harmless.

A Fable to Make the Point

Once upon a time there was a little mouse who lived in a house with a family that had no pets. One day a stray cat moved in with the family. The mouse, never having seen a cat before, ran away in fright.

The next day the mouse spotted the cat again. But instead of running away as before, he stayed at a safe distance and watched the cat at play. The next day, feeling even safer, the mouse walked within a few feet of the cat as it drank milk from its saucer, though the cat never had

11

occasion to look in his direction. So the following day, the mouse scurried directly up to introduce himself to the cat, hoping to become friends. The mouse was quickly eaten. The moral: Beware of dangerous things that appear harmless!

****

Excuses appear harmless. Quite harmless. That's one of the reasons why they're so dangerous. But they aren't harmless. Like the cat to the mouse, appearance and reality can be two different things. Excuses are destructive to your company in ways that you usually don't suspect and that you often don't see coming.

What Follows

In the remainder of Part I, we will lay the foundation by looking at what excuses are, why they happen, and what makes them so important and so dangerous. In Part II we will take a look at the scope of the problem of excuses in our corporations by examining how they influence a company's culture, leadership, planning processes, and teamwork, as well as how they infect bureaucracies in general. In Part III we will guide you step by step through the process of diagnosing the excuse-making virus in your company and of applying the most effective treatment, which we've seen work with great success in many companies of all sizes.

If you find yourself thinking from this point forward that excuses are relatively harmless, at first that may be because we will be discussing fundamentals. Beware, however, if that thinking persists, for this is your first clue that your relationship to excuses may be like that of the mouse to the cat. You and your company may be in danger and you may not know it!

On the other hand, you will know that you are in a position to get out of danger when a little voice inside of you says, "Aha! I see." At that point, half the battle against the destructive influence of excuses will be won, because you will begin to recognize the real enemy. We will then be able to show you how to gain complete victory, including all the strategies you will need to become number one!

Notes and Quotes

An excuse is worse and more terrible than a lie: for an excuse is a lie guarded.

Pope

3

Excuse-Making:
What Is It?

Definition

Ex-cuse, n. 1. A plea or explanation offered in defense of one's conduct. 2. A release from obligation, duty, etc. 3. That which excuses, that which extenuates or justifies a fault, or is intended to do so. 4. A pretended reason for conduct; **pretext.**

Definition

Pre-text, n. Pretense; false appearance; ostensible

15

reason or motive assigned or assumed as a cover for the real reason or motive.

We All Make Excuses

We all dislike it when other people make excuses. Yet we do it ourselves. We've all run into complications resulting from the excuses we've made. Yet excuses have also bailed us out of some tight situations. What is this thing that we call "making an excuse," really? Is it the same as telling a lie? Is it a "white lie"? What is a white lie? Is an excuse a rationalization? If so, how does that differ from a lie or a white lie?

Lies

A lie is a falsification of the truth that is usually intentional. It is a lie when someone who earns $25,000 a year tells others that he makes $50,000. It is a lie when a person who drives an automobile to work reports that she commutes on her bicycle. It is a lie when someone says that he worked for his previous company for ten years when in fact he worked there for only three. A lie is an intentional distortion of reality.

White Lies

A white lie is also an intentional distortion of the

truth. What distinguishes it from other lies is that (1) it is of little if any consequence, or (2) it is uttered with "positive" intent. Dick, a conscientious manager, is supposed to have an important report on his vice president's desk by 9:00 a.m. on Monday morning. At the appointed hour, the report is not finished. Dick goes to his vice president's office, expecting to be reprimanded for not having the report ready. He learns instead that his boss won't be in until after lunch. Relieved at the news, Dick works frantically and finishes the report by lunchtime. When his vice president returns, he calls Dick to thank him for having the report finished on time. "No problem, sir," Dick replies. "It was on your desk bright and early this morning!" This is a white lie of the first type. It is an intentional falsification of the truth where, at least by all appearances, there is no consequence for having said it.

The second type of white lie is the one that is said with "good" intentions. John has an office mate, Chet. John is bothered by Chet's tendency to spend many hours a week engaged in social telephone conversations. John has complained to his supervisor, and he knows that Chet will be confronted about it in his upcoming six-month review. Chet senses that John is upset about something, but John denies it when asked. "Oh no, everything is fine. I've just been a little preoccupied lately." John's intention is positive. He doesn't want to hurt Chet's feelings by telling him that he's about to be reprimanded. John has just told a white lie. And who hasn't?

Rationalizations

A rationalization is a close relative to a white lie,

but with one fundamental difference. White lies can be told to protect yourself *or* someone else. Rationalizations are unconscious, and they are *always* self-protective in nature. They are distortions of reality that serve only one purpose: to protect you and you alone. The sales manager asks you, "Why didn't you land the new account you've been working on lately?" Truth: you didn't build a good relationship with the prospect while someone else did, so he gave the account to another company. Your answer: "The other company invested more money in the cost of the sale than we did"—which is also true. But this is a rationalization because you are avoiding the real reason for the loss of the account: *your* failure. You are giving rationale to protect yourself from being reprimanded.

Excuse-Making

Excuse-making is more akin to rationalization than it is to lying. Yet there is a difference between an excuse and a rationalization. They are like fraternal twins—the same, yet different. That difference, though minor in appearance, is of major consequence. The concept of rationalization is quite specific. It is on Freud's original list of unconscious defense mechanisms. A rationalization is a psychodynamic principle of self-defense. It is a therapist's tool to identify and work with weak egos in a clinical setting.

Excuse-making, on the other hand, is a more generalized concept. Like rationalization, it serves a self-protective function. But it is much broader in nature—a way of thinking, a mindset. Excuse-making is characterized by the general tendency to externalize rather than internalize the reasons for our emotional discomfort. It is the difference between two distinct attitudes one can assume when faced with the possibility of criticism, blame, or failure: "Johnny made me do it" or "I did it."

Excuse-making is a *way of being* that is rampant in our culture. It is a *way of thinking* that is in our homes, in our institutions, and in our corporations. It is a silent and slow-progressing social ailment that wreaks its havoc in ways that go mostly unnoticed. It is largely invisible, yet extremely corrosive. Like carbon monoxide, excuse-making is colorless, odorless, yet extremely dangerous. In ways that are chronic and unspectacular, excuse-making costs many companies in this country literally billions of dollars every year.

A Helpful Chart

Lie	White Lie	Rationalization	Excuse
Falsification of the truth	Falsification of the truth for "good" reasons	Self-protective statement	Self-protective statement (generalized)
Usually Conscious		**Usually Unconscious**	

Figure 3

In other words, excuses are rationalizations that are generalized and diluted, watered down from the extremes that express themselves in the therapist's office. In this less obvious yet pervasive form, excuses make their way from the heart of our living rooms, to the desks of our class-rooms, to the corridors of corporate America. Excuse-making is a cultural condition—one where excuses are common to the point of being almost socially acceptable, and where consequently their danger goes mostly unrecognized. Excuse-making has become part of our social fabric, a condition that we refer to occasionally as *excusitis*.

Again, the lethal nature of excuse-making in this country lies in its commonness and pervasiveness. Where there are people, there are excuses. Excuses cut across class distinctions, whether economic, social, or educational. They cut across political, ethnic, gender, sexual-orientation, and religious-preference lines. They cut across age, rank, and serial number. They are everywhere in our culture. And while we can sometimes catch glimpses of the damage done by this excuse or that excuse, rarely do we see or comprehend the overall cost of excuse-making as it concerns getting results, whether in our personal lives or in our organizations.

Excuses Take Their Toll

Nowhere is this principle more true than in our corporations. The ultimate purpose of any for-profit business or company, however altruistic its goals, is—at a minimum—to stay in business, and ideally to show a profit. Success is measured by that bottom line.

Yet, as we will explore in this book, for most companies that bottom line is a much smaller number than it might be because of that invisible nemesis that is as old

20

as humankind—**excuses.** Even in corporations where the profit margins are acceptable, excuses in the workplace tend to cause countless problems and endless managerial headaches. Managers, as we all know, manage budget line items: gross profit percentages, revenue per employee, advertising expenses, production percentages, accounting fees, commission percentages, and the like. But there is no line item for managing the cost of excuses. The result is that excuse-making goes unmanaged. The problem is that unmanaged excuse-making has the potential to grow into bigger problems that lurk beneath the surface until they present themselves in ways that obscure the original excuses. And in whatever ways the consequences of excuses finally surface—whether as staff conflicts, break-downs in communication, excessive absenteeism, or what-ever—they *must* be managed, often at great expense to the company.

Excuses Hide Problems

The purpose of any excuse is to hide the true nature of a problem. Whether in one's personal life or in the workplace, excuses mask the truth either from oneself or from others. Whenever the true nature of *any* problem is hidden, there is a good chance that the original problem may compound itself many times over.

For example, the greater the number of people that are affected by an excuse, the more complicated the original problem may become. It is a simple matter of arithmetic. If one makes the same excuse to two people, and they each make the same excuse to two other people, and so on, it isn't long before the original excuse could have far-reaching

21

ramifications. We'll have much more to say about this in Part II when we look at how excuse-making can spread its poison in our companies.

Cleaning Off the Spindle

This chapter is about the nature of excuses. Before looking in the next chapter at why excuses happen, there are still a few loose ends to wrap up, some of which are review and others of which are miscellaneous items.

• Again, most excuses are subconscious. This means that we are typically not aware of the fact that we are making an excuse when we do so. And since excuses are usually subconscious, they tend to become serious roadblocks to truthful communication, problem resolution, and the achievement of desired results.

• Since most people are unaware of the excuses they make, their excuses sound like perfectly logical reasons to them. This is *precisely* the danger. **Excuse-making can become a logic in itself**, a way of thinking that is the basis of a creeping social ailment in our country, as well as in our corporations. It is the social ailment we call excusitis.

• Speaking of excuse-making becoming a logic in itself, let's look at the difference between excuses and explanations (or reasons), since these terms are often confused, and even used interchangeably. There is always an ulterior motive when an excuse is given, namely, to protect oneself. Excuses deflect responsibility; explanations and reasons, on the other hand, can be given *while still accepting full responsibility* for any wrong done. Therefore, the same statement can be an excuse *or* an explanation, depending on (1) whether the speaker is accepting responsibility or not, and (2) whether he or she is willing to do whatever is necessary to correct any wrongdoing. We will say more about this in Chapter 17.

• We have not yet specifically discussed "half-truths." Let's go right to the dictionary. **Half-truth**: *A statement or account containing only some of the facts, the rest being purposely left out with the intention of deceiving.* Technically speaking, a half-truth is not a lie, since nothing is falsified. Also technically speaking, a half-truth is not an excuse, in that half-truths are purposeful (which implies consciousness and intentionality) whereas excuses are mostly unconscious and unintentional. However, the real purpose of a half-truth is to deceive, as is also the case with a lie or an excuse. In that sense, then, we will consider half-truths as being closely related to excuses, and will therefore use them interchangeably hereafter.

• There is nothing devious about the excuse-making process. It is a natural phenomenon, a normal functioning of the human mind. But then, that leads us to the next subject: "The Source of the Disease."

Notes and Quotes

We are all manufacturers—making good, making trouble, or making excuses.

A .V. Adolt

4

The Source of the Disease

Time out for a brief lesson in pain and how human beings deal with painful situations.

Excuses Can Help a Person Feel Better

Nobody likes to hurt. This is true physically, mentally, and emotionally. We human beings have many wonderful mechanisms built into our system to defend ourselves against feeling pain. The state of shock after a person is injured in an accident is a classic example. While in shock, one may not feel any pain for several hours while the body rallies its defenses to handle the trauma that it has just experienced.

The same principle is true of us as psychological beings. Experiments have been conducted where a special pair of glasses is used to invert a person's field of vision so that everything is seen as upside down. In a relatively short period of time, amazingly, a person wearing these same glasses will begin to see everything right side up! What's more, when the lenses are removed the world appears once again temporarily upside down. Soon, however, the person will begin to see the world right side up.

The point is that the human mind is a miraculously powerful thing. It does whatever it can to insure our survival in this world. Since pain in a human being of any kind always signals danger, it is the job of the various systems of the mind and body to put a stop to the feeling of danger by eliminating the source of the pain. Psychologically speaking, this means that whenever possible the mind will do whatever it can to keep from hurting. One of the ways our minds have figured out how to do this is to—you guessed it—*make excuses.*

How It Happens: Example #1

Let's take a closer look. Mark, a well-mannered new salesperson on the job, is not meeting quotas. For five consecutive months he has fallen short. His sales manager has informed him that in order to meet his required level of sales, he must make a minimum of five cold calls every day. Mark hates cold calls, so he doesn't make them. But listen to what he tells his wife when she complains that he's not earning enough money to support the family. "I can't help it that my sales are down. I just don't have a good territory!" This is an excuse on Mark's part. Why did he make an excuse rather than tell his wife the real reason that his sales are insufficient? Because it kept him *at that moment* from hurting. Mark was avoiding two potential sources of pain—one that might come from his wife's response, the other from what he would feel if he admitted the real reason to himself.

How It Happens: Example #2

Sally is, in general, a talented and valuable member of an office staff. Her office manager has asked her to give a joint presentation on some newly acquired word processing capabilities to the engineering department. Sally agrees to co-present with her supervisor, though she is petrified of having to speak in front of a group.

On the morning that the presentation is planned, Sally calls her manager to report that she was very ill in the night, and that she will not be able to help with the presentation. The fact is that she didn't sleep well because she was so concerned about having to stand up in front of the engineers. But if she told her manager the truth, it would hurt. Instead, she made an excuse in order to protect herself from the pain.

Notice one additional dimension to Sally's inter-action with her supervisor: *The excuse she gave is one that her boss will accept.* The fact that an excuse is acceptable in the eyes of the person to whom one is making it adds tremendous power to the potential for excuse-making.

We will visit this notion again later.

Our Potential for Making Excuses Is Inborn

We don't need to be taught to make excuses. As part of the self-protective nature of the brain, we are born with the raw materials necessary to make spontaneous, appropriate, ingenious, and instantaneous excuses. It has nothing to do with having evil thoughts or being a bad person. Put an individual in an experience where the truth about himself might hurt, and there you have an excuse in the making.

We Also Learn to Make Excuses

To say that we don't need to be taught to make excuses is not to imply that we aren't also taught. Indeed, we begin to learn which excuses to make, and when to make them, at a very early age. Two-year-old Jimmy sees his four-year-old brother Scott getting away with not eating the vegetables he doesn't like with the excuse, "I'm full, Mommy." Thus it is that Jimmy learns quickly that excuse-making is allowed. So he tries it out for himself. "And Jimmy, why aren't you eating your vegetables?" "Because I'm full, too, Mommy!"

It doesn't take long for our young brains, already predisposed to make excuses whenever possible in order to sidestep pain, to learn exactly when and how to do it. Excuse-making is the way the young child learns to maneuver in his or her world. We need only get away with making an excuse one time for the process to be reinforced and for the excuse-making mindset to be put into motion. In the words of Sven Wahlroos, in his book *Excuses: How to Spot Them, Deal with Them, and Stop Using Them,* "If children are allowed to get away with using excuses, some of which may originally have been deliberate, the excuses will become automatic reflexes by the time they reach adulthood" (1981, p. 6).

What he doesn't say is that in the average child's life, he or she is allowed to get away with excuses on many, many occasions. Dad sometimes makes excuses to Mom, Mom sometimes makes excuses to Dad, parents on occasion make excuses to their children, children learn to make excuses to their parents. The patterns become well-rehearsed at an early age. This is why we may refer to excuse-making occasionally as **four-year-old behavior**. Because by that age we have all been well-prepared to function in the world—a world where excuses are not only allowed, but are also unknowingly encouraged and rein-forced.

Excuses and Not-OKness

This is an aside, but we think an important one. A whole chapter, perhaps an entire book, could be given to this subject, but a quick overview is all we have space for here.

Many a child is raised hearing from time to time that he or she is worthless, no good, inferior, "in the way," to be seen and not heard, a "bad" boy or a "bad" girl. The conclusion many children reach as a result is that they are Not OK persons. Suppose that a child's mother and father are under extreme financial stress. In a moment of intense frustration Dad shouts at Mom, "I wish the kids had never been born—they cost too damn much money!" What does a small child conclude in this situation, especially if this statement—powerful because it was made in an emotional moment—is never corrected? Sometimes what's not said speaks louder than what is said.

Nor does the problem stop in the home. The same phenomenon carries forward to school and society. For example, schools typically view failure by children as unacceptable rather than as a valuable learning experience. Consequently, when a child fails at something, he or she is usually disciplined rather than encouraged. Far too often in this situation children conclude that they are Not OK, and much damage is done to their young psyches.

When a child concludes that he or she may be Not OK, it hurts a lot! It hurts so much that it may lead the child to grow up making excuses whenever telling the truth could bring on the feeling that, deep down, he or she may be Not OK. An excuse helps one in that moment to feel OK.

Excuse-Making as Normal vs. Abnormal Behavior

This is where the line between rationalization and excuse-making gets a little fuzzy. When we feel Not OK about ourselves at some deep level, weak egos—and therefore an abundance of rationalizations—set in. The deeper the pain, the more pronounced is the rationalization. In its extreme forms, one doesn't have to be a trained psychologist to spot this kind of behavior.

A man had been bragging incessantly about his boat to an acquaintance. Tiring of the story, his acquaintance asked the man if he could see the boat. The man replied that he would love to give him a ride in his own personal 150-foot luxury yacht. The problem was, it was *so* big that it had to be anchored several miles off shore, too far out to be seen from land. It seems that the motor on his smaller boat that he used to get to it was broken down, so he was sorry, but the offer would just have to wait until another time.

Most people would not have difficulty recognizing this story as an untruth. But it is more than just a lie. It is a blatant rationalization used to cover the fact that the man didn't have a boat of any sort, although reporting that he did helped him feel more OK at the time.

This example is purposely used to illustrate that when we mention excuse-making in this book, we are not referring, as with this man, to some pathological condition whose source is a deep-seated feeling of Not-OKness. Most people feel OK enough about themselves that they don't have to rely on extreme rationalizations or outright lies to keep from hurting emotionally.

Normal People Don't Like to Hurt Either

Nevertheless, it is important to keep in mind that "normal" people, the vast majority who feel mostly OK themselves, don't like emotional discomfort, either. But the rationalizations of normal people are qualitatively different from those of the man and his luxury boat. They are much less obvious, and far more invisible, pervasive, and commonplace. They form a language all their own—the *language of excuse-making*. It is a language that, by and large, is an acceptable language in our culture. Its power, and its danger, lies in its invisibility and subtlety. It is a language we all learn at a very young and formative age. It is a language that expresses a chronic disease of the times—the disease of excusitis. And it must be eliminated in the workplace if we are going to fix corporate America.

And Last

Thus it is that we become skilled at making excuses early in our lives. Sadly, that same skill continues to develop throughout life because it continues to find fertile soil in which to grow and multiply. One of the places where the soil is most fertile for its expression is in the corporations of this country. Let's press on and look more closely at what this means.

5

Excuses Indicate Other Problems

When it comes to excuses, the world is an interesting place. It is a bit of a paradox. A high premium is placed on responsibility, at least in terms of lessons taught. Parents give us important messages about responsibility. "Pick up after yourself, Jane." Teachers tell us it is important to take responsibility for ourselves. "Make sure your homework assignment is completed, students." Boy Scout and Girl Scout troop leaders teach us to be responsible individuals. "Do a good turn daily." Priests, pastors, nuns, church schools—more lessons about how important it is to be a responsible person.

But in practice, the world doesn't always work that way. Not only are excuses allowed (remember Sally and her excuse about being ill and therefore not able to present to a group of engineers), they also are encouraged and re-inforced. That they are allowed is somewhat easily under-stood. Personal illness is an excellent case in point. Rarely is sickness questioned so long as it is not overdone. But what of the fact that many companies actually have acknowledged "sick days" as part of their benefits package? Since people aren't paid extra if they don't take them, are we thereby encouraging people to take sick days without really being sick? Are we making it easier for people to make excuses?

A Common Situation

Let's take a closer look at the suggestion that the workplace may actually encourage and reinforce excuses.

Richard is a sharp individual. He began his career in middle management at a sizeable corporation on the East Coast within weeks after he graduated from an Ivy League business school. His superiors recognized early on that Richard had great potential for moving up the management ranks in the business world. He showed considerably more initiative in solving problems than those who had preceded him. He was the envy of others in middle management with whom he worked. After 18 months on the job, he was promoted. Nine months later, a second promotion. After four years, Richard found himself already in an upper management position. While Richard had numerous skills and talents in the corporate environment, including being a natural leader and communicator, his real forte had always been, and still is, his ability to identify and solve problems.

Today Richard is 53 years old. He is the CEO of another large company. But there are problems. He has been divorced twice, unable to sustain his marital relation-ships in large part because of the long hours he puts in at work. His health is failing under the weight of the never-ending stress of his job. Now, as always in the past, he is heavily burdened by the problems that confront him daily in his business. He voices his concern in terms of how much easier things would be if the managers who report directly to him would take more responsibility in solving some of the problems that he is left with. "They just don't seem to take any responsibility around here," is a comment he has been heard to say on more than one occasion.

Richard's story is not an uncommon one. He is but one of thousands of executives who are good people, strong leaders, respected individuals, hard workers, but who experience trouble brewing at some level that is difficult for them to put their finger on. It is the source of considerable frustration. In addition, they know it is costing their companies a great deal of money.

What Richard and the countless numbers of exec-utives like him don't know is that he may be unwittingly encouraging and reinforcing the very cause of his own problem. Think about it a minute. Richard fought his way to the top through his ability to solve problems. How is he going to assure himself and others that he has what it takes to *stay* at the top? Inside, he feels that he must continue to perform well at the same skills that got him there. **He must continue to solve problems.**

****

It is impossible to solve problems unless there are problems to be solved. To say it bluntly, Richard must have problems in order to function.

35

The Return to Four-Year-Old Rules

When the unspoken corporate ethos, or culture, is that Richard must have problems to solve in order to function well in his position, two things will happen. First, though unaware of the fact that he is doing so, Richard will surround himself with—to one degree or another—*dependent* people who know quite well how to play by the rules. Second, these same people will arrange for Richard to receive more than his share of problems. Why? To please their boss. How? *All they have to do is play by the same rules that they learned as four-year-olds.* Make excuses— it works every time. I couldn't do it because it was this department's fault. This department couldn't do it because it was that department's fault. I blame you. You blame someone else. They blame yet someone else. And so on, sometimes without end.

The consequence: problems do not get solved, matters do not get handled, desired results are not achieved. No one person in the corporate structure can be held responsible because there are so many interdependent parts. One by one, the problems get passed up to Richard's desk. By the time the problem gets to Richard, it is surrounded by so many excuses that he has a difficult time understanding what the real problem is. The real problem may be that X didn't get done. But the excuses relate to its being Y department's fault. So Richard may concentrate on Y and miss the heart of the real problem.

Thus it is that Richard gets more than his share of problems. It is sometimes overwhelming. He tries to figure it out. He thinks he sees the problem, and he even tries to fix it. "They just don't make managers like they used to." Fire this one. Train that one. Hire yet another.

Ultimately, none of his solutions work. Why? Because he has only been able to see pieces of the problem rather than the bigger picture. What is happening in that bigger picture? Is it Richard's doing? Yes and no. Is it his managers' fault? Yes and no. Is it the people downline for their unwillingness to take responsibility? Yes and no. It is all of the above, and more. It's the mixture of many elements coming together in such a way that the results are less than desirable. It is excuse-making run rampant, and corporations surviving, even if barely, in spite of themselves.

Excuses Point to Other Problems

There are two fundamental reasons why we set forth the hypothesis that excuse-making is so critically important as a core issue in corporate America. We will discuss the first of these reasons here, the second later.

Wherever excuses exist in the workplace, there we will find in existence several other related—and usually invisible—destructive forces in operation, forces that interfere directly with achieving desired results. Excuses are like the tip of an iceberg: fairly big in and of itself, but only a small chunk compared to the rest that lies beneath the surface. For all that we see, there is much more that we don't see.

Those who navigate in waters where icebergs exist are well aware that the danger to their ship is the part of the iceberg that lies beneath the water and out of sight, not the part that shows. This is exactly the way it is with excuses. It is the parts that don't show, the ones you don't readily see, that you need to be concerned about the most.

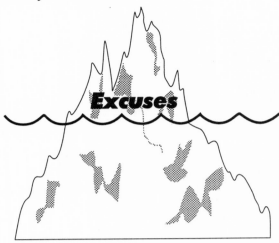

Figure 4

Let's take a look at some of these destructive forces that form the body of the iceberg beneath the surface of excuses.

Victimization

Where there are excuses, there—if we poke around a bit—we will invariably find hiding what is known as a "victimization mindset."

Definition

Vic-tim-i-za-tion, n. The state of being victimized; the attitude that one is a victim of influences *outside of one's control,* thus robbing an individual of the personal power to change his or her set of undesirable circumstances.

An Example from the Olympics

Our society is a veritable hotbed of the victimization mentality. We were reminded of that again by the recent 1994 Winter Olympic Games. The United States' own Nancy Kerrigan was edged out for the gold medal by Aksana Baiul of the Ukraine by the narrowest of split decisions. Immediately afterward, where was the American press? Noisily interviewing each other trying to convince themselves of Kerrigan's victimization. After all, Ms. Kerrigan did two combination jumps, including a difficult triple-toe, triple-toe loop. Baiul did only one combination, a double-double. Some Kerrigan supporters pointed out that the Ukrainian judge was the father of Baiul's ex-coach. Get it? *Some judge victimized Nancy because he was partial to her opponent!*

****

And thus we showed the world our way of thinking: **It must be someone else's fault.**

Victimization and the Legal System

Another example of the victimization mindset in our society can be found in our legal system. One could debate whether the system encourages and supports people to think as victims, or whether it is simply responding to the way people think on their own. Probably some of both is true.

Either way, the victimization mentality certainly reaches deep into our system of jurisprudence. *It must be somebody (or something) else's fault.* Few would argue against the premise that we are the most lawsuit-happy nation in the world. For example, here is a man who, in a state of inebriation, crosses the center line in his vehicle and collides head-on with a car carrying a family of five. All five people in the other vehicle are killed. The inebriated driver experiences whiplash, and for several months thereafter, chronic neck pain. What happens? The drunken driver sues the bar and bartender for being responsible for his drunkenness, the collision, and the whiplash. What's even more interesting? He wins!

Procrastination

Where there are excuses, there—if we poke around a bit—we will invariably find hiding something known as procrastination. Typically, it can be found just beneath the surface, as with the iceberg. In other words, procrastination is rarely open and obvious. But when one finds it in operation, you can bet on the presence of excuses as well!

Definition

Pro-cras-ti-na-tion, n. The act of putting off doing something until a future time; postponing or deferring action; delaying from day to day; waiting until tomorrow to do that which could be done today.

Procrastination in Operation

George is the vice-president of operations at a $75-million-per-year midwestern trucking firm. In January he was asked by the senior vice-president to research the reasons why the drivers had been receiving an inordinate number of fines for carrying cargos that exceeded the normal weight limits. George agreed to take on the project, and promised to present the results at the next monthly meeting.

Subsequently, George was asked for the results of his study at the February executive committee meeting. He replied that he had been very busy, and that he would have it ready for the March meeting. His senior vice-president accepted George's answer, apparently unconcerned about what had now become commonplace (and therefore acceptable) at his company: the *procrastination excuse*—one of the most commonly used excuses in business. At the March meeting the report still was not completed. George was asked why. "I'm sorry, sir. I was so busy that I assigned it to Frank, and Frank hasn't been able to get to it yet. He is working hard to complete another project. I'll do my best to have him submit it by next month."

****

*Earlier we pointed out that **when you get excuses, you don't get results.** George is a classic example of this principle in operation.*

Reactive Thinking

Where there are excuses, there—if we poke around a bit—we will find hiding what is known as "reactive thinking" and "reactive people" (as opposed to "proactive thinking" and "proactive people"). It probably won't be open and obvious, but if there are excuses, there will be reactive thinking. You can count on it.

Definition

Re-act-ive, adj. The state of responding to a stimulus; being affected by some influence, event, etc. **Re-act-ive Think-ing**: a way of conceptualizing experience such that one's behavior is seen as a function of conditions *outside of oneself* rather than as the result of one's own decisions and/or choices.

The Language of Reactive People

Stephen R. Covey in his bestseller, *The 7 Habits Of Highly Effective People*, states:

> The language of reactive people absolves them of responsibility. "That's me. That's just the way I am." *I am determined. There's nothing I can do about it.*
> "He makes me so mad!" *I'm not responsible. My emotional life is governed by something outside*

my control.

"I can't do that. I just don't have the time." *Something outside me—limited time—is controlling me.*

"If only my wife were more patient." *Someone else's behavior is limiting my effectiveness.*

"I have to do it." *Circumstances or other people are forcing me to do what I do. I'm not free to choose my own actions.*

That language comes from a basic paradigm of determinism. And the whole spirit of it is the transfer of responsibility. *I am not responsible, not able to choose my response.* (1989, p. 78)

Fundamentally imbedded in the reactive thinking syndrome, where the password is "I-am-not-responsible" thinking, will be considerable "if-only" language. If only the economy were better, if only we had more team players, if only my boss were person-centered and not task-centered, if only I didn't have all this paperwork, if only this, if only that. **Excuses, excuses, and more excuses!** It is poisonous, self-limited, handicapped, victimized thinking. It is a monkey on the back of the corporate structure, and it must be driven away if we expect to get results.

Entitlement As a Way of Thinking

Wherever there are excuses, there—if we poke around a bit—we will invariably find hiding an attitude of "entitlement." In Judith Bardwick's provocative book *Danger in the Comfort Zone*, she writes:

43

> *Entitlement* is the name I have given to an attitude, a way of looking at life. Those who have this attitude believe that they do not have to earn what they get. They come to believe that they get something because they are owed it, because they are *entitled* to it. They get what they want because of *who* they are, not because of what they *do*.
>
> Entitlement is what I have been seeing in American corporations: people not really contributing, but still expecting to get their regular raise, their scheduled promotion....Entitlement destroys motivation. It lowers productivity. In the long run it crushes self-esteem...it is epidemic in this country. (1991, p.3)

And later she adds:

> We are more likely to sustain Entitlement in people when...we see [them] as victim[s]. (1991, p. 153)

Here it is again: excuses in the making. When people think in "victim" terms, they believe they are freed from having to take responsibility. They are entitled to *whatever* simply because it is owed to them, not because they've earned it. And once things are owed to them, excuses *must* follow. There is no other possibility. It goes with the territory. "I shouldn't have to do this or that in order to get what I want. I am entitled to it."

Entitlement thinking is a logic in itself. It swims in the same stream of logic with reactive thinking, victimization, and **excuses, excuses, excuses**. It is too often *the* American corporate logic. It's what Dr. Bardwick calls in her subtitle "the habit that's killing American business."

Where there are excuses, there will be undesirable results! The habit of excuse-making is the habit that is breeding entitlement thinking. It is the same habit that is killing American business!

****

The Projection of Blame

Wherever there are excuses, there—if we poke around a bit—we will invariably find hiding the projection of blame. Implicitly or explicitly, projection of blame is a partner of excuse-making. Remember George, whose report was due at the March meeting. It wasn't his fault—he was just too busy (in addition to procrastination, *projection of blame* onto busyness). So he passed it on to Frank. It must have been Frank's fault (*projection of blame* onto Frank). Of course, Frank was too busy (*projection of blame* onto Frank's busyness). And so it goes. It is always easier to blame our behavior on someone or something other than ourselves. Remember what we said in Chapter 4 about pain and trying to avoid it? Blaming our shortcomings on ourselves is painful. Projecting blame onto others is relatively painless, as well as automatic, instantaneous, and predictable. And not easily changed unless that change is planned.

And Much More

We could go on at considerable length pursuing

similar hidden connections. For example, wherever there is blame, there we will invariably find hiding an abundance of externalization ("Johnny made me do it"). Where there is externalization, there we will find hiding an abundance of can't-do thinking ("I can't do that because..."). Where there is can't-do thinking, there we will find hiding an abundance of irresponsibility. Where there is irresponsibility, there we will invariably find little, if any, accountability. Wherever there is no accountability, there we will find helpless thinking, self-deceit, mistrust, hidden motives, etc., etc., etc.

It would not be difficult to further unravel each of these scenarios—just as we have done with victimization, procrastination, reactive thinking, entitlement, and the projection of blame—to show that excuses are the common denominator of every major problem in corporate America. We won't, however, because we hope by now the point is clear. **Excuses are an indicator of most—if not all—of the chronic problems in corporate America. Where we find excuses, we will always find some combination of the others. They all lurk in the larger body of the iceberg that is hidden beneath the surface of the water. Each of them points to the presence of all the others. They go together in ways that are almost impossible to separate. If we have one, we have them all, in varying degrees. Taken collectively, they make it almost impossible to get the results we are looking to achieve!**

What are these chronic corporate problems that excuses are always in the middle of? The following diagram reveals some of the more common behaviors and problems that hide beneath the presence of excuses—each of which significantly interferes with the accomplishment of desired results.

Figure 5

The Enemy Is Elusive

The point is that these various blights on American companies are bacteria of a similar strain. They are cousins that travel together. Where you find one, you are likely to find many others, if not all.

Which leads us to the *second* reason why we see the elimination of excuse-making as so vitally important to the cure for our corporate ailments. It has to do with the difficulty, the frustration, the futility of trying to get a grip on such things as victimization, helplessness, procrastination, reactive thinking, irresponsibility, accountability, entitlement, and the like. They are—like a marine recruit's hair after the first cut—nearly impossible to get a hold of.

The same is not true, however, about excuses. Once recognized, they can be quantified, measured, remedied, and eliminated. Excuses are real and tangible things. They can be taken hold of while the problems they point to tend to elude our grasp. Yet by getting a grip on excuses, we can get a stranglehold on every problem that perplexes our companies! Excuses can be fixed! And wonderful outcomes occur—that is, the other problems go away—when the proper machinery is set into place for a company to be able to follow the maxim: *No Excuses in the Workplace!*

In Summary

We have seen that there is a way of thinking that has gradually, insidiously, silently, and methodically crept its way into the mainstream of American thinking. It is an

48

attitude that has many faces, most of which lie beneath the surface of awareness in the same way that most of an iceberg lies beneath the surface of the water.

Despite the many elusive forms and figures this family of problems can twist and bend itself into, there is one that is distinguishable above all the others. It is one that we *can* get a clear look at (though we must *learn* to see it, since it takes a unique vantage point to do so). It is one that *is* possible to get a firm hold on. That one, of course, is **excuse-making.**

Excuse-making is *the* major roadblock to achieving the outcomes we desire. The longer we fail to recognize it, the longer we wait to get a firm grip on it, the longer it goes unattended, the more problematic it becomes in terms of getting the results we want.

One Last Thought

We have shown how many of the problems that perplex our companies today tend to travel together, like wolves in a pack. We have further touched on how one of those problems, namely excuse-making, gives us access to the *entire family of problems* in ways that none of the others can. Excuse-making is like the lead wolf in the pack. It shows first.

What we haven't yet looked at in any detail, however, is a unique quality about excuses that allows us to exterminate the whole family by eliminating just one of its members. That is, when we get rid of excuses, we have not just shot the lead wolf. Rather, we have blown up the entire family of problems, both the visible *and* hidden parts, and thereby have annihilated the complete pack!

Let's therefore take a closer look at how it's possible to eliminate all of the troublesome relatives of excuse-making in one fell swoop by simply eliminating excuses. After that we will head into "Part II. The Scope of the Problem: How Excuses Manifest Themselves in Corporations."

6

Kill Many Birds with a Single Stone

It is generally true that what we think about **X** determines how we function in relation to **X**. That is to say, our beliefs define the parameters within which we are able to take action. How we see something defines and limits what we can do. For example:

Beliefs of Old: #1

There was a time in the course of human history when it was commonly believed that the world was flat. That belief defined and limited our choices regarding how

51

to be at sea. Man would venture out on the water only so far as land remained visible. Then he reversed his course and returned home. He was afraid that if he sailed any farther away from the shore, he would fall off the edge of the earth, never to be heard from again. His behavior was consistent with, and limited by, the beliefs he held about the world *at that time*.

#2

It was only a little more than 100 years ago when those who demonstrated "abnormal" behavior were thought to be possessed by the devil. Such behaviors as drunkenness, infidelity, or sudden outbursts of emotion were handled in ways that today would be considered barbaric and inhumane. Some of the customary treatments were whipping, lowering slowly into poisonous snakepits, forced feedings of a mixture of sheep manure and wine, public ridicule, noise-making, and unexpected icy baths. The objective was always the same—to "scare the devil" out of a person, a saying that remains with us today. Our behavior for dealing with people who acted abnormally, though perfectly logical given the frame through which we viewed it, was limited by our way of thinking about abnormal behavior *at that time*.

#3

During the Industrial Revolution, children worked long, hard hours—12- and 14-hour days—in the emerging industrial plants. If children were forced to labor by those same standards today, we would consider it unusually cruel and abusive treatment. Yet such behavior was commonplace then because it was consistent with the beliefs about the role of children in the family. It was a value that carried over from the farmlands where for centuries children had been expected to work long hours in the fields to help support the family. The forced employment of the young was defined, and limited, by the beliefs about the role of children *at that time.*

More Recently

We need not look so far into the past to see this same principle at work. Consider the issue of women in the workplace. It was popularly believed by many in the past, and by some yet today, that a woman's place is in the home. Let's go back a mere twenty years. Only 3 percent of the attorneys in this country in 1972 were women. In addition, it was nearly unthinkable for a woman to travel overnight. It was believed that if she did, the other men's wives would be jealous and would not tolerate it. So as a general rule, women didn't travel overnight. Our behavior was limited and defined by the beliefs that we held.

Today, the beliefs about women in the workplace have changed considerably, and therefore so have our behaviors. In 1993, 41 percent of the practicing attorneys and 47 percent of the enrollees in law school were women. Furthermore, women travel overnight as common practice in the business community. *Beliefs set the parameters on our behavior, on how we do things, on how we function. Simply put, **we are limited by what we believe.***

Athletic records furnish many interesting examples. When it was believed impossible for an individual to run one mile in four minutes or less, runners mostly didn't challenge that belief. Their behavior was consistent within the accepted paradigm. The goal was to *approach* four minutes, but *exceed* it? Never! And then came Roger Bannister, a man who believed differently. Through his belief that a four-minute mile *was* possible, the limits of his behavior were expanded, new possibilities arose, and new horizons were reached. And now to run one mile in four minutes, though still a tremendous feat, is nevertheless fairly common.

And so it is with every new world record, every new invention, and every new technique that betters the old way of doing *anything*. **All progress begins with a belief that something can be better, a mental framework that sees it differently from the accepted and customary way of seeing it, a perspective that is out of the ordinary.**

Perception Affects Reality

The point is that it has been true throughout the course of human history, and it will probably always be true, that our view—our perception—of anything determines the limits within which we can, and will, deal with that thing. Our behavior is, generally speaking, logical and consistent within the context of the lens through which we are looking. Change the lens, the paradigm, the mindset, the belief system, and amazing new opportunities arise.

When we were able to perceive the world as round rather than flat, whole new horizons opened up for world travel. When we changed our view that abnormal behavior was caused by mental and emotional factors rather than by demon possession, new and effective opportunities for treating the mentally ill emerged. When we changed our perception of the role of children in the family, tremendous new strides were made in our definitions of fair treatment and education of the young.

Re-examining the Lens

Similarly, the time has arrived in the course of corporate development to update and upgrade the lens through which we are accustomed to looking at problems in the workplace. Our experience continues to demonstrate that the current paradigms are not as effective as they might be. They are often too narrow and too limited to fix the problems that have a stronghold in organizational structures today. This book is about a shift to a powerful new way of looking at corporate problems, and the amazing new possibilities that such a shift opens up for fixing those problems.

Relationships Between Things

There are three ways to view the relationship between any two or more things. The relationship might be **causal**, it might be **coincidental**, or it might be **mutually coexistent**, also known as **systemic**. While the distinctions between these may appear at first glance to be a bit academic, it is very important to understand their differences in order to (1) grasp the basic premise of this book, and (2) use these concepts to fix your company's problems.

Causal Relationships

A causal relationship is one in which something (the cause) sets in motion something else (the effect). Eye strain causes headaches. Viruses and bacteria cause infections. Poorly maintained equipment causes shutdowns. Shutdowns cause loss in production. Ineffective management causes low levels of human performance. All of these are examples of cause and effect relationships. Headaches are related to eye strain *causally*, equipment breakdown is related to poor maintenance *causally*, etc. In simple terms, one thing causes the other to happen.

Coincidental Relationships

A coincidental relationship is one in which something is related to something else by chance. There is no particular rhyme or reason why something happened in a certain way; it just happened. A car passes another car on the expressway. The relationship between the two cars is coincidental. It just happened that way. The director of computer operations is out of town on the same day that the system breaks down. The relationship between the two events is coincidental.

Mutually Coexistent (Systemic) Relationships

When the relationship between two or more things is mutually coexistent, they are related neither causally nor coincidentally. That is, one does not cause the other, nor are they related by some chance happening. They simply go together as parts of the same system. Arms don't *cause* hands and fingers, nor is it merely a coincidence that where we find one, we also find the others. They are part of a system where one part "goeswith" the others. They are mutually coexistent. Porcupines don't *cause* their quills, and the relationship between porcupines and quills is not just by chance. Quills simply "gowith" porcupines. They are part of the package. Managers don't *cause* workers, nor are they related by chance. Management and labor go together. They cannot be separated. So with trees and leaves, heads and tails, up and down. All of these things are examples of mutually coexistent relationships—things that "gowith" other things. Coexistent relationships are those where something exists as part of something else, mutually, necessarily, **systemically.**

The Current Corporate Paradigms

Traditionally, we have looked at and analyzed problems in the corporate world either through the lens of cause/effect, or through the lens of coincidence. In the first case, we have viewed this or that problem as being caused by something, and then we have set about trying to change that thing (the cause). For example, if we think that the problem of diminishing productivity is *caused* by inadequate teamwork, the usual method of fixing the problem is to try to build better teams. If shrinking sales is *caused* by poorly trained salespeople, then the solution is generally either to hire trained salespeople or train the old ones. This is far and away the most commonly used paradigm for analyzing and fixing corporate problems. It is *the* accepted corporate perspective.

We also tend to view some corporate problems as coincidental. That is, some problems pop up here and there, not from any obvious causation, but more or less by chance. In a sense, causal and coincidental explanations are closely related, the only real difference being whether or not we think we can identify the cause of some event. When we can, we use causal explanations. When we can't, we tend to see it as a coincidence.

For example, Sam in accounting is irritable and argues often with his assistant. There is some possibility that we'd look for departmental stressors as a cause of that problem, but more often we're likely to see Sam as short-fused, someone who "just hasn't been himself lately." Either fix Sam or tolerate him. This is an example of coincidental analysis of problems. The problematic situation appears to be isolated and unrelated to other things. When this is the case, the fix is usually *very* narrow in focus, even more so than with remedies based on causal explanations.

A New Way of Seeing the Problem

By themselves, these traditional ways of looking at corporate problems are inadequate and outdated. Limiting our analysis to cause/effect and coincidence explanations is analogous to thinking the world is flat, or that the patent office should close because all that can be invented has been invented. They can vastly limit exciting new opportunities for fixing the problems.

It is our experience that the stubborn problems in corporate America today can be most effectively addressed and resolved by looking through the lens of mutual co-existence as an explanatory model. It is our view that most of the problems in organizations today "gowith" other problems. Attempting to resolve those problems through cause-and-effect or coincidence models will nearly always fall short for the same reason that dropping people unexpectedly into icy baths didn't solve the problem of abnormal behavior. The paradigm doesn't fit the reality of the situation.

The secret—the key to the vault that holds the treasure—is to seek out the family of problems that travel together as a *system.* Having done that, the next step is to identify and isolate the part (or parts) that most affect the other parts that "gowith" it. If this can be done, then the task is to choke off that one essential component that governs all the others until one by one the other parts perish. It is rather like cutting off the head of a chicken. The chicken will run around for a few seconds as if still alive once its head is severed. But all of the parts that "gowith" that component—its legs, wings, feet, heart, lungs, etc.—soon die without the essential part, the head.

Excuses: The Essential Part

This book is about severing the head from a whole body of problems in corporate America so that, one by one, all of the problems will die. Our experience has taught us that the head of the chicken in terms of corporate problems is **excuse-making**. It more than any other single factor indicates, perpetuates, and dominates other problems in the workplace. It is the one common denominator of the troubles that perplex our organizations. By isolating and eliminating this single phenomenon, all the other problems that accompany it are rendered impotent. Let's change our analogy of the iceberg with all of its underwater components to that of a buoyant mine, the kind that blows up ships on contact. Let's say, also, that the trigger points that explode the mine are excuses.

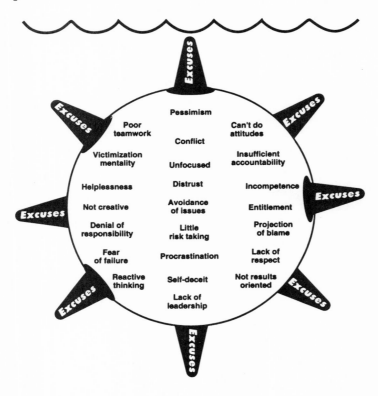

Figure 6

If we remove the spikes, the trigger points, from the mine, there would be nothing to set the mine off. It would be harmless, just another small object floating in the water.

Since there would be no way for the explosives to be denotated, every other corporate troublemaker would be rendered inert.

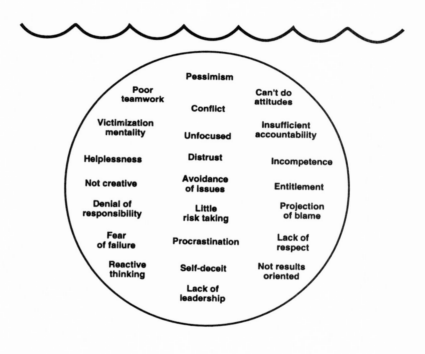

Figure 7

We will explore in some detail why this is the case—that the same stone that removes excuses from the workplace kills all of the other pesky "birds" that go with them, as well. And we will examine closely what comprises the bigger family of problems to be eliminated.

As you are about to see, *most*, if not all, of the problems that perplex the corporate world today are members of that family of birds. And for the first time, there is a systemic approach that will wipe out *all* of the problems, not just one here and one there, as has been true in the past.

****

When you eliminate excuses, *you get rid of all the other problems.* *When you get rid of the other problems, you make room for the positives.* *When you make room for the positives,* **you get results!**

****

Traditional Strategies

It will also become clearer as we go along why the traditional methods of addressing the problems in our companies do not produce long-term improvements. Consulting and training programs that approach the solution through conventional cause-and-effect or coincidence paradigms usually *cannot* effect any lasting change. How could they? It would be like filing down the claws of a tiger who had just clawed someone to death. The fix would be temporary because claws grow back; and it would be ineffective anyway because there are other ways a tiger can kill people. The point is that when corporate problems are addressed from a cause-and-effect paradigm, there generally can only be a series of shifts in the system, and it isn't long before the old problems recur.

Furthermore, even when we do try to fix problems in organizations through cause-and-effect approaches, we usually try to fix the people first. We tend to think that if we just had very talented people (cause), the problems will be solved (effect). So what do we do? We try to make superstars, extraordinary people, and we bring in all kinds of trainers and consultants to make this happen. But listen to Peter Schutz, former CEO of Porsche AG:

> The secret of success in business rarely consists of finding a group of superstars. The secret actually lies in getting extraordinary performance out of ordinary people. What makes an extraordinary person is an extraordinary organization, and an extraordinary process.

We submit to you that the way to have an extraordinary organization and an extraordinary process is to break out of the cocoon of cause-and-effect and coincidental thinking, and fly high with the wings of systemic thinking.

We are not saying, nor would we want to be mistaken to mean, that some of the time-honored programs out there such as total quality management, leadership training, interpersonal communications, sales training, trust building, team building, empowerment, and the like are unimportant or totally ineffective. *Certainly they are not.* It is more a matter of timing and integration. To attack any problem while looking through a lens that doesn't properly focus on that problem is like trying to see Mt. Everest through a microscope. It just doesn't work! Once properly focused, there most assuredly is a place for some of the traditional programs. Again, the problem is not with the corrective measures taken to date, but with the cause-and-effect perspective from which they almost always approach the problem.

We realize that the concept that it is important to look at problems from a different point of view is not new. What is new, however, is the discovery of *this powerful systemic perspective from which to look at corporate problems.* It is powerful because **it works to get results!** It works to get results because it elicits extraordinary performance from ordinary people. Therein lies the future of corporate success.

Part
II

The Scope of the Problem

How Excuses Manifest Themselves in Corporations

7

In the Corporate Culture

Nearly everywhere you turn in corporate America these days, someone is talking about "corporate culture." And well they should be. The concept of culture is more than just current and fashionable. It is positioned critically in the center of all that is unhealthy about our companies today. If the corporations in this country are going to compete and win in the global marketplace, we must become acutely aware of the seriousness of the cultural issues that exist in our organizations. The heart and soul of the message to be learned and applied from this book rests in the very center of the cultural issue. To put it bluntly, what you're about to read is the guts of what you need to pay attention to.

What exactly is this thing that we refer to as "corporate culture"?

Definition

Cor-po-rate Cul-ture. The spoken and unspoken rules in an organization that set the standards for how things are to be done. The company ethos. The characteristic ways of thinking, feeling, and behaving in any given occupational group. The prevailing attitudes, values, beliefs, and actions of the people within a company.

In Other Words

All companies have a culture whether they know it or not. That is, every place of business has its characteristic ways of thinking, valuing, making decisions, and behaving. Whatever these standards are determine how people look at situations, interpret information, communicate, and act. Culture even sets the emotional tone, or feeling state, by which people function within that organization.

Corporate culture is, in effect, the personality of the company. Like people, corporations have different personalities. There are some companies where if you stand in front of the door at five o'clock you're likely to be trampled. There are other companies where people filter out slowly over the course of two or three hours. In some companies people address each other formally, in others informally. There are some companies where the work pace is quite intense and others where it is fairly relaxed. You can often sense the personality of a corporate culture from the atmosphere when you first walk in the door. Some corporate environments are light and fun-loving, others serious and professional, even intimidating. Some inspire confidence, some don't. Some are electric and draw people, making them feel welcome. Others are boring; still others are cold and unfriendly. Some companies respond to calls from their customers with nothing but excuses. Other companies meet their customers only with solutions.

How Does It Happen?

What makes a company's culture what it is? How can one company's culture be so different from another's?

The Role of Tradition

Tradition plays a large part, not only in establishing corporate culture, but also in perpetuating it. When Nick was hired as an accountant in a large midwestern furniture company, he was told that he was expected to report to work by 8:00 every morning. He noticed when he read the policy manual that it said the same thing. His first day on the job, Nick arrived at 7:45 a.m., happy to be in his new position and eager to get started. He couldn't help but notice, however, that the four other accountants in his department arrived between 8:30 and 9:00. Nick was a bit puzzled, but didn't think too much of it until the same pattern continued for several weeks. By the end of the first month, Nick found himself arriving at work around 8:15 a.m. He was nervous about it at first, but was relieved when nothing was said. Now, of course, after several months on the job, Nick arrives between 8:30 and 9:00 along with his colleagues.

In countless similar ways, the tireless voice of tradition speaks loudly in carrying on the culture of any company. And the problem is not just that the cultural values get passed on from one employee to another over a period of years. What's equally important is that companies tend to hire people who fit naturally into their present culture. Like attracts like. The result is that hiring people of a similar bent serves to feed the prevailing culture, since all such hirees will, to varying degrees, bring with them the same values that are already reflected in the company.

Taking a Broader View

An attempt to get a handle on what corporate culture is all about inclines one toward taking too narrow a view. People are used to associating culture with the framed mission statements, company slogans, motivational sayings, and handbooks that are visible around the workplace. Equally, corporate culture is thought of as whatever people in the workplace say it is. *Culture is much, much more than what is framed, written, or spoken about in a company.* Culture consists also of all that is unframed, unwritten, and unspoken. In fact, just as in Nick's company, **corporate culture is *mostly* what is unframed, unwritten, and unspoken.**

70

Let's explore more closely what we mean by looking at a few examples.

Reactivity vs. Proactivity

Very few people today would take issue with the notion that it is important to be proactive in business—to make things happen rather than wait for them to happen. Many gurus on the subject, including Stephen Covey, have done an excellent job of helping companies become aware of how important proactivity really is. But our experience in the corporate world continues to suggest that any actual implementation of the concept of proactivity too often stops at the level of precept. That is, proactivity is a wonderful *rule* to believe in. It is a profound maxim for governing corporate conduct. Not uncommonly, CEO's, corporate executives, and managers stand in front of their people and preach the message of proactivity. "We want this company to be more proactive! If we don't become more proactive, we may not be around in five years." Some company leaders strongly recommend reading certain books on the subject. Others buy copies for everyone in management and make it mandatory reading. (Not a bad idea, really.)

The problem is that *saying you believe in* proactivity, suggesting that people read the latest best-seller about it, and even making proactivity a formal written part of your corporate culture will not by themselves make people more proactive. *You must also change what they do, since it is the **behavior** of your people that defines your culture.* It doesn't matter how much you persuade your people to *believe in* proactivity, for example, if—in their behavior—they remain more focused on short-term goals than on

71

long-term goals. If they are focused on short-term goals, they are probably in more of a reactive mindset than a proactive one, *regardless of what you'd have them believe about proactivity.*

Warren Bennis in his book *On Becoming a Leader* quotes television producer and writer Norman Lear as saying that short-term thinking is "the societal disease of our time." Why? Because when we are focused on the short term, we rarely take into consideration the long-term consequences of our decisions and our behaviors. And those long-term consequences could be very damaging.

Bennis agrees with Lear. He thinks that short-term thinking is seriously holding back business in this country. Listen to his words:

> I think Lear is absolutely right. American business has become the principal shaper and mover in contemporary America—even more than television—and has, in an odd irony, by zealously practicing what it preaches, sandbagged itself. Having captured the heart and mind of the nation with its siren songs and instant gratification, it has locked itself into obsolete practices. American business has never been more popular and less successful . . . Dick Ferry, president and cofounder of Korn/Ferry, agrees, and he is not optimistic. "Corporate America may talk, on an intellectual level, about what it'll take to succeed in the twenty-first century, but when it gets right down to decision making, all that matters is the next quarterly earnings report. That's what's driving much of the system. With that mind-set, everything else becomes secondary to the ability to deliver the next quarterly earnings push-up. We're on a treadmill. The reward system in

this country is geared to the short term." (1989, pp. 22-23)

****

Again, *corporate culture is mostly what is unframed, unwritten, and unspoken.* If the people in your company are more focused on the short term almost to the exclusion of the long term, the corporate culture is one of **reactivity**, not proactivity, regardless of what everyone would like to think to the contrary!

An Example of How This Works

Long-term strategic planning for one's job is an exercise in proactivity. When was the last time you saw an evaluation form or appraisal process that gave any credit to the employee for being able to do long-term strategic planning? Usually, the evaluation process focuses on how well the person handled some specific assignment or duty in the short term.

If you want to improve *anything*, you have to measure it. How can we measure proactivity when little attempt is made to quantify what it is that constitutes proactivity? Let's say you want your salespeople to "proactively" seek larger accounts. So you ask them to do market research on large companies before going in. That way they will know what the company is all about and they will impress the potential customer as being well-prepared and well-informed. This would be an example of proactive selling.

Clearly, to actively seek larger accounts is a long-term process. You can't just have your people throw aside everything they're doing and tell them to spend the next three months researching big clients in order to go out and make the calls. In addition, you can expect that this will take them out of their emotional comfort zones and cause considerable distress. So your people need to be taught how to blend this proactive project into their weekly goals program and their weekly accountabilities program. Ask them to identify perhaps four major accounts they want to land in the next year. Then have them set up benchmark measuring points for the year to determine their progress in terms of specific goals—doing research, action plans, etc. These goals are then built into their accountabilities system, and so on. More about this later.

****

Similarly, when was the last time you saw a sales professional's appraisal in which one of the appraisal issues involved (a) how well this person developed his sales plan, (b) how well he followed his sales plan, and (c) whether his sales plan used creativity and proactivity to attack the market? These are things we rarely look at to evaluate. If we aren't going to evaluate them, how can we expect our people to perform to those standards? *As long as our evaluations and accountabilities are set up on a short-term basis, we're not going to have a proactive corporate culture, no matter what is said at the meetings, no matter what books are recommended, and no matter how the mission statement reads.* Short-term thinking and proactivity are contradictory concepts.

The Same Example Extended

So here is Larry, a better-than-average salesman for eight years with a leading computer software company. The company has had shrinking profit margins for the past two years, and the CEO is concerned. He knows that something must change. He recently attended a week-long workshop that emphasized, among other things, the importance of salespeople's proactivity in the marketplace. He discovered that being more forward-looking was necessary not only to get ahead, but maybe even just to survive.

The CEO returned, excited about what he had learned. He called a meeting of his regional sales managers, who in turn called meetings with their respective salespeople, to sell them on the idea of becoming more proactive. He handed out a popular book on the subject to everyone. He insisted that the words "BE PROACTIVE" be made into some attractive posters and placed generously around the workplace in clear view of everyone. He even appointed a committee of top managers to re-examine the company's mission statement and build the concept of proactivity into it.

Larry was inspired. His CEO and his sales manager both did an exceptional job of impressing on him the importance of this new approach. At first, Larry's excitement was expressed in the form of some new-found energy in making his sales calls. He had a one-month and three-month sales quota to meet, and he was fired up about it. Little more was said to him about becoming proactive by the CEO and sales manager until the next semi-annual sales meeting, at which time the company's "buy-in" to the concept of proactivity was restated and reinforced in the various speeches given by management.

Nothing else changed. There was no effort to build proactivity into Larry's goals, evaluations, or accountabilities. The demands placed on him to meet short-term quotas soon overshadowed any excitement he might have had for becoming proactive. Larry did the best he could to be more proactive, at least by his limited understanding of the whole notion. Mostly, in retrospect, what proactivity meant to him was to actually *do* what was expected of him rather than *to put things off*. Since the whole concept was never clearly explained in detailed, practical terms, nor built into his accountabilities in a way that could be measured, Larry was not able to meet the "proactive" expectations of his superiors. "Proactivity" became a precept to believe in, but it had no meaningful behavioral significance.

And It Fails

As could be expected, the whole proactive agenda was lost in the flurry of short-term activities. So what? Consider the possible consequences. At the end of the fiscal year when the company profits have further fallen, will Larry be more likely to accept the blame or project it onto someone or something else? Will his attitude be more optimistic or pessimistic about the next management strategy that comes along? Will he be respectful of his superiors, or disrespectful, especially if the CEO places a good chunk of the blame for shrinking profits on the sales force for not being proactive enough? Would the resulting stress in the sales department express itself as conflict between Larry and his colleagues? Will Larry feel like he has the power to change things, to make things happen? Or will he feel like a victim? What if he didn't quite make his one-month and three-month quotas because he was, in fact, spending some of his time doing long-term, proactive planning? Would he be rewarded for that behavior, or would he be punished? If he were punished, would he tend to become more positive in his sales efforts, or more negative?

More to the point: **Here come the excuses**. "Larry, why didn't you reach your monthly goal?" "It's been a tough month, sir." "Larry, what have you done to become more proactive in the marketplace?" "I've tried to do more reading at night, sir, to become more informed about product knowledge when I'm with a customer." "Larry, this company is sinking, fast. What can you do to help?" "I'll try harder next month, sir." "Larry, I notice that your attitude has been slipping. You've been really negative lately." "Things have been rough at home recently, sir." "Larry, what's the problem between you and your colleague Steve?" "He's been hard to get along with lately, sir." "Larry, why wasn't your last monthly report submitted on time?" "I've been very busy trying to be more proactive, sir."

****

One reason people don't get results is because they are *allowed* to make excuses. Another reason people don't get results is because they are *encouraged*—almost "forced" by the system—to make excuses. **When the system is set up in such a way that failure is inevitable, excuse-making is unknowingly encouraged in that company.** This is because, given the choice between admitting to failure or making an excuse, most people most of the time will automatically give an excuse to spare themselves the pain. Again, excuses are an indicator, a warning signal, of a systemic problem (or problems) in the company. Where there are excuses, there—if we poke around a bit—we will find hiding other problems. Excuses never travel alone.

The Arithmetic Factor

Now multiply this one simple example about Larry by the entire work force of 239, or 1800, or however many people are in the corporation, and you have what is commonplace in our companies: **an excuse-laden corporate culture.** Again, it is not a question *of whether* excuse-making happens (since virtually every business is infected to some degree), but *how much* does it happen? Those companies where excuses are the most commonplace are the ones that are in the most trouble. Those companies where excuse-making happens the least are leading their respective industries.

The Point

Always, **when you don't get results, you get excuses.** *And you can't get results unless the desired outcome is purposely and carefully built into the evaluation and accountabilities process.* A long-term, proactive approach often requires the acceptance of possible short-term sacrifice. No amount of corporate-culture preaching or propaganda, no fancy posters or motivational plaques, no eloquent speeches at national sales meetings will eliminate excuses from the workplace—*unless* the desired behaviors (and reasonable expectations) are built into the appraisal process. **But as long as there are excuses, there will not be results!**

The Problem Is Systemic

It is important to note that, though our first example was about reactivity vs. proactivity, we could have started with any behavioral problem listed in the base of the iceberg (figure 5) and arrived eventually at the same place, namely, the excuse-making process. For example, and in a much less detailed way, let's look at pessimism vs. optimism. Pessimism is one of the ingredients that is at the core of cultural issues. How can you have proactivity if you're not optimistic? Optimism is about the future; pessimism is rooted in the past. How can you be focused, or have good teamwork, or take risks, or trust, or have harmonious relationships, or lead, or feel empowered, or not fear failure, or stretch yourself to meet commitments, if you are pessimistic? And now the key. *Pessimistic people will always be making excuses. Optimistic people rarely make excuses. Therein lies one of the important control factors.* ***We won't eliminate pessimism in the workplace unless or until we get rid of excuses!***

Why? Again, wherever there is short-term thinking, there is reactivity. Wherever there is reactivity, there is the lack of stretching to keep commitments. Wherever there is lack of stretching to keep commitments, there will be little risk-taking. Where there is little risk-taking, there will be fear of failure. Where there is fear of failure, there will be can't-do attitudes. Where there are can't-do attitudes, there will be victimization. Wherever there is victimization, there will be helplessness. And where there is helplessness, there will be pessimism and procrastination. Where there is procrastination, there will be the loss of creativity. And where there is loss of creativity, there will be following instead of leading. Where there is following instead of leading, there will be denial of responsibility. And where there is denial of responsibility, there will be *excuse-making*, just as surely as the sun will come up tomorrow.

And So On

To make the point as clear as possible, we used one example about reactive thinking, and another about pessimism. Notice how the issues began to overlap one another. This is the way it is with tracking *any* negative characteristic in a corporate culture. The real problem is systemic in nature, so no matter where you begin, you soon return to the place where you started. It is like the circumference of a circle. No matter where you start, your journey will always take you back to the point of departure.

Furthermore, as you make the journey around the circumference, if you look to the inside of the circle, the midpoint will always be the same. It is the stake in the ground from which all points on the circle are determined.

Figure 8

So does every negative corporate culture have a midpoint from which all the characteristics of a negative culture can be measured. That midpoint is always, excuse-making.

Figure 9

Because excuses are at the midpoint, they are of central importance. They may or may not show while their cousins hide, and vice versa. But just as with a circle, if there were no midpoint, there would be no circle. Similarly, if there were no excuses, there would be no more negative culture. It would be gone, in one fell swoop! The remedy, the cure, the fix that really works and actually lasts, is to develop a corporate culture—not just in word, but *in deed*—where there are no excuses in the workplace!

In Review

• Understanding the concept of corporate culture is instrumental to fixing the problems that exist in our organizations.

• Every company has a culture. Usually, that culture is much more than what people in the organization think it is. Culture involves all the subtle rules of how to think, feel, and behave in a company. For most organizations, this involves much that is not said, not written, and not framed on a plaque.

• Tradition plays a large role in passing culture on to the next generation. Corporate behavior perpetuates itself.

• Many companies have excuse-laden cultures. The context in which excuses abound consists of many negative characteristics that point to one another, each of which are poisonous to the overall effectiveness of the company.

• These poisons include, among others: denial of responsibility, projection of blame, procrastination, reactive thinking, self-deceit, pessimism, victimization thinking, entitlement attitudes, and the refusal to be accountable.

• Sometimes excuses are evident and these other problems

tend to be hidden. Sometimes it is just the opposite—excuses are difficult to recognize while their relatives are not. A valuable rule of thumb is: (1) If you detect any of the above poisons in your company, you can be sure there are excuses; and (2) If you detect excuses, you can be sure the other poisons are there, too. *The problem is systemic; excuses and their relatives "gowith" each other.*

• If you want results, then excuses must go. By ridding yourself of this one corporate ailment, all the related problems—the poisons—are also cleaned out of the system. The result will be not merely a surviving but a thriving business. And you will be well on the way to becoming number one again!

Notes and Quotes

It is easy to make excuses when we ought to be making opportunities.

Warren Wiersbe

8

In Leadership

Leadership has never been such a hot topic in corporate America. It ranks at the top of the list of developmental programs on which organizations are currently investing large sums of money. Why? Because there is a desperate need for more effective leadership in our ailing companies. Warren Bennis again:

A few years ago a scientist at the University of Michigan listed what he considered to be the ten basic dangers to our society. First and most significant is the possibility of some kind of nuclear war or accident that would destroy the human race.

The second danger is the prospect of a worldwide epidemic, disease, famine, or depression. The third of the scientist's key problems that could bring about the destruction of society is the quality of the management and leadership of our institutions. (1989, p. 14)

****

Leadership is the cornerstone of the whole improvement concept. Leadership is where all progress begins. Without the proper leadership, all of our institutions are in serious trouble.

****

What Is the Problem?

The problem is not that there is an alarming shortage of good, strong people in leadership positions in our corporations. There are plenty. The problem has more to do with how "leadership" has been understood—or more precisely, misunderstood. The tendency in most American businesses has been to see leadership as equivalent to management and administration. This is a huge mistake, as we will discuss in detail later on. The point here is that our misconceptions about leadership have played a major role in causing our middle-of-the-pack performance in world competition.

The problem is that as long as we have an outdated understanding about what constitutes an effective leader, we will continue to invest in obsolete remedies. It would be like investing our money in surgical knives if we still believed that the best cure for infection was to bleed people. The cure is not to keep replaying the old solutions, but to see the problem in a new way. So in this chapter we will look at a new understanding of what true, effective leadership is.

Definition

Lead, v. To guide or conduct by showing the way. To precede; to introduce by going first.

The Leader As an Example

Lee Iacocca, in his book *Iacocca, An Autobiography*, said it well:

> Leadership means setting an example. When you find yourself in a position of leadership, people follow your every move. . .when the leader acts, people watch. So you have to be careful about everything you say and everything you do. (1984, p. 229)

Including how you handle excuses. As the leader goes, so will others follow.

We have made it clear that the winners in the corporate race will be those companies that make purging their culture of excuses an absolute top priority. This task falls directly on the shoulders of the leaders. Ultimately, *it is the responsibility of the leaders to provide the impetus necessary to establish and maintain an excuse-free culture.* The definition of leadership *must* include this one, central theme. Only this kind of leadership can keep the employees of a company from regressing to the excuse-making mode, a mode—you will recall—that is built into people by nature to help them protect themselves. This understanding of leadership is the only way to regain and hold the winning edge in the current marketplace.

Leadership Culture vs. Employee Culture

Technically speaking, a corporation cannot have a culture short of the people who make up the company. A company's culture will always be a combination of the culture of the employees and the culture of the leaders. The leaders may well not be directly responsible for causing a company's culture. Often, the corporate culture was inherited by leaders when they joined or took over the company. But *always*, as the leaders assume control, they are responsible for (1) deciding what type of culture they want, (2) identifying the culture that exists, (3) deciding in what ways they want to intervene to bring the company to the desired culture, (4) implementing the developmental programs to bring the desired results, and (5) measuring the results of the intervention(s) to ensure that they are working. Again, when this is not properly taken care of, excuses will grow as rapidly as weeds. *The company that is not working through strong leaders to avoid an excuse-making culture is a company with an excuse-laden culture. If you don't work to prevent it, you will by default end up with it.* And with the excuse-laden culture will come the whole family of excuse-related characteristics.

The First Problem

As we said, the biggest single problem about leadership in corporate America today is confusion about what constitutes a leader. Many organizations don't differentiate between leadership on the one hand, and management and administration on the other. However, management and administration are the antitheses of the concept of leadership that is required to regain pre-eminence in the global marketplace. The work of those in managerial and administrative positions is defined by their titles. Administrators administer *past* policy, and managers manage *existing* conditions. Certainly, these functions are important in any organization. But they are not to be equated with leadership. Leadership is futuristic by its very nature. Leaders *show the way, precede, and introduce by going first.* Leadership is, by definition, proactive. It is grounded in can-do attitudes, courage to face issues, creative thinking, empowered behavior, optimism, stretching to meet commitments, risk-taking, internalization of responsibility, and long-term focus. In other words, leadership involves excuse-free behavior.

How Is the Confusion of Management and Administration with Leadership a Problem?

In most companies, one of two things is true about

89

the leaders. Either there is no differentiation between leaders, managers, and administrators—in which case leaders function in the same way as managers and administrators; or, if they have been differentiated, the leaders in the company *have been promoted from within the ranks of* management and administration.

An Example

Allen graduated with his MBA from a relatively unknown business college in the Northwest. At age 23 he was hired into a middle management position at a growing manufacturing company. Allen was a conscientious manager. He took his job seriously and, by and large, performed admirably in his various areas of responsibility. His managerial skills were recognized and appreciated, and he was rewarded by working his way through the usual promotion process within the company as it continued to grow. Twenty years later, Allen was offered the position of senior vice-president in charge of operations. Of course, he accepted the job. Why wouldn't he? He had worked long and hard to get there. It was the payoff for his stellar work over the years as a manager.

But what was Allen trained to do? And what was he good at doing? *Managing, period!* His skills were superb at managing existing conditions, which is what a manager does in his company. A leader, remember, is future-focused. A leader's mindset is on what is coming, and his energy goes into figuring out how to lead others into and through that maze. Allen was not trained as a leader. He did not function in any of his work experience as a leader. He did not think as a leader. In fact, he wasn't even aware of how a leader differs from a manager in job responsibility.

It is now five years later. Allen is 48 years old. What might we suppose about the profile of this company under Allen's leadership? Is the corporation likely to be on the cutting edge of innovation in its field? Is it likely to be gaining market share or losing market share? Is it pro-actively seeking larger accounts, or is it more focused on managing the accounts that they currently have? When projections aren't met, is Allen of the mindset to take responsibility for that, or does he hunt for the perfect scapegoat?

Allen isn't a make-believe character. He is real, and here are the facts. Every year for five consecutive years Allen has fired one or more of the four VP's who report to him. Why? Because every year Allen would go to the CEO and make his projections on what the company profits would be—and every year the company fell short. So every year he fired at least one VP. He projected all of the blame for the company's failure onto the VP's. The first two or three years, it was easy to think there might be some validity in Allen's behavior. Now, however, after five years of the same thing over and over, Allen is in trouble. The CEO is beginning to catch on. He has stopped wondering why the company was losing good people. He sees that Allen is firing VP's because of his unwillingness or inability to admit that he's the person who is responsible for the failure(s). **Allen is making excuses!**

It Is Not Entirely Allen's Fault

Let's talk about how Allen made it through twenty

years as a manager. Chances are that he did it by playing the game of corporate politics and by keeping his nose clean. Many times over those years Allen witnessed a recurring phenomenon. Some manager in the company would show a few signs of leadership by taking a risk here and there, and occasionally failing. As problems developed up the executive ladder, Allen observed that the person who took a risk was scapegoated and let go or forced out of his job. He learned quickly that the emphasis was on placing blame rather than learning from mistakes.

So you see, the Allens in corporate America don't necessarily get to the top through superior performance. Often they get there by not taking risks, by not being proactive, by being average, by continuing to do what's been done in the past, and by learning how to stay out of harm's way. Such behavior serves to keep them out of trouble, and therefore they manage to survive while others around them take the fall. Because they have survived, they are the only ones left with any seniority. So natually, they get the promotions.

By the time the Allens finally make it to the top, they have totally absorbed this corporate way of thinking. It is only natural, and to be expected, that they will handle problems from the top exactly as they saw them handled all the years they were coming up the corporate ladder. When problems develop that they should be taking responsibility for, they will find the necessary scapegoats and get rid of them. Typically the goats will be those individuals who have demonstrated a flair for being proactive, for making a few waves by showing some initiative, and by taking an occasional risk. Risk-takers will always have some failures, and their failures usually show. When their mistakes are visible, they unfortunately become easy to hunt down and kill.

And then we wonder, where have all the leaders gone?

****

So Where Is the Problem?

We've seen that the problem is not entirely with Allen. In fact, if the CEO fires Allen thinking that letting him go will solve the problem, he will likely only repeat the cycle and promote someone into that position who also came from the ranks of management. That person will likely be someone who did well as a manager, but who nonetheless has a managerial thinking pattern, just like Allen. In time, the problem can only repeat itself. This is because the problem is built into the corporate system. It is like inbreeding in a family. If one child proves to be maladapted in some way due to genetic distortions from the inbreeding, what good will it do to boot him out of the family and raise another child to replace him? The next one is likely to be maladapted, as well. And the next one. And the next one. And so on. Firing the person who manifests the symptoms is rarely the best solution. In fact, rarely is it anything other than a very temporary solution. The symptoms will repeat themselves again and again until we recognize what the real problem is and fix it.

The Formula for Corporate Victory

In the quest to become number one again, the edge

will go to the companies that do whatever it takes to develop excuse-free cultures. This will happen only when we begin to train, hire, and promote people who either have leadership skills already, or who demonstrate the clear potential for developing into leaders. The difficulty has been that we've never identified what leadership skills are in relation to eliminating excuse-making from our companies. So not having identified them, we haven't been able to recognize or evaluate or foster those skills. It's just never been a goal to shoot for. But that's about to change.

The Scope of the Problem

How many Allens are there in corporate America? How many billions of dollars does it cost our companies because of all the Allens out there? How many billions more will our companies lose by allowing the problem to continue? If the current system of hiring and placing so-called leaders is allowed to continue uninterrupted, our corporations will continue to be plagued by excuse-laden cultures. And you can be absolutely sure of the following two things:

• If excuses are made and tolerated by "leaders" at the top of an organization, then excuse-making will permeate the culture from top to bottom. This is because an example has been set that excuse-making is permissable. President Truman made popular the saying, "The buck stops here." Many CEO's pride themselves by displaying a similar motto in their offices. Rarely do we think to ask, however, that if the buck stops at the top, why was it allowed to get that far up the ladder in the first place? "Passing the buck" is nothing more than a colloquial expression for the passing of blame, the refusal to accept responsibility, and the making of excuses. "The buck stops here" implies that it doesn't stop before it gets all the way to the top. If this is true, then excuses must have been allowed. And when excuses are allowed, they will be like rats in the warehouse: For every rat you see, there are hundreds, maybe thousands, that you don't see. Similarly, for every excuse that you see at the top of an organization, there will be hundreds, maybe thousands, of excuses down the ranks of that organization that may go unnoticed. Why unnoticed? Because excuse-making is a way of thinking. It is the logic of much of corporate America. It is commonplace, and what is common goes mostly unnoticed.

• If excuses are allowed at the bottom of an organization, they will bubble all the way up to the top of the organization. Why? Because as people are promoted up the line, they carry the culture with them. As with Allen, the way he saw it done is the way he learned to do it. And it is the way he will continue to do it. This is the meaning of tradition and the powerful role it plays in perpetuating a company's culture.

And Let's Not Forget

Where there are excuses, there will be projection of blame, entitlement attitudes, reactive thinking, can't-do attitudes, poor teamwork, pessimism, non-risk-taking, incompetence, disrespect, avoidance of issues, lack of focus,

helplessness, self-deceit, procrastination, non-results orienta-
tion, lack of creativity, absence of stretching to keep
commitments, distrust, conflictual relationships, fear of failure, non-accountability, denial of responsibility, follower
mentality, victimization mindsets, short-term focus, and
much, much more. *These are the viruses that are sapping
the energy—and the vitality—from corporate America. The
good news is that they will all die off when we eliminate
excuses from the workplace.*

The Point

Those in leadership positions determine what the
corporate culture will be. When companies have a negative
culture (i.e., an excuse-making culture) and those at the top
are moving in the same direction due to tradition, you have
companies that are, or soon will be, in trouble in today's
economy. On the other hand, when companies have a
negative culture and the leaders are moving in the direction
of an excuse-free culture, you have companies hard at work,
well-focused, and destined to achieve the winning edge in
the marketplace.

Again, the only way to achieve the latter of these
two alternatives is to start by recognizing that leadership
and management/administration are very different concepts.
Does it make sense to assume that an outstanding defensive
end in professional football would be an effective head
coach for some football franchise? Defensive ends and
head coaches are quite different beings. Not that one can't
become the other in some instances, just as some good
managers become effective leaders in corporations. But to
assume that being effective in one position makes you

unquestionably effective in another is simply invalid.

The point is, *to assume either that good managers are automatically promotable to leadership positions, or to assume that good managers and administrators **are** the leaders in your company, is to unknowingly participate in an excuse-making corporate culture, the cost of which in dollars is astronomical.* Effective leadership—the type that will provide the impetus to lead your company into the winner's circle by creating an excuse-free organization—does not happen through allowing the wheels of tradition to grind on and on. Effective leaders must be sought out, hired, promoted, rewarded, developed, and trained. This is no small task. But it is certainly possible once the problem is recognized.

How do you recognize a true leader according to our specific definition of leadership?

1. First and Foremost, a Leader Has Vision

Vision is a guiding purpose that propels a leader forward. He knows where he wants to go; he thinks futuristically; he looks forward. His vision serves as a beacon, and nothing will deter him from the accomplishment of that vision. There is no room for excuses in a leader's primary purpose. Excuses will only get in his way. He simply doesn't have time for them. Jimmy Johnson, the ex-head coach of the Dallas Cowboys who guided his team to two consecutive Super Bowl victories, had a vision of winning the Super Bowl when he took over the reins of a failing football organization. His first year he won very few games. But he was never deterred from his vision. Despite his many differences with owner Jerry Jones, the

97

same ones that led to his eventual departure, he refused to let those differences interfere with where he was going. They never became an excuse for not realizing his vision.

2. A Leader Has Respect for Authority

This surprises most people because we tend to think that leaders *are* the authority and that they don't need to have respect for it outside of themselves. But whether a leader's authority figure is a supervisor, a customer, a checkbook, or even God, you must have respect for an outside authority, whoever or whatever it is. Let's look at an example of one outside authority that you always have in business, namely your customers. If you're not respectful of their authority, you soon begin to lose them. And if you lose too many, you're out of business. Suppose an important customer isn't receiving delivery of a critical product when he needs it. Do you call that customer and give him the excuse, "I'm sorry, but my production people haven't been doing their job lately," or do you respect the authority of that customer and figure out how to get him what he needs, regardless? *It is not possible to respect authority and make excuses.* The two just don't go together. There is a job to get done, and excuses cannot be allowed to get in the way. It is people who *don't* respect authority who give excuses. They are busy projecting the blame elsewhere.

3. A Leader Is Self-Confident

People who are self-confident don't make excuses—

not because they never fail, but because they are willing to admit to their own mistakes. Those with a high level of self-confidence will not be afraid to follow their guiding vision. They see failure as a valuable learning experience, not as the end of the road. Self-confidence is something that is pervasive. It relates closely to self-esteem. The leader who isn't self-confident and doesn't feel good about himself won't be given the opportunity to lead for very long. People who would otherwise follow soon sense the leader's lack of self-confidence, and they abandon that person to gravitate to some other individual who *is* self-confident—someone to whom they can attach themselves.

4. A Leader Is Enthusiastic

Enthusiasm, self-confidence, high self-esteem, and optimism are all closely related concepts. The enthusiastic leader is someone whom people look forward to being around. He is someone who will maintain an even keel in an organization and not allow moods to get low. He can sense it when people are having down moments, and his enthusiasm will help pick them up. Enthusiasm is infectious, and those who have it are those whom others return to for a boost to their batteries when the going gets tough. Enthusiasm attracts people, and this is what makes those who have it such effective leaders. People with enthusiasm are people who generally take responsibility, don't project blame, and don't have time for excuses. They are proactive people who are typically on the move toward achievement of their goals. They have things to do, places to go to, and people to see. Their rule is "let's get it done" rather than "let's make excuses."

5. A Leader Has a High Energy Level

Energy is a direct descendent of the optimism of people who are looking forward. Leaders cannot be looking backwards. They must be continually focusing on their objective, and this requires—and generates—high levels of energy. Energy is not just the *speed* at which people work, but also the *length* to which people work. Many individuals want to get ahead in life, but too often they don't want to do what is necessary to make that happen. Success requires long, hard hours. It takes a high energy level to maintain this activity. There have been numerous studies that have linked physical fitness to success in the workplace. There is a direct correlation between physical fitness, high energy, and success. Energetic people have the ability to go into afterburn. Good leaders are people who, when they find themselves in very difficult situations without much time to act, can call on their energy, fire the afterburners, and go into the hyperdrive speed that allows them to do whatever has to be done in a limited period of time.

6. Leaders Focus on the Big Picture

The difference between vision and focusing on the big picture involves the issue of not being sidetracked. Many people have vision, but they aren't effective leaders because they lose sight of the big picture and let the small issues distract them. Once a true leader is focused on the bigger picture, he's not going to be sidetracked or daunted by small failures or problems along the way. He realizes that it is acceptable, sometimes even necessary, to lose some battles in order to win the war. Therefore, the leader will take the smaller setbacks in stride, and he will have no compelling need to rationalize, project blame, externalize, or make excuses.

7. A Leader Is an Intuitive and Inductive Decision-Maker

He surrounds himself with a wealth of information from which to make his decisions. He trusts his intuitive powers to help lead him in the right direction. And he has developed a decision-making process that allows him to see trends and make accurate predictions based on particular facts. An intuitive and inductive decision-maker is pro-active rather than reactive, and therefore has little need or room for excuses, either from himself or others.

8. Leaders Expect Success

Good leaders create an expectation of success in whatever they undertake. They expect it from themselves, and they expect it from those whom they lead. If you expect success from others, then by definition you will not accept excuses. The expectation of success propels you through all the diversions. It is the antithesis of excuse-making. It is no-option behavior. Don Shula, head coach of the Miami Dolphins, expects his players to play penalty-free games. As a result, the Dolphins lead the league year after year in fewest penalties.

Leaders don't expect to fail, so they "backstop" themselves for failures along the way. The concept of backstopping involves the recognition that, like all human beings, the leader has certain weaknesses and shortcomings that need to be compensated for in the people around him. The leader must leverage his strengths, and hire toward his weaknesses. That in itself is the direct opposite of excuse-making. The leader expects to succeed, so he does not allow cracks in which excuses can grow.

9. Leaders Are Self-Disciplined

No matter what the job, no matter what the task, there will always be elements that are distasteful. The ability to have the self-discipline to do the unpleasant means that you are going to accept responsibility for the end result. People who don't have self-discipline will always be able to find an excuse for not doing the difficult, unpleasant, and distasteful things.

10. Leaders Are Willing to Take Risks

You can't risk unless you are willing to fail (even though you expect to succeed). You're not willing to fail unless you have the self-confidence to face that failure. You can't face failure unless you are willing to take responsibility for your actions, and you're not going to take responsibility for your actions if you project blame by making excuses. Good leaders will take risks, and they will have managers and administrators around them to serve as checks and balances to help mitigate any loss from dangerously high risks.

In addition, effective leaders will take the risk of allowing others around them to experience failure. When the leader is focused on the big picture, he sees that a few small failures by those whom he leads are of little significance. Yet the lessons learned from those failures can make a huge difference in the development of his people. A true leader understands the distinction between "failing to learn" and "failing, to learn."

11. A Leader Has Mental Toughness and Emotional Stability

This entails a wide range of things, but basically what it says is that a person has himself or herself together and does not feel easily frightened or threatened by situations or personalities. If you have emotional and mental strength, you are willing to face your shortcomings and your weaknesses, try to understand them, and do what is necessary to overcome them. You are also willing to confront issues, including criticism that others may make of you. You are willing to hear the bad news. Mentally tough and emotionally stable people do not need to rely on excuses. They can look at things the way they really are. This characteristic is essential for leaders because they must lead through the waters of "what really is," not what he or others unrealistically hope or wish things to be. In other words, leaders have the mental toughness and emotional stability to be grounded in the reality of the situation, whatever that situation is.

12. Leaders Will Recognize the Need for Additional Knowledge

Effective leaders never profess to know it all. They realize there is always more to learn and there are different ways of doing things. They are willing to submit themselves to the stresses and strains of a mentor relationship. They are willing to admit that they don't always know what to do. People who are willing to accept the fact that they need to learn more are also willing to admit to failures and inadequacies, and to subject themselves to discomfort in trying something new and different. And this is not the sign of someone who is an excuse-giver. Quite the opposite is true.

13. A Leader Is a Good Listener

There is a very ironic twist here. Most people perceived as leaders are those who are giving inspiring advice in their attempts to lead people to greater things. But let's face it, the best teaching method—and a good leader has to be a good teacher—is through self-discovery. This means encouraging others to use their own minds and develop their own problem-solving skills. A leader can do this by listening to the ideas and opinions of his subordinates. *The first sign of greatness in a leader is the ability to develop greatness in others.* You cannot develop good leadership qualities in others unless you are a good listener.

We've seen many CEO's who think they are good leaders because they are good "tellers." But the problem is, as soon as they are out of the picture, their organization is incapable of effective operation because their people have turned into followers. A leader who leads by telling breeds followers. And breeding followers invites excuses when the followers can't operate without their leader.

14. Leaders Are Lucky

Effective leaders tend to have good luck. Ineffective "leaders" tend to have bad luck. Luck is a funny thing. When Gary Player was at his peak as a professional golfer, someone said to him, "You're a very lucky golfer." He responded, "Yes, the more I practice the luckier I get." Luck is a perception of others more than anything else. Good leaders will admit to luck, while poor leaders tend to take credit for luck. Luck is the result of persistence, observation, the ability to focus on the right thing at the right time, and the absence of excuses. If you do these things, you're going to get lucky and you're going to win. Sometimes you're going to win for reasons that you don't understand at the time, and this is what most people call luck. *Luck is when preparation meets with opportunity, and the opportunity is recognized and seized.* If a person prepares enough, is persistent enough, and refuses to be an excuse-maker, he will get lucky sooner or later.

15. A Leader Is Introspective

Good leaders are those who are willing to look at themselves and face their failures without externalizing and making excuses. Leaders must always be improving, and the way they're going to improve is by examining themselves and admitting their weaknesses and failures. Introspection takes time. It is a discipline that requires from one-half to one hour a day to really perfect. Introspection is vitally important to effective leadership because, in a sense, it continuously hones all of the other leadership qualities.

16. Leaders Have Integrity

Integrity is more of a personal trait than anything else. People with integrity are honest, they are trustworthy, and they do the things that are right regardless of the personal consequences to themselves in many instances. Because of this, people with integrity are consistent in the way they deal with certain circumstances. To help see the importance of integrity in a leader, look at a person without integrity. This person shirks responsibility and avoids admitting to weakness or failure. He will project blame, make excuses, and refuse to accept responsibility. Anyone who has tried to follow the lead of an individual without integrity knows what an impossible task that is.

17. Leaders Have Control

Many people in leadership positions feel as if they are out of control, often even admitting to that fact. The primary reason a leader goes out of control is because he is unable to differentiate between real issues and excuses.

There is one behavior that a leader must be in control of above all others, and that is excuse-making behavior. As soon as a leader accepts excuses, he surrenders control. At that point, the excuse-making disease has taken control over the operation of that leader's company (or his unit in the company).

18. A Leader Is Decisive

People within companies often can't make decisions because those in leadership positions can't, or won't. It has never been more true than in corporate America today that *he who hesitates is lost.* Being decisive wasn't as necessary in the past. Corporations could use their momentum to run over the competitor that challenged them. Today, however, time is of the essence. A company can go from market dominance to collapse in a few years as opposed to a few decades. Never before has it been so important that our leaders be decisive.

19. A Leader Is a Good Communicator

Traditionally, an effective communicator was one who was good at "telling." To communicate meant to inform. The good communicator typically could write or speak clearly, if not eloquently. The leader that is capable of demanding excuse-free behavior, however, places more emphasis on mutual understanding than on his eloquence. His goal is to make sure that those he leads comprehend his vision and understand his expectations. Otherwise, his plan won't work. When people don't understand, they are set up to fail. And when failure is imminent, so is excuse-making.

20. A Leader Is Sensitive

To what? To other people's feelings. A leader must not embarrass or humiliate those whom he leads. People tend to become self-protective—even to the point of being dishonest—if they are not treated with dignity and respect. The effective leader assumes the self-worth of others, and works to build trust with them. Only in this context will it be safe for employees to not give excuses when faced with threatening situations.

The Point, Once Again

Leadership and management/administration are, by definition, different concepts. When leadership is understood in a company as the same thing as management and administration, or when those in positions of leadership have been promoted from the ranks of managers and adminstrators, *the "leaders" will likely not be prepared to lead the company into an excuse-free culture unless they have been properly trained to do so.* And such training is rare.

Remember, if you want to change the culture of an organization, you must begin with the leaders. It is their responsibility to bring about the desired changes. But to effectively change the culture, your leaders must be *true* leaders. That means that the majority of the criteria just discussed must be met, or the results will be—whether you like to think so or not—an excuse-ridden culture.

Essentially, to ensure that you have the leaders who can make your culture excuse-free, you have one of two choices. Either you train the people you currently have according to the accurate definition of what constitutes an effective leader, or you move the current people out and hire new leaders who possess the appropriate qualities. It's that simple.

In Review

• A corporation that is burdened with excuses is less than a fully functioning company. Megadollars are being lost that could otherwise be made.

• An excuse-ridden culture can only be changed with the proper leadership.

• The first step toward making that change is to recognize that the problem is both spawned and perpetuated through confused perceptions of what leadership is.

• One of the major reasons that our corporations have become excuse-infested is because the source of the problem is built into the very heart of the corporate system. This is why until now it has gone mostly unrecognized. That problem is the promotion of people into leadership positions who have been trained to think like managers and administrators. This statement is not intended as an attack on managers and administrators. Far from it. *Effective managers and administrators are indispensable to the successful operation of a company. It's just that they may not be as effective at managing change (i.e., leading) as your culture requires.* Managing change demands different skills, different beliefs, different goals, different traits. Managing policy and managing change are as different as night and day.

• *The elimination of excuses from the workplace begins and ends in leadership.* There are only two options. Either train those who are currently in leadership positions to be leaders, or replace them with people who have strong leadership qualities. There are no other choices if you want your company devoid of reactive thinking, can't-do attitudes, poor teamwork, conflictual relationships, short-term focus, denial of responsibility, projection of blame, and so on. When leaders target the elimination of excuses, all these other corporate poisons are flushed out. When this is accomplished, results will certainly happen. And your company will be well on its way to recapturing first place.

9

In Planning

Two of the biggest problems in corporate America today are *lack of focus* and *lack of consistency*. Goal-setting and planning are intended to prevent these problems. The fact that many companies still struggle with these issues suggests that the entire planning process is often fraught with excuses.

That being the case, it is important to explore some of the reasons why and how this is true. If we can grasp the dynamics of how excuses manifest themselves in the corporate planning process, we will have taken a giant stride toward seeing the immensity, the subtlety, and the destructive potential of the problem of excuses in the workplace. Not the least of these is the fact that excuses cost our companies literally billions of dollars every year.

Definition

Plan, n. An outline; a draft; a map. A scheme for making, doing, or arranging something; a project; a program; a schedule.

Definition

Plan, v. *The act of developing* an outline, draft, map. The act of developing a scheme for making, doing, or arranging something, etc.

The Problem of Confusing the Two

We invite you to take a long, hard look at the fact that the word "plan" is both a noun and a verb. That may seem insignificant at first, but in the corporate world it is anything but insignificant. The confusion by leadership between the noun and verb meanings of the word "plan" leads to difficulties of far-reaching proportions in the workplace. "Plan" as a *noun* is a thing, a document, a product, a blueprint, a map. "Plan" as a *verb* is a process, an action.

If you ask company owners, presidents, and CEO's the question "Is planning important?" the majority would answer that it is. Yet what "the planning process" means to most of them is that they must somehow end up with a written document that they can thereafter refer to as "the plan." This is exactly what "plan" means in the noun sense of the word. Consequently, most companies have one or more of the following:

- a strategic plan
- a business plan
- a sales and marketing plan
- an operations plan
- a product development plan

In many cases, large sums of money have been invested to develop such plans. Yet most of them are not living, breathing entities. Odds are that they are sitting on a bookshelf collecting dust or are neatly filed away in some obscure drawer or cabinet, out of sight and all but forgotten.

Why Does This Happen?

As a general rule, smaller companies create plans because of some external influence. For example, the SBA, the bank, or the shareholders may require it. If it's not an external factor that is requiring it, it is an outside source that is influencing it. Or the CEO may read a book that inspires a desire to generate a plan, or he may overhear other CEO's talking about their business plans. As a result, unfortunately, the vast majority of plans are driven by external pressure to prepare them.

It may well be the case that an outside source, such as the bank, may want planning to occur as a *process*, as in the verb sense of the word. The problem is that when those who prepare the plans are only fulfilling a requirement from the outside, they place relatively little value on it. The result is that the plan becomes a product (noun) rather than a process (verb). The purpose of the plan in the preparers' minds may be simply to impress those who will be reading it. As a result we have a multitude of independent consultants who specialize in putting together business plans for companies, or in helping companies put together business plans for themselves. Since business plans are sometimes judged on the basis of volume and appearance, the resulting plans are too often little more than window dressing.

Now this is not an inexpensive process. Companies can spend many thousands of dollars to get such a plan done. But even more importantly, the plan will have very little value to the company beyond satisfying the needs or requirements of the outside source. There is no attempt to systematically communicate the plan throughout the ranks, there is no buy-in by the employees of the company, and there is no way to measure progress or regress with regard to achieving the goals as set forth in the plan. So what happens to it? On the shelf it goes, thus making the whole project a waste of time and money. This is a perfect example of what we mean by "plan" in the noun sense of the word.

In Bigger Companies

In mid-sized and larger companies, planning might be done for some of the same reasons—for example, to meet the expectations of the board of directors. An additional motivation in bigger companies, however, is that planning is one of those things that corporations are just supposed to do.

Imagine for a moment that we pay a visit to The

Average Corporation, USA. We seek out all the executives, managers, and administrators. Then we ask each of them separately (and confidentially so it doesn't upset the boss) the following question: "What do you think of the planning process around here?" Most of them would probably admit that they see very little value in it.

Why? Because the plan was prepared for the wrong reasons—to create a product that ends up on the shelf. Since it is not perceived as having any real value, efforts to revive the plan will not be taken seriously, and the plan (noun) becomes even less valuable. While those asked might agree that coming up with a plan is an important thing to do (because the boss tells them it must be done), they also see it as a time waster and as a distraction from their daily work routines. They will generally look at it as something that the boss handed down to them, but that is going to have little if any consequence to the company.

Subsequently, for the majority of people the whole planning process becomes an exercise in futility. Sure, the plan will be prepared as required, and it will probably look good. People will generally put their most optimistic projections into the plan to put the best face on it. But when it's all finished, chances are that it will be set aside to collect dust, right beside the plans from last year and the year before that and the years before that. And it will more than likely never be reviewed again, not even at year's end—which further magnifies the feelings of futility among all who had a hand in preparing it.

What Does This Have to Do with Excuses?

Whether a company approaches the "plan" as a

product or as an active process is a function of the culture of that company. *The "plan" is nothing more nor less than the solidification and the manifestation of the corporate culture.* If the culture is reactive, we will find the plan sitting on the shelf—except when it is dusted off for the purpose of finding out who to blame. If the culture is pessimistic, or tolerates procrastination and irresponsibility, or is short-term focused, or exhibits poor teamwork, or demonstrates can't-do attitudes, *we will find the plan sitting on the shelf.* And if you find a company plan sitting on the shelf, you will also find an abundance of can't-do attitudes, short-term focus, procrastination, denial of responsibility, and so on in that company. Count on it! They always go together.

In short, *wherever there are strategic plans, business plans, sales and marketing plans, **any kind of plans** that are collecting dust or filling drawer space, there you have an excuse-making culture.* And because that is true, you also have all of the members of the family that go with excuses living in your corporate environment, whether or not they are welcome, and whether or not you like it. That's just the way it is because of the systemic nature of the problem.

Corporations Tend to Encourage Excuses

Earlier in this book we pointed out the tendency of corporations to allow and even indirectly encourage excuses. Nowhere is this more true than in the planning process. Let's look more closely at how this phenomenon happens.

Corporation XYZ goes through a yearly planning

process. Bill, the CEO, mandates that the process is to begin on November 1 and must be concluded by December 21 in order to get it out to all the employees by the beginning of the January-through-December fiscal year. This same planning procedure has happened for several years at XYZ. So Bill's only real job is to remind the management staff in October that the date is soon approaching and to get ready to go through the process. He may do this by copying last year's memo, penciling in the new date, and having his secretary retype it and distribute a copy to each manager.

The planning process itself is built around a departmental questionnaire that was introduced by an outside consulting firm six years ago, for which the company paid a sizeable fee. The manager of each department is expected to collect the information through meetings with his people, build it into a departmental report, and submit it to the CEO's office by December 21.

Here We Go Again!

Every year the planning process happens in approximately the same way. The managers grumble about the extra workload, but of course don't say anything to Bill, since he's the one who mandated it. They postpone tackling the project until the last possible minute, at which time they call a few quick departmental meetings with the people they manage. Most of the people in each of the departments gripe and complain about having to "do this stupid questionnaire one more time," wondering what good it does. Like Bill, they hunt down last year's material and make a few small changes here and there before photocopying it.

In the end, the reports somehow get completed and are submitted to Bill on time. He reads them over, consolidates them, and thereby builds his plan for the upcoming fiscal year.

On December 29 a newsletter from the CEO's office is released to each of the managers, forecasting the market and making projections for the year. Finally, after several narratives, comes the bottom line: "WE EXPECT THE MARKET TO TAKE A SLIGHT TURN DOWNWARD THIS YEAR. WE ALL MUST TIGHTEN OUR BELTS AND FIND WAYS TO CUT COSTS. IF WE DO THAT AND WORK TO MAINTAIN OUR CURRENT LEVEL OF SALES, WE WILL ACTUALLY SHOW PROFIT OF AROUND 10 PERCENT OVER THE NEXT YEAR." The report concludes with a few pages of numbers detailing how much each department can spend, and what the sales numbers will have to be.

Once the managers have received the newsletter from the CEO's office, it now becomes their responsibility to communicate this "plan" to the employees at their first departmental meeting in January. And they do. And everyone hears it. And everyone says, "Fine, okay." And the plan goes on the shelf and stays there, collecting dust.

Now if this example is a bit trite, it is also more than a bit accurate. It represents the way that many, many companies go about the so-called "planning process." It is based on "plan" as a noun. The attitude seems to be, "Let's get a document, a product, that we can circulate throughout the company, and then be done with it."

Now Come the Excuses

Let's jump ahead to October of the same year. Nine of the ten departments have overspent their budgets. Bill confronts the managers of each of these departments and asks what happened. This is what he hears:

- "I told my people. They just don't listen."
  (Denial of responsibility, projection of blame,
  victimization, externalization.)

- "Costs have gone up over what was projected. We
  could only cut out so much and still function."
  (Denial of responsibility, projection of blame,
  victimization, externalization.)

- "It will improve over the next couple of months,
  promise." (Self-deceit.)

- "We did the best we could." (Helplessness.)

- "Your projections might have been a little too
  optimistic." (Denial of responsibility, projection of
  blame, externalization.)

- "A couple of our people were spending way over
  their budgets. But we got rid of them when we
  found out what was happening." (Reactive thinking, projection of blame, denial of responsibility,
  externalization.)

Do you see what these are? These are all excuses, and, as such, they point to the dangerous conditions in the parentheses, which are the same ones that lie beneath the the waterline in the iceberg. These conditions—denial of responsibility, projection of blame, and so on—seriously jeopardize the overall effectiveness of the corporation.

So What Does This Mean?

When corporations proceed with the planning process as if "plan" were a noun, that process both *expresses* and *spawns* an excuse-making culture. Most companies believe that the plan (noun) should forecast what will happen in the coming year. Yet projections in the plan will inevitably be unrealistic because changes will occur during the year—changes in the market, changes in product, changes in personnel, and so on. Because of these changes, it is unlikely that people will be able to live up to all the expectations spelled out in the plan.

Hence employees are "forced" to protect themselves against criticism and blame, and they do this by making excuses. This is what we mean by saying that corporations tend to encourage excuses. There is nothing devious about it on either side. Making excuses is an automatic, spontaneous, instantaneous reaction by individuals—managers and employees alike—to avoid emotional pain, including the criticism of not meeting the expectations as spelled out in the plan (noun).

When Planning Is a Verb

Planning in a proactive, creative, optimistic, can-do, stretching, responsible, long-term-focused company is a verb. It is something that you not only *develop* proactively, you also *implement* it proactively. It is an ongoing process from the beginning of the year to the end, and then it begins anew. If a plan isn't a working plan, it is no different from an architect's blueprint that never gets pulled out of its cardboard tube. Or a professional hockey player's playbook that never once gets opened. We don't build skyscrapers or professional athletic teams with noun-type plans. How can we expect to build healthy organizations that way? Blueprints and playbooks are dog-eared, wrinkled, soiled, and spotted with coffee stains and chewing gum. They are used—frequently, if not daily. They are living, breathing documents that reflect the pulse of those whom they serve. This is what a "plan" must be if we are to rid our companies of the fatal disease of excuse-making. And it can be done!

Planning and Goals

It is not uncommon for corporations to think of "planning" and "goal-setting" as two separate entities. This is because of our tendency to look at "plan" as a noun, as a product, as something to create and then forget about.

Now along comes the task of motivating people. One way to do that is to have them set goals. So time management seminars and goal-setting workshops are conducted to help people reach for something higher. But they

121

don't work—and they won't work, because these strategies are not integrated into the larger "plan." The notes and other materials from such programs, therefore, just become something more for people to put on the shelf, thereafter to collect dust.

The point is that goal-setting is a meaningless concept unless it is married to the planning process. A viable plan must begin with input from all those affected by the plan. It must proceed with buy-in by everyone and sign-on to the program. Next comes the process of interpreting company goals into departmental goals, again with input from all affected, and buy-in by everyone into the plan. Then comes the interpretation of the departmental goals into individual goals which each employee negotiates with his or her supervisor. Finally, the goals must be benchmarked, monitored, measured, upgraded, and adjusted, until they are living, workable periodic goals. Then and only then do you have a "plan" in the healthy, excuse-free sense of the word.

Imagine for a moment what can happen in a company when the business plan is translated into every employee's individual work-related goals, where everyone is responsible for and accountable to those goals, and the progress toward achieving them would be continuously measured and rewarded. What would happen to employee morale? What would happen regarding motivation, incentive, and productivity? Ultimately, what would happen to the bottom line? Clearly, this would be a workplace where there is no room for excuses. Where there is no room for excuses, there is no room for all of its negative cousins, either, and subsequently, *there will be results!*

Planning and Implementation

Often the problem with implementing the corporate plan is not due to the plan itself. Many plans are well conceived and well thought out, often under the guidance of a consulting firm that specializes in corporate planning. The problem, rather, is in the absence of a plan to implement the plan. Without such a "metaplan," no one is given ultimate responsibility to see it through. The result, of course, will be more excuses. Since there is no accountability for the implementation of the plan, before long it will take a back seat to one crisis or another, and will soon be forgotten. The point is that *there must be no excuse for making excuses about not implementing the plan, even if that means revising the plan.* Never should a company follow a plan (noun) to its own grave. Rather, it must be committed to the planning process (verb), and that ongoing process might well include changing the plan as needed.

Planning Is a Team Process

A plan—like a chain—is only as strong as its weakest link. Too often we have plans that fall apart because just one individual failed to provide his necessary "link." By definition, a plan is something that is all-encompassing. It brings together multitudes of departments, disciplines, and types of people. But while the planning process is usually a team process, the execution of the plan is too often assumed to be an individual process. One of the breakdowns of plan implementation is that individuals who are left to execute the plans are not held accountable to the team that helped make those plans. This opens the door to all kinds of excuse-making when the plan eventually fails.

Long-Term vs. Short-Term Plans

The planning process consists of two broad categories: long-term and short-term. One of the difficulties companies run into is the incongruity between short- and long-term plans. This relates back to the discussion in Chapter 7 about corporate culture. In an excuse-laden culture, short-term thinking is prevalent. Short-term is where the crises are, and crises always capture immediate attention. This makes long-term planning almost impossible. Furthermore, if any long-term planning does occur, it will typically be at odds with the short-term focus that results from reacting to one crisis after another.

A Diagnostic Tool

One clear indicator of an excuse-laden company is that virtually everything has top priority. Everything is a crisis. It is a mentality of constantly fighting brush fires. There is no primary direction and purpose, so it's impossible to set priorities. A company that doesn't set priorities is a company that's not planning effectively. And a company that's not planning effectively is a company full of excuses.

Where Should Plans Start?

There has been a good deal of debate lately as to whether plans should start at the top of an organization and negotiate their way down, or whether they should start at the bottom and accumulate as they go up until they become a master plan. The truth is that it probably doesn't make any difference where the planning begins. What *does* make the difference is whether or not there is buy-in and ownership (acceptance of responsibility for one's own part) at all levels. If you don't have ownership, excuse-making will naturally happen.

Here is an example we see time and again. Corporate headquarters will set a budget. Nobody in the various divisions will say anything as to whether the plan is good or bad, achievable or not achievable. They just shrug their shoulders, and then halfway into the fiscal year they say things like, "We're never going to make that budget." "They don't know what it's like in the field." "They don't understand that we can't get our workers to produce at that level for the amount of money we're allowed to pay them." "It wasn't realistic in the first place." "We didn't set it. In fact, they never even consulted with us." "We don't have to worry about it. We don't even have to take responsibility for it."

What is this except one excuse after another? Ownership is a big chunk of what it takes to get rid of excuses. If you have ownership of a plan, you have the basis for being able to take excuses out of performance.

125

Measurement and Adjustment

Another reason why the planning process can fail miserably is because of the lack of measurement to evaluate whether or not the plan is being achieved. Periodic measurement helps to keep "plan" as a verb. People, if left to their own devices, don't like to have a plan. They are more than happy to let the plan lapse into its noun form. Goals frighten and stretch us, and move us out of our comfort zones. Goals keep people from doing things the way they've always done them in the past.

The point is that the loftiest of plans and the best of goals will die on the vine unless there is accountability to the plan through measuring the progress and adjusting behaviors as necessary along the way.

"Plan" As a Verb Is All-Encompassing

In order for "plan" to be a verb rather than a noun, planning must (1) penetrate vertically throughout the organization, and (2) include things that are usually not thought of as part of the planning process: personal planning, written goals, agendas for meetings, interest in what will happen in the future of the company as it relates to one's job, and so on. Without these, planning cannot be a living, breathing function of the organization. And where it is *not* a living, breathing function of the organization, there will not be results, but there will be plenty of excuses.

In Conclusion

• "Plan" as a verb always has value even if the goals are not always reached. Much of the value of planning is in the process, during which everyone in the company takes an active, responsible role. The planning process is as important, if not more important, than the final written plan.

• "Plan" as a noun has value only if it is the result of a carefully designed planning process. In terms of results, perfect execution of an ill-conceived plan looks much like poor execution of a well-conceived plan. It is important to make sure that your plan is properly prepared, because therein lies your only hope for proper execution. Otherwise your people are set up to fail, and they will be "forced" to protect themselves with excuses. And where there are excuses, there will be a multitude of other corporate sins. Plan on it.

The Scope of the Problem

Notes and Quotes

We have forty million reasons for failure, but not a single excuse.

Rudyard Kipling

10

In Teamwork

Teamwork in organizations was a relatively obscure concept a few years back. Today, everybody in corporate America is talking about it. Why the big emphasis on work teams in recent years?

Definition

Teamwork, n. 1. Joint action by a group of people, in which each person subordinates his or her individual interests and opinions to the unity and efficiency of the group; coordinated effort, as of an athletic team. 2. Work done by or with a team.

129

Why Have Teams?

The trend for corporations in today's economy is to downsize. As of the writing of this book, about 3,000 people per day are being let go from their jobs in this country. This downsizing trend is designed to cut the fat from organizations, to go "flatter," as they say. This flattening effort is aimed particularly at cutting out layers of middle management so there are fewer people between the top layers and the bottom layers of a company, thus "flattening out" the organization.

In the past, it was not uncommon for the typical manager to manage from two to five employees. Now, because of downsizing and flattening, the typical manager is managing between 20 and 40 employees. Because of this, there is less opportunity for managers to interact with, supervise, and direct their people. This is the first reason why teamwork has become so important in our companies. It is a way to compensate for the direction that was previously furnished by management.

The Age of Specialization

A second factor that has required better use of the team concept is the movement in our society away from generalists and toward specialists. As a result of this trend, very few people know a lot about many different things. Instead, most people know a lot about some specific thing.

So in order to accomplish a specific goal or task, it is often necessary to employ the talents of numerous people in some type of team setting. If you look at the average company today, the level of expertise within the company has increased tremendously over the past few years. The technical skills required and the technical abilities available have dramatically increased. This means that each player generally brings more to the table now than in the past. There is more innovation today than at any other time in history. These new ideas are coming less often from CEO's and more often from work team members.

Effective Teamwork vs. Ineffective Teamwork

It is fairly easy to recognize good teamwork: the result is that the job gets done. Through cooperative and coordinated effort, a good work team is notably productive and efficient. A group that works well together is indeed a thing of beauty.

What's maddening in the corporate structure are those situations when the job *doesn't* get done through teamwork, and the results are *not* there. While it is easy to recognize an ineffective work team, it is *very* difficult to recognize the cause of the ineffectiveness. Poor teamwork can be the manifestation of several possible problems.

Why Teamwork Fails

1. Bad work teams will generally do such a good job of externalizing and excuse-making that it is almost impossible to see the real problem. Furthermore, the whole team can come to a consensus on an excuse. (This is not devious, remember—it is an unconscious function, in this case, of

131

the group.) Therefore excuses tend to be accepted even more as "explanations" or "reasons" by the sheer force of numbers. So when a team gives an excuse, it naturally has more validity than when an individual gives an excuse.

2. There may not have been a clearly defined, understood, and *accepted* set of accountabilities for each member of the team. This is sometimes due to a lack of clarity about what exactly the entire team is supposed to accomplish. But more often, it is due to ambiguity in the determination of individual responsibilities: who is supposed to do what, how, by when, etc. When the specifics are not clearly spelled out, most teams will weaken. When the team members report back for progress, something important will have been left out, or will have fallen through the cracks. Again, this is because the particular task wasn't originally conceptualized as part of the charter, or it wasn't clearly understood which team member (or members) were responsible for it.

3. As team members jockey for power (as people tend to do), they will sometimes overcommit and accept too much responsibility, or accept responsibility for something they aren't qualified to do. A team situation sometimes creates a level of enthusiasm in the group that is difficult for any one individual to maintain apart from the group. It is the tendency for any group to take on, shall we say, a temporary "personality" of its own. This temporary personality will fade as the enthusiasm of the group fades. When this happens, the result will be failure in one form or another. And where there is failure, there will also be externalization of the problem, projection of blame, and more excuses than you can shake a stick at.

4. Teamwork implies working among your peers. Peers are less likely to hold each other accountable than are managers. There is a certain insecurity in trying to hold a peer accountable. It tends to bring up all the old, negative messages from childhood about being a tattletale. Yet by not holding a peer accountable within a group, you help disguise the real issues. That is, you allow for excuse-making.

5. It is not uncommon for a team to have one person who tries to dominate, control, gain power over, or in some other way negatively influence the group. Sometimes you can see that this is a person who is utilizing the team to gain his own power base. Whether his motivation is low self-esteem, lack of self-confidence, revenge against someone in management, or some other reason, such a player may cause a team to fail. The other team members may resent such behavior and begin to work at cross purposes. Some team members may even intentionally sabotage the team's effort and cause it to fail so that the power-hungry person would look bad. This type of scenario is a real hotbed for excuses, since no one will give the real reason for the lack of results.

6. One of the inherent problems with the teamwork concept is that, by usual standards, it requires players who fit the middle of the spectrum. That's what a team player is expected to be. The individuals on the extremes are generally not good team players. Yet often it's the people on the extremes who have the most to offer. The best teams are not made up of clones, but of a diversity of people. Yet when someone selects a team, he generally picks people with whom he's comfortable and who are similar to him in many ways. By so doing, the differences, the extremes, will be overlooked, and this could have a devastating effect on the total team effort. Since the team concept is important for the future of our corporations, we need to find ways to include those people on the extremes and make them a functional part of the team process. We must stop finding excuses for leaving out of the teamwork effort some of our most valuable resources.

The Point

Teamwork is a concept that is easily misunderstood, so it's possible to approach the whole subject from the wrong direction. A popular belief is that if your team isn't working well together, it helps to put the players in some type of experience where they must depend on each other for their safety. Weekend trust walks, ropes courses, climbing exercises, and similar programs are famous for this. The strategy may be, for example, to put the team in a dangerous situation where they have to depend on each other to keep from getting hurt.

These experiences tend to create an adrenalin rush that leaves everybody feeling good about what happened. But they are unreal—not grounded in the real problems of everyday life. So on Monday morning these same team members find themselves back at work facing the identical problems that they left behind on Friday. And, all too often, the team handles those problems in exactly the same way as before. Why? Because such team exercises rarely address the *real* reasons—the six just discussed—why teamwork doesn't work. Until those reasons are properly addressed, any team, because of the very nature of the team concept, is at risk of failing on a regular basis.

A Point to Remember

It merits a moment's review to say again what happens when people face the possibility of failure. To protect themselves from embarrassment, criticism, blame, or emotional hurt in any form, people will automatically, unknowingly, and yet very creatively *make excuses.* This behavior is a self-protective mechanism that is born into us. It is part of being human.

Therefore

When a team is failing, or has failed, no one is likely to step forward and take full responsibility. Instead, each of the team members will probably be called in individually by their managers, free to make their own excuses *apart from the team* as to why the effort failed. And you can be sure that the excuses will take the form of blame projected onto someone or something else.

That this happens is one of the factors that allows for, if not encourages, the breakdown of the team effort. This closed-door posturing with management is likely to evoke excuses and fingerpointing by each of the players, which in turn creates animosity among the other team members. The greater the animosity, the more likely other members are to give additional excuses to protect themselves, and the problem snowballs. The result is that everyone involved (management included) gets steered off course, and the real problem ends up not getting fixed at all—or at best the solution is greatly delayed.

In Conclusion

Many of our traditional views of teamwork create a context in which people in the workplace make excuses. Excuses are systemic in nature, remember. They "gowith" certain other conditions (insufficient accountabilities, procrastination, pessimism, etc.), and they will occur whenever any (or all) of these conditions prevail. *One of the secrets to getting results instead of excuses is to eliminate the conditions in which people are allowed and/or encouraged to make excuses.* We will be giving considerable attention to this principle in Part III.

Suffice it to say here that teamwork is important, and it is necessary. It will no doubt be on the corporate scene for many years to come. But until we come to grips with the real issues that are involved in the team process, we are likely to continue to have high rates of failure from team efforts, along with an abundance of excuses, rather than high-level results.

11

In Bureaucracies

Like cancer in the human body, excuses are such an insidiously destructive force in our corporate bodies that we must seize every opportunity to identify them, expose them, and systematically destroy them. In this chapter we will provide an opportunity to look at how excuses manifest themselves in bureaucracies. Since most corporations are, by definition, bureaucratic in nature, we think this information will help you identify excuses in your company. Like it or not, what you're about to discover is that bureaucracies are to excuses what swamps are to mosquitoes: they provide a fertile environment in which to multipy. And multiply they do!

Definition

Bu-reauc-ra-cy, n.   Administration of an organization through departments and subdivisions managed by sets of officials following a typically inflexible routine.

Their Source

Where do bureaucracies come from? Probably very few people, if any, have ever intentionally set out to create a so-called bureaucracy, yet they exist in abundance. Most people in the corporate world are caught smack in the center of them, yet not everyone recognizes that fact. It's like not being able to see the forest because of all the trees: bureaucracies are so close to us that we can't see them clearly. They *are* us, which is a big part of the problem. So how did we get in the middle of this bureaucratic mess? Why do bureaucracies have to be a part of the workplace at all?

The Life Cycle of a Business

After working for twelve years at an odd assortment of jobs, Ed decided to start his own industrial detergent business in the basement of his home. That was over thirty years ago. Like so many individuals who venture into the business world on their own, Ed did virtually everything himself in the beginning. He emptied the wastebaskets, did the accounting, handled all the marketing and selling, answered the phone, and serviced his customers. On top of all that, he alone was responsible for the production. At the time, Ed was totally in tune with his customers' needs and wishes. He was, as Barbara Walters on the television series "20/20" is fond of saying, "in touch." He knew everything that was going on in relation to his business, and there was never any question as to whether or not he was responsive to the market's needs. He could respond quickly to any situation because he was a one-man show.

Ed's business began to flourish. As he became more and more successful, his workload became overwhelming. There was much more to do than one person could possibly do well. So Ed made two important business decisions: it was time to move into a larger facility and it was necessary to hire a few people to help him run his business.

The Policy Manual

It wasn't long before Ed came to realize something that most entreprenuers discover when they take on their first employees: The people he hired had a difficult time thinking as he did. Ed soon figured out that he needed to give some attention to managing his help. So he wrote a policy manual. As Ed knew when he wrote his first one, a policy manual is a book of company rules and regulations. What he wasn't cognizant of, however, was that that same manual was also the first stage of an emerging bureaucracy in his company.

As time passed, Ed's company continued to grow. There were more orders for industrial detergents than he and his employees could manufacture and deliver. So he hired more people. Before long, Ed realized that he was unable to manage all of his people by himself. So he singled out some of his more conscientious employees and promoted them to the ranks of management. It would be their job to enforce the policy manual in each of their respective departments. He assigned one manager to oversee sales and marketing, one in manufacturing, one in finance, and one in the office. In terms of reducing the stress on Ed, it proved to be a wise decision. But again, Ed did not see the subtle shift in priorities that was taking place right in his own company. He did not realize the focus was gradually moving from "Are we responding to the marketplace?" to "Are we following company policy?" Though Ed did not know it at the time, his company was becoming a bureaucracy.

The Conflicts

As the bureaucracy swelled within his company, Ed became increasingly detached from the realities that were going on in the market. He found himself handling conflicts and grievances that resulted from people not following company regulations. Slowly, quietly, invisibly, yet surely, the bureaucracy was growing. Ed was now becoming an enforcer of rules as opposed to a creator of policy designed to respond to the needs of the marketplace.

In the gradual development of Ed's company, there was another distinctive shift occurring. The managers were getting nervous about a phenomenon that often happens in bureaucracies called "kill the messenger syndrome." As you know, in ancient times it was not uncommon for a person who brought bad news to the king or emperor to be put to death. Somehow that was supposed to make the problem go away. In corporate America that same phenomenon gets translated into: if someone up the chain of command doesn't like what he or she hears, get rid of the person who said it!

The point is that the managers who reported to Ed didn't want to be "killed" for bringing the bad news. Bad news could be of two types. It could be something unpleasant about the marketplace, or it could be bad news about policy being broken by employees. Either way, they learned how to hide such things to protect themselves. Consequently, Ed became less involved with the kinds of issues that would lead to increased productivity in the company, and more involved with things that would get in the way of reaching that goal.

And the Bureaucracy Continues to Grow

Jack, one of Ed's original employees, is no longer performing well. Ed doesn't want to hurt Jack, and he doesn't know how to get rid of him. So he moves him into a specially created position. When Ed looks in on Jack four weeks later, he finds that the position is filled not only by Jack, but also by an administrative assistant, a secretary, a file clerk, a copy machine, and a coffee pot. To justify his existence, Jack is usurping the time of other people by creating reports and other paperwork.

****

And so it is that the bureaucracy continues to grow.

The Dark Days of Winter

It is now thirty years since Ed began his business. His company is fraught with problems. Sales are up for three years in a row, but profits are down over the same period because of shrinking margins. The competition has become so keen that the only way the company can survive, and then not for long, is to continue to lower prices.

What has happened to Ed's company over the last thirty years is precisely what has happened with so many big and aging companies in our country. They have lost touch with the marketplace. They have developed so many insulating layers that their entire focus has moved in the direction of ruling themselves rather than fulfilling the needs of their customers.

Herb Kelleher, CEO of Southwest Airlines, realizes the importance of staying in touch with the needs of the customers. He believes that time spent behind his desk is nonproductive time. He purposely tries to gain as much exposure with his customers and employees as possible. Rather than travel on the corporate jet, he flies commercially so as to deal with line personnel, flight attendants, passengers, and so on. It should come as no surprise that Southwest Airlines has the highest profit margin in the business.

The larger an organization becomes, the more it tends to accumulate secondary responsibilities to the point that it is unable to focus on its primary responsibilities and purposes. This is because the people who need to be "in the know" often become—by the nature of the system—the ones who are the most removed. Such is the nature of any bureaucracy.

A Current Example of the Birth of a Bureaucracy

The amount of information that is now available through the use of technology is absolutely overwhelming. Management teams cannot begin to keep up with it.

****

Five years ago, Mike ran his business on the basis of five key financial indicators that he monitored weekly. Today he has an entire staff of people who are providing to him 98 key indicators on a weekly basis. Of course, each person thinks his key indicator is the most important. Mike was taxed trying to keep up with five, and now it is absolutely impossible for him to deal with 98. To try to prevent the loss of any gold nuggets in the endless flow of information, he hires more and more administrative assistants to keep track of these 98 indicators. These assistants, by the way, need copy machines and coffee makers, and they must be managed and led.

Now Mike, like most CEO's, is a very busy person. With corporate meetings and all, there are heavy demands on him approximately 70 percent of the time. So only about 30 percent of Mike's time is discretionary. He gets thirty-page monthly reports from his reporting offices, each of which takes an average of 20 hours per month to prepare. When Mike is at his best, he can only analyze and absorb a very small piece of it.

When we think of the compounding effects of all this, what we have here is an executive who is getting a lot of information that he's not using—some of which may be very valuable. And we have a large number of man-hours put into preparing paperwork that is never effectively used by management. We also have a growing staff of people to be managed. What we have, really, is a sprouting bureaucracy, a special type called an "information bureaucracy." This phenomenon is bound to become more common, with many companies not yet realizing that it is already happening to them.

What Does This Have to Do with Excuses?

Everything! First, we've just seen, through the examples of Ed and Mike, how a bureaucracy tends to build layer upon layer of insulation between a company and the marketplace that it serves. What are those layers of insulation really insulating? The unfortunate answer is: reality, truth, *the way it really is* in the world that the bureaucracy was intended to serve. By nature, bureaucracies obscure and water down the truth. Obscured truth is the womb of half-truths, lies, rationalizations, and excuses.

Second, and this may be another way of saying the same thing, remember how Ed's managers disguised the bad news, first to protect Ed, but mainly to protect themselves? If they couldn't tell Ed the whole truth, that means that they felt forced by the system to say something less than the whole truth. Even though Ed's managers would think of themselves as truthful individuals and not liars, nevertheless by the nature of the system—the bureaucracy—they were forced to protect themselves, which they did by making *excuses*.

Which leads us to point number three, perhaps the most important. In any organization, whether public or private, profit or nonprofit, service- or production-oriented, large or small: *when excuses are allowed at the top of an organization* (and this is almost always the case with bureaucracies), *they will be allowed and encouraged throughout that organization.*

Let's say it differently. *Bureaucracies breed excuse-making cultures.* As a general rule, people will make excuses in order to survive at the top levels of a bureaucracy. Yet where there are excuses at the top, there is going to be an abundance of excuses throughout the rest of the organization. That's why we've said that bureaucracies are to excuses what swamps are to mosquitoes. Excuses will multiply and infest the entire corporate environment.

In Review

The bad news is that unless there is some strategic intervention, bureaucracies—like lemmings marching to their death at sea—will continue to travel down their self-destructive paths. The evidence is clear. Comparing the lists of the top ten corporations in this country in 1980 and then again in 1990, only one company made both lists. In the global marketplace, many companies that held top ratings for decades have slipped considerably in the standings.

The good news is that this trend does not have to continue. It is reversible. Some companies have made progress, but they have not yet recaptured the lead in world competition. To do so requires looking through a different lens that makes it possible to see the problem in a new way. Otherwise it's like trying to find a blue line on a piece of paper while looking through a blue lens. It would be nearly impossible to see. That's the way it is with excuses. We haven't seen their destructive potential because we've been looking through an excuse-colored lens. We've been looking through cause/effect and coincidental modalities, and it is impossible to see the enemy from either of those perspectives.

The problem of excuses in the workplace is a massive, systemic problem. Excuses are everywhere. They are almost as common as the air we breathe. Like air, excuse-making is invisible, unless you have the proper instruments with which to spot it. Learning to recognize the problems caused by excuses is like learning to look at three-dimensional art. You can stand in front of the mat and look for quite some time before the hidden picture lifts itself off the screen and comes into clear view. Then, once you've seen it, you wonder how it could have been so difficult to find.

The point is that recognizing that excuses *are indeed* a problem is the first half of the battle. Once that is accomplished, the remedy is not all that far away. Excuse-laden cultures are like alcoholism, which is a disease of denial. For the person with a drinking problem, half the battle is to recognize and admit that he has a problem. So it is with bureaucracies, corporations, cultures, leadership teams, departments, and so on that are infected with excuses. *If we can just see the problem, and admit to it, we can fix it. Until we see it, there is little hope for complete recovery.*

****

In Part II we have addressed how excuses manifest themselves in culture, leadership, planning, teamwork, and bureaucracies. The same infection may be found in customer service, sales departments, production, community relations, and even the boardroom.

Our purpose has been to give you a new perspective on the source of the problem, and to see what happens in companies that have the disease. You cannot know yet to what extent your company is infected, or what to do about the problem. We will tackle that in Part III.

To this point, we have wanted you to see more clearly how devastating excuses can be in the corporate setting. The problem of excuse-making is systemic—once in the company, it can easily infect the entire corporate body. And whether the corporate body is ailing from excuse-making in whole or in part, either way it is very difficult to achieve winning results. This, again, is because *where there are excuses, there will not be desired results.*

Notes and Quotes

He that is good for making excuses is seldom good for anything else.

Benjamin Franklin

Part
III

The Solution to the
Problem

How to Eliminate Excuses
from the Workplace

12

The Commitment Step: To or Not To?

As beneficial as it would be to have no more excuses in your workplace, you may be wondering whether it is really possible to achieve such a state. Perhaps to do so seems like a corporate utopia, rather like trying to achieve a sinless world. You may be asking yourself the question, "How do I know whether or not to move ahead with such a project?"

The purpose of Part III is to help you discover *your* answer to this question. By the time you finish it, you will have a much clearer understanding of whether or not it is something you want to undertake. In this chapter, we want to discuss some preliminaries to actually getting started.

What Does "Excuse-Free" Really Mean?

We've spoken often of helping you achieve an "excuse-free" organization. However, technically speaking, it may well be impossible to reach this goal because *being totally excuse-free is an ideal state.* As long as there are human beings, there will be excuses. We will likely never totally eradicate this self-protective mechanism from the workplace. But that should not deter us in our efforts to *reach for the goal* of becoming excuse-free in our companies. Olympic gymnastic or diving champions rarely achieve perfect scores, but they never stop striving for perfection in their quest for excellence. *It is the striving for the ideal that makes them number one.*

The effectiveness of ridding your company of excuses might be likened to the Richter scale method of measuring the power of an earthquake, only inversely. An *increase* of 1.0 on the Richter scale multiples the power of the quake by 10; a *decrease* in the number of excuses by 1.0 multiplies the effectiveness of your company by 10 or perhaps more. The point is, a company doesn't have to be totally excuse-free in order to take giant strides forward in getting results. But it does have to be consciously—and constantly—striving toward the *goal* of becoming excuse-free.

Why?

Let's suppose you start a company from scratch. Intentionally, you make it company policy that excuses are acceptable in your organization, which means that everyone

152

is allowed to deny responsibility, to project blame for their own mistakes, to procrastinate on the accomplishment of tasks, and so on. You would probably agree that this would be a ludicrous and unproductive thing to do, and that the company would have big problems before long.

Yet this is precisely the condition that many of our companies are in today. They are excuse-infested. Not, of course, because excuse-making is part of company policy, but because ridding themselves of excuses is **not** part of company policy. *It is critical to understand that excuse-making is the default position for people if clear corrective measures are not taken by leaders and management.* To default is to "fail to do," and this is exactly what has happened to our organizations, if not our country. It is why we haven't yet recaptured the lead. Excuses are like quack grass or dandelions in our lawns. When we fail to manage their growth, they quickly take over. In much the same way, when we fail to manage excuses, our cultures become excuse-infested.

Said Differently

Excuse-making has generally been ignored in corporate America. People in corporations have simply never before realized its destructive power. Since the management of excuses has never been a line item on the budget, since it's never been evaluated, since it's not information that has ever been gathered from customer surveys, since it's not included on employee evaluation forms, we've just assumed that excuse-making isn't all that important an issue. Failing to recognize that excuses are a problem is what makes them such a *big* problem.

153

This must change.   And it will only change by effectively managing excuses, which means to consciously—and constantly—strive toward the goal of becoming excuse-free.   The closer an organization comes to reaching this ideal, the more effective will be its results, and the further ahead of the competition it will be.

****

Let's discuss (1) what it takes for a company to be able to change; and then, if those conditions are right, (2) what a company actually has to target for change.

The Necessary Ingredients for Change

Generally speaking, there are three prerequisites that are necessary for any company to make significant, gainful, and lasting change: (1) the leaders must be *ready* to change; (2) they must have an *intense desire* to win; and (3) they must be *willing to make the commitment* to do whatever it takes to become number one in their field. These characteristics are so important that they each deserve a closer look.

Readiness

The first rule of change is that no company changes until its leaders are ready. You may have heard the saying,

154

"When the student is ready to learn, the teacher will appear." By the same token, when the company's leaders are ready to change, the answers will appear.

Readiness to change is always a function of discomfort—that is, disliking things the way they are in your company and wanting them to be different. Contentment breeds complacency—and ultimately, defeat by the competition. Discontent breeds initiative, creativity, proactivity, invention, progress, and ultimately, victory. Hence the saying, "Necessity is the mother of invention." Necessity grows from discontent. If you are less than content with the present state of affairs in your company, you may be ready to change.

Desire

You must truly want to lead the competitive race in your market. If you are content with anything less than aiming for first place, then adopting this powerful new formula won't help. It won't help because it won't happen. Though there are rare exceptions to the rule, we all know that champions *at anything* are made, not born. Show us any champion, regardless of his field of endeavor, and we'll show you an individual—or a company full of individuals—with a fierce desire to compete, to excel, and to be number one.

Commitment

There are millions of people in the world, and

hundreds of thousands of business owners, who would like their situations to improve. There are far fewer who are committed to doing what it takes to make the changes necessary for improvement.

Genuine commitment (as opposed to lip service) can be measured in four ways: *(1) the willlingness to change* (assuming there is readiness); *(2) the willingness to risk; (3) the willingness to invest time; and (4) the willingness to invest money.*

Some people like to talk about how committed they are to one thing or another. But if you want to know what someone is *truly* committed to, look at what he does, not at what he says he wants to do. *The commitment to win is evident in action,* not intentions.

What Has to Be Targeted for Change?

Traditionally, companies have placed importance on developing vision statements, mission statements, and, more recently, values statements. Our experience is that these concepts are easy to confuse, since they overlap each other to some degree. But they are also clearly distinct from one another in important ways. You must understand these distinctions in order to know what to target for change.

Before addressing the distinctions, though, we want to make it clear that we are *not* authorities on vision, mission, and values statements. Much helpful information is available to you on these subjects if you are looking for the opinion of experts. Our only purpose here is to provide working definitions to any reader who may not be familiar with the terms so that you will better understand what comes next.

Vision Statements

A vision statement is a statement about *where* you want your company to be in the future (as compared with where it is now). A vision statement is, in effect, an expression of a long-term goal or goals. Vision statements can be made for the entire company, for a department, and for individuals. They are usually expressed in "we will" (or "I will") language. For example, a *company's* vision statement might be any (or all) of the following:

- *We will* be a $100-million company by the year 2000.

- *We will* have a broad base of customers with no single customer exceeding 3 percent of our annual revenue.

- *We will* service every zip code in the United States within the next five years.

- *We will* open ten new satellite offices within the next three years.

The vision statement of a *division* or *department* might be:

- *We will* have less than 5 percent quality defect rejection by 18 months from now.

- *We will* have a totally computerized inventory system within the next year.

And for an *individual*:

• *I will* be the number one salesperson (gross sales) within two years.

• *I will* be promoted to a senior management position within three years of starting to work for this company.

Notice, in each case, that the vision statement is a projection into the future. This expression of *where* a company, division, department, or individual wants to go is the distinguishing mark of a vision statement.

Mission Statements

A mission statement is a statement of *how* the vision will be achieved. It is a set of objectives to be accomplished in order to achieve the long-term goal(s). Functionally, the objectives serve as short-term goals. So a mission statement generally answers the questions "*How* are we going to get there?" and "*What* has to be done to accomplish our vision?" Mission statements are typically stated in "by" language. For example:

As a *company* we will attain our vision statement of being a $100-million company by the year 2000:

• *by* having the highest-quality products on the market.

• *by* having a better-trained sales force than all of the competition.

• *by* maintaining price advantage.

• *by* extending markets geographically into two new locations per year.

As a *department*, we will attain our vision of having less than 5 percent quality defect rejection within 18 months:

  • *by* closely monitoring purchases and assuring quality control of purchased components.

  • *by* rewarding workers for a combination of high quality and high production rather than high production alone.

As an *individual*, I will accomplish my vision statement of being promoted to a senior management position within three years:

  • *by* ensuring that all reports are filled out on time.

  • *by* presenting at least one new idea to management every month.

These are only a few examples of the kinds of issues to be addressed in order to put together an effective mission statement. The point here is that a mission statement defines *how* you are going to make your vision statement happen; it lists the steps you will take to bring your vision to reality.

Values Statements

Values statements exist on quite a different plane from vision and mission statements. A values statement expresses the *standards of behavior* to be followed by the people within a company as they work to bring their vision and mission statements to fruition. Vision and mission statements deal with *things to do*; values statements deal with *ways to do* those things.

By comparison, suppose you had a "to do" list. Let this be the equivalent of your mission statement. Now you ask yourself, "In what way will I do the things on the list?" For example, will you do them as fast as you can, as slowly as possible, or at a pace that feels comfortable to you? Will you do them carefully or recklessly? Will you strive for perfection on each of the tasks, or will you want only to complete them, regardless of quality? These are questions of value. Values statements answer the question, "What are the *rules for our behavior* as we proceed?"

Values Statements in the Workplace

Let's look at this in a business context. In dealing with customers, is our behavior going to be relaxed or formal, light or serious, friendly or aloof? Are we going to work so intensely toward our goals that we ask our employees to work forty-five hour weeks until our goals are achieved? Or will there be periods of play time and relaxation built in to renew our people along the way? Are we going to listen closely to what our customers tell us they need and respond accordingly, or are we going to project what we think the customer will need and gamble on our predictions?

As before, this is only a small sampling of the sorts of questions that must be addressed in putting together a values statement. The point here is that values statements deal with the question *"What is important to us in terms of our standard of behavior—our rules of conduct?"* as we move toward achieving the goals in our vision and mission statements.

Values Statements and Corporate Culture

Corporate culture, you will recall from Chapter 7, is: *The spoken and unspoken rules in an organization that set the standards for how things are to be done; the company ethos; the characteristics and distinguishing ways of thinking, feeling, and behaving in any given occupational group; the pervasive attitudes, values, beliefs, and actions of the people within a company.*

Values statements, as just discussed, are: *The standards of behavior in a company; the ways to do things in the workplace; the rules for conduct.*

****

It should now be clear that "corporate culture" and "values statements" are closely related concepts. The culture of a company is defined far more by its values statements than by its vision and mission statements. Corporate culture is the sum total of the values of a company.

Why Is This Distinction So Important?

Many companies are well-practiced at putting together vision statements and mission statements. Usually under the guidance of a trained consultant, and often at considerable expense, companies spend endless exhausting hours putting these statements together to guide them forward.

The mistake that many companies make is to assume that their culture is determined by their vision or mission statements. This is simply not the case.

Again, vision statements tell where a company is going. Mission statements—how you are going to get there—flow logically from the vision statement. Values statements, on the other hand, define the standards of behavior for getting to where you are going. They do *not* flow logically from either the vision or the mission statement. They are independent of the others. Values statements express an altogether different dimension of the corporate experience. They are codes of conduct to be superimposed over both vision and mission. In other words, values statements alone establish your culture.

****

We've said before that to rid your company of excuses, you must develop an excuse-free culture. We've also said that the way to do this is to manage excuses. What couldn't have been said with any degree of clarity until now is that *the only way to manage excuses effectively is to **commit** yourself to the values statement: **This*** *company will have an excuse-free culture.*

Why This Must Be Done Now

One of the big problems in corporate America today is that the rate of change in the business environment is much greater than it has ever been. And this rate of change is going to increase geometrically as technological development continues to accelerate and information becomes more and more readily available. The result is that too often vision and mission statements have little meaning in today's marketplace because of the tremendously fast-changing conditions. By the time some vision and mission statements are put together, the business has so radically changed that the statements are no longer completely valid—if they are still valid at all.

This is not to say that vision and mission statements are no longer important. On the contrary, they remain a necessity. But they are not *as* important in today's business climate as a well-defined values statement.

For Instance

A company can have perfect vision and mission statements and yet fail miserably if the values statement creates a culture that cannot respond to fast-changing market conditions. Conversely, a company that may not have the perfect vision and mission statements but which has a solid values statement (and therefore a good culture of people) can succeed because of its responsiveness, proactivity, creativity, optimism, acceptance of responsibility, and so on.

Example #1

Let's suppose Company A has the following vision statement: We will have the most technologically superior products in the marketplace in five years. Its mission statement reads: We will accomplish this by introducing one new product every 12 months.

Even though these statements may be otherwise realistic, the vision could crash if there is no values statement that guarantees a proactive mindset of the people in research and development. How can they ever become technologically superior as stated in the vision statement if their way of being—their standard of behavior—is *reactive*? By definition, reactive people are always at least one step behind whoever is in the lead. And, no doubt, they will have plenty of excuses for not being the most technologically superior, because where there is reactive thinking, there will be excuses. Always.

****

If excuses are not managed in an organization through a clear values statement that demands excuse-free behavior from its people, the culture will automatically default to the excuse-making syndrome. This will be true regardless of the clarity of the vision statement, and regardless of the specificity of the mission statement.

Example #2

Here is Company B with a vision statement of having customers in every zip code in the country by the year 2000. Its mission statement is to hire enough salespeople to accomplish that market coverage. But if in their rapid growth they hire salespeople who tend to externalize their failures ("It's someone else's fault") rather than internalize them ("It's my responsibility"), it is unlikely that the vision statement will ever be achieved.

This is because there is not a strong values statement that insists on internalization rather than externalization from its employees. The culture will be excuse-infested because the proper values statement is not in place that will drive excuses out of the culture. If and when the going gets tough, the people on the sales force will therefore likely be projecting blame and shirking responsibility rather than doing whatever is necessary to get the desired results. Externalization and excuses are kissing cousins. Externalization can only thrive in an excuse-laden culture. And where there are excuses, there won't be results.

Conversely

Company C has a vision also: to be number one in the marketplace with their product line within the next four years. Their mission statement: to accomplish this by doing whatever it takes to achieve their vision. (This mission statement, by the way, would fail nearly every consultant's test—it's not specific, not measurable, and so on.)

Yet if company C's values statement is that it will

have an excuse-free culture, then it will only hire people to be leaders who meet the criteria of leadership (according to the clear understanding of leadership as spelled out in Chapter 8). This means that the company will end up with a team of people who want the organization to be number one. Even though they may not have any idea at that point how they're going to make their vision a reality, the point is that the values of their people will be so strong—so excuse-free—that they will indeed become number one, whatever it takes to get there.

The strength of the core values of a company is closely tied to the strength of the leaders of that company. It is excuse-free leadership that allows this approach to work. However, excuse-free leadership is not something that just happens by itself. *It is something that must be aggressively pursued, and this aggressive pursuit flows directly out of the values statement of the company.*

The Point, Once Again

As we said, you should not conclude that vision and mission statements are useless. However, as you look to what the future of your company should be, it is important that you focus not only on products and services but also on developing and maintaining the proper culture.

The only culture that can respond to—and win in—the markeplace is the culture that is proactive, creative, optimistic, responsible, accountable, stretching, trusting, helpful, focused, risk-taking, blame-accepting, internalizing, and so on. ***This is the excuse-free culture that grows out of your commitment to an excuse-free values statement.*** *This is the culture required to surge ahead of others and*

166

become the leader in the daily race of the marketplace. This is how to become number one again.

What to Do Next

At this point, you do not have to appoint special committees who will wrestle for months with the questions "How do we want our people to behave, and what do we want our values statement to be?" *Step one is simply a matter of committing yourself to adopting the values statement:* **This company will become excuse-free.** This is far more important than the development of your products and your services, your visions and your missions.

If you do this, your people will develop your business for you. By getting rid of excuses, you will foster all the positives that are the derivatives of an excuse-free environment. And those positives will give you a corporate team that is strong enough to take your company to any height that you would like it to go, even to being (and remaining) number one.

Your Involvement Is Crucial

An excuse-free culture can only be achieved when those at the top express their commitment by (1) making the decision to proceed, and (2) actively involving themselves in the process. When this is not done, others in the organization will perceive the non-involvement of top management as a statement that achieving an excuse-free culture is unimportant (since actions speak louder than words). Also, any reason given for the non-involvement will be taken as an excuse in itself, whether or not it really is an excuse.

Either way, when it comes to eliminating excuses from the workplace, it will do little good to tell others to do something that you are not willing to be involved in yourself. *Real* commitment, remember, involves the willingness to change, the willingness to risk, the willingness to invest time, and the willingness to invest money. The third of these—the willingness to invest time—does not just mean the time of others. It means your time as well.

When it comes to ridding your company of excuses, direct and active involvement by the decision-maker(s) is mandatory. Right from the start it gives an important message to your people that you are serious in your commitment to bring your values statement to reality, and to have your company become excuse-free.

In Review

• An excuse-free culture represents an ideal. The secret is not to become totally excuse-free as much as it is to *continuously strive for that ideal*. The closer a company comes to becoming excuse-free, the further it will move ahead of the pack, outdistancing by far those who do little or nothing to manage excuses in their company.

• In order to accomplish *real* change, a company must be *ready* to change, must *want* to change, and must be *committed* to change.

• Being committed to anything means being willing to

change, risk, invest time, and invest money.

• Establishing vision statements, mission statements, and values statements must be part of the planning process for all companies. Of the three, a company's values statement, far more than the other two, defines that company's culture.

• To win in today's economy, you must be committed to making your values statement the guiding light for action in your company, even more so than your vision and mission statements.

• Specifically, the values statement that you must commit yourself to is to become excuse-free.

• If you do this, you will automatically foster a corporate culture that attracts, develops, and keeps the people necessary to help your business grow. It will consist of a group of people who: insist on being in touch with the needs of the customer; are able to adjust quickly to a fast-changing business climate; are optimistic, proactive, coura-geous, risk-taking, and so on; and settle for nothing less than becoming number one again.

Notes and Quotes

Whoever wants to be a judge of human nature should study people's excuses.

Hebbel

13

The Diagnostic Step: Are We Infected?

Once there is commitment at the top to develop an excuse-free culture, the next step is to determine to what degree your company is infected.

Before You Begin Your Diagnosis

We have made a point of saying that the culture of every corporation is unique to that company, just as personalities are unique to individuals. It is probably fair to say that no two companies have identical cultures.

171

But the question of how the culture—the collective values—of your company is unique from others is not the real issue here. The diagnostic question you need to focus on is: *To what degree is my unique culture infected with the excuse-making virus?* That is, to what extent are excuses and excuse-fostering behaviors manifesting themselves within my company?

This Is Really a Three-Part Question

Your company is made up of three distinct components: the organizational structure, the processes, and the people. The **organizational** component of a corporation is literally the way the company is organized. It is the organizational flow chart. It is the determination of what the various divisions and departments of the company are, and who reports to whom. The **processes** are the various systems used by the company to accomplish necessary tasks. For example, planning is accomplished through the planning process, employee evaluation through the evaluation process, and so on. The **people**, of course, are individuals who fill the positions within the company.

So the question "Are excuses manifesting themselves in my company?" is really three questions:

• "Does the organizational structure of my company create conditions under which people are allowed, encouraged, or 'forced' to make excuses?"

• "Do any of the processes used in my company breed excuse-making behaviors?"

• "After the organization and processes are fixed, are any of the people who work here still excuse-makers—*especially* those in leadership positions?"

In order to diagnose the excuse-making virus in your company, you must examine your organization, your processes, and your people. The problem of excuse-making is systemic. It can invade your company at many different levels in very subtle ways. Like cancer in the human body, we must look for excuse-making in the corporate body wherever it might be growing. So all three components must be thoroughly examined in order to make an accurate diagnosis and prescribe the most appropriate treatment.

Technically speaking, the organizational and process components of your company cannot *make* excuses; only people can do that. But the organization and the processes can have built-in weaknesses that encourage excuse-making, just as a weakened immune system allows viruses to spread through the body. So when we talk about examining your organizational structure and your processes, we aren't really looking for excuses, but rather for the weakened condition—the context—in which excuses happen.

The Rule

In order to get rid of excuses, you must first get rid of the reasons why people make them. You must imple- ment a systematic approach to change your company into an *extraordinary* organization with *extraordinary* processes in order to get extraordinary performance out of ordinary people.

173

The Solution to the Problem

So the rule is: *Never start your diagnosis at the "people" level. You can't know which excuses are related to individuals until you know which ones result from the organization and the processes.*

Approach the Diagnostic Process with an Open Mind

We cannot emphasize enough how difficult it can be to recognize the problematic nature of excuses as such. Seeing what's really there is one of the toughest jobs you'll have to do. *This is not because excuse-making is inherently difficult to see.* In fact, once you know how to spot it, it is quite easy to identify.

The problem is that we tend to be blind to excuses because of our perspective. When we're inside a paradigm, it's almost impossible to see outside of it—that is, to look at it objectively. This relates to our discussion in Chapter 6 about beliefs. For example, if we believe that everything that can be invented has been, we'll be ready to close the patent office. The point is that we tend to see only those things that fit inside the parameters of our paradigm.

A Common Example

Ron, the northwestern regional sales manager for a large retail fitness equipment company, asked Pete, one of his 16 salespeople, to prepare a proposal for a sizeable commercial job. The prospective customer was eager to get the job installed for their grand opening. The day before the proposal was due for Ron's approval, Pete asked for another two weeks because he had "simply been too busy to get to the proposal."

The "I'm too busy" excuse is one that is used commonly in the workplace. One of the reasons it is so often used—and generally so quickly accepted by others—is that it is seen from inside a specific paradigm that *busyness is a positive thing.* Think about when you ask someone, "How are you?" Often the response is "Busy." This is a respectable answer. Perhaps it's a carry over from the Protestant work ethic: that hard work is good, and if you're busy, you must be working hard. Whatever the reason, the commonly accepted paradigm in our society, and therefore in our companies, is that busyness is a virtue. Besides, it is easy enough to identify with the person who says, "I'm too busy," because we're all so busy most of the time ourselves.

But this is exactly the point. When we are inside of the "busyness is a virtue" paradigm, it is very difficult to have another perspective. Yet outside of that paradigm is another reality: the proposal is not completed on time, the competition may have just gained a huge competitive edge, and the deal may be lost. Worse than that, the prospective customer's trust may have eroded because what was said would be done in a certain time frame wasn't *in fact* done. This may negatively impact any attempt to get future business with the firm—and perhaps even with others if the word gets out that this fitness equipment company doesn't make good on its promises.

A Reminder

Remember what we said in the Preface about how

little material we were able to find on the subject of excuses. Information about excuses is conspicuously missing from the literature. This could only happen in the context—the paradigm—that excuses are *not* all that important and certainly *not* all that destructive.

But outside of that paradigm is another possibility. That possibility is exactly the new management theory we are advancing in this book: *Excuses are extremely important; they wreak havoc in our corporations when it comes to getting results; and they stand in the way of recapturing our number-one position in the marketplace.*

Switching Paradigms

We are asking you to step from one paradigm, where excuses and their relatives are mostly ignored, into another paradigm—the opposite one, really—where you realize that excuse-making causes problems almost everywhere you look. Making this shift isn't easy to do. It takes a little time, a little patience, and a lot of open-mindedness.

And yet, the elimination of excuses from the workplace is not all that difficult once you recognize (i.e., diagnose) the real problem. *It is in the recognition of the size of the problem that your first major challenge lies.*

So look closely with open eyes and with an open mind as you proceed with your diagnosis, or you may miss what there is to see. Keep your eyes open to new possibilities, or you may inadvertently slip back into the old paradigm where the chances of distorting the accuracy of your diagnosis are high.

The Audit as a Diagnostic Tool

Traditionally, problems in corporations have been identified by means of the audit. The purpose of the audit is to work through a checklist of questions to determine whether and where your company may need help. The most prevalent is the financial audit. Also high on the list is the audit where procedural efficiency is examined. There are other audits as well: security audits (which study the security of data in computer systems), billing-record audits, etc.

The Traditional Audit Won't Work to Diagnose Excuses

Audits are very useful tools for identifying certain kinds of problems. They look at hard data—data that are specific, objective, factual, measurable, and usually numerical, such as dollars in sales, days missed on the job, profit margins, material costs, and employee turnover.

The problem is that a company's culture, its collective value system, is *not* hard data. It is intangible and therefore more subjective than objective. It is the manifestation of human behavior within the corporation, and human behavior is "soft" data, not hard. This is why the traditional audit will not be effective for diagnosing the excuse-making virus in your company.

The 360-Degree Audit

The key to accurate diagnosis of anything that is

intangible and subjective is to look at it from as many different angles as possible. This is why there are several members on a jury. The accuracy of the judgment for or against the defendant lies in the collective perception. It is the same reason that we have judges in such sporting events as boxing, diving, gymnastics, and horse shows. Usually the judges place themselves at different angles to the event. They need to see it from as many perspectives as possible to insure accuracy.

So it is with the 360-degree audit. It is a valuable tool because the accuracy of the score is based on the concept that the aggregate perception is the one closest to reality. Upper management, for example, will see something from one perspective, middle management from quite another, and line workers from still another.

Which brings to mind a fable by John Godfrey Saxe (Stevenson, 1953) to help make this point:

It was six men of Indostan, to learning much inclined,
Who went to see the Elephant (though all of them were blind)
That each by observation could satisfy his mind.

The first approached the Elephant, and happening to fall
Against his broad and sturdy side, at once began to bawl:
"God bless me! but the Elephant is very much like a wall!"

The second, feeling of the tusk, cried "Ho! what have we here
So very round and smooth and sharp? To me 'tis mighty clear
This wonder of an Elephant is very like a spear!"

The third approached the animal, and happening to take
The squirming trunk within his hands, thus boldly up and spake:
"I see," quoth he, "the Elephant is very like a snake!"

The fourth reached out an eager hand, and felt about the knee.
"What most this wondrous beast is like is mighty plain," quoth he:
'Tis clear enough the Elephant is very like a tree!"

The fifth who chanced to touch the ear, said: "E'en the blindest man
Can tell what this resembles most: deny the fact who can,
This marvel of an Elephant is very like a fan!"

The sixth no sooner had begun about the beast to grope,
Than, seizing on the swinging tail that fell within his scope,
"I see," quoth he, "the Elephant is very like a rope!"

And so these men of Indostan disputed loud and long,
Each in his own opinion exceeding stiff and strong,
Though each was partly in the right, and all were in the wrong!

The Point

Two important things are accomplished by the 360 audit. First, it prevents the "wrong"—or more precisely, the *narrowness*—that can result from any single perspective in the corporate environment. Second, it takes all the "partly rights" and, by putting them all together, it collectively builds the most accurate picture. That is why the 360 is such a necessary and valuable diagnostic tool.

Whereas the 360 can be used in many different ways to measure corporate behaviors, it is crucial that you use it to diagnose the excuse-making syndrome in your organization. Remember, excuses and their partners are next to impossible to identify in ourselves. They are designed to protect, and are therefore invisible to those being protected. You must rely on the collective perception to spot both excuses and the weaknesses in the system which allow them to grow.

In figure 10 (p. 186) we will introduce you to a sample 360 audit that you can use to diagnose excuse-making in your company. There are some other things, however, that need to be discussed first.

The Solution to the Problem

The 360 Audit Isn't New, but When, Where, and How to Use It Is

Three-sixty surveys are becoming common practice in companies. Almost all of the 360's currently in use survey specific individuals. That's fine. *But in order to get rid of excuses you must survey your organization and your processes first.* Again, with regard to eliminating excuses from the workplace, ***never start your diagnosis at the "people" level.*** *You can't know which excuses are related to individuals until you know which ones result from the organization and the processes.*

The Importance of Anonymity

For the 360 audit to work effectively as a diagnostic tool, those who participate in it must be guaranteed anonymity if they desire it. Otherwise people will be frightened of the process and will not furnish accurate information. Since in the first stage you are looking for information about your organization and your processes rather than your people, knowing specific names isn't necessary. So don't require them.

In some companies, people will insist that they want names on all 360's. When this happens, it can force a lot of introspection, progressive thinking, and benefits. But only if that is what *everyone* wants. Putting names on the surveys can be a choice, but in the first stage it is clearly not necessary.

The Clear Understanding of Purpose

Everyone must be given a clear understanding of the purpose of the survey. There can be no mystery about it, or people will feel uneasy.

The purpose of the 360 diagnosis in the beginning stage is to assess accurately to what degree your organization and your processes allow the excuse-making virus to live and spread in your company. It is *not* to identify certain individuals as being excuse-makers.

You want your people to feel safe so they will be totally objective and give you accurate information about your organization and your processes. To accomplish this, make sure that (a) no one is required to put his or her name on the 360 diagnostic sheets; (b) people are reassured that the purpose is not to hurt anyone, but to eliminate excuses from the workplace so that the company will be as healthy as possible; and (c) the information is processed by an outside, objective firm.

Whom to Include in the 360

Again, the purpose of the diagnostic step is to determine at what levels and to what degree your organization and your processes are infected with excuses. To insure an accurate diagnosis, it is important to seek a summary of observations from several levels both inside and outside of your company. You need to include at least these four levels in your 360 diagnosis:

- Oneself
- Leadership/Management Team
- Employees
- Outside Sources

Each of these layers is distinct and provides a valuable perspective. Let's look at each category.

Oneself

We mean a diagnosis, not *on* oneself, but rather *by* the "top dog" in any given unit. His 360 survey will be *on* the organization and the processes within that unit. If the unit being diagnosed is the entire company, this would be by the owner, president, or CEO. If the unit being diagnosed is the division of a company, it would be by whoever is in charge of that division, such as the division manager. If the unit under observation is a satellite office, it would be by whoever directs that office, such as the branch manager.

Leadership/Management Team

Here, again, we mean *by*, not *on*, everyone who is in a leadership or management position. What your leaders and managers will be surveying is the organization and the processes in the unit being diagnosed. Depending on the number of people involved, it may be helpful to divide this group into various levels of management, such as upper and middle management, department heads, line supervisors, and so on, to get the unique perspective of each level.

Employees

This would include anyone who is not in a position of management or supervision. If the company is small enough and if the numbers are manageable, it would be best to have every employee do a 360 evaluation on the organization and the processes. The larger the company, the more important it will be to randomly sample the various populations of workers. Of course, the larger the number of employees surveyed, the more accurate the collective perception.

Outside Sources

To elicit the most accurate response from outside sources about your organization and your processes, they must be clearly informed as to what you are trying to accomplish. This takes courage on your part. Many companies have struggled with this because they hate admitting their weaknesses, especially to their customers. The irony is, your customers are probably more aware of your weaknesses than you *or* your company are. It's just that, in the end, customers have a peculiar way of telling you: They just quit calling.

The Solution to the Problem

Which Outside Sources to Select

There are any number of external sources you might go to for help on the 360. In some ways, these outside agents can furnish the most valuable information of all. How those outside your company view your organization and your processes may speak the loudest as to the presence or absence of excuses in your company.

Possible sources include: suppliers, customers, banks or other financial institutions with which you do business, prospective employees, former employees, competitors, other business leaders, community leaders, and community members. Which of these to invite into the project will depend on the size and location of your company, availability of outside agents, and the appropriateness of each to your particular situation. Obviously, it would be impractical—and unnecessary—for a company of any size to approach all such sources. The rule again is this: within reason, *the broader the base of perception, the more accurate the diagnosis.* Also, the larger the company, the more likely it is that a random sampling will suffice.

As before, those outsiders who agree to help furnish the information must be totally protected by making their 360's anonymous and confidential.

A Useful Rating Form for the 360

Figure 10 (p. 186) is a rating form you can use to get the initial raw data you will need to make an accurate diagnosis. The list is a small representation. There will be many items that you need to add or delete, depending on your circumstances. You will notice that the items listed

184

are excuse-related behaviors (for example, projection of blame, procrastination, and so on) rather than excuses themselves. The reason, remember, is that excuses can disguise themselves in many different ways, so we need to look for as many of those disguises as possible.

You will also notice that the items are the same ingredients that were listed in the body of the iceberg beneath the surface of the water in Chapter 5. These are the problems that tend to hang around each other in companies. They are "birds of a feather that flock together." They all "gowith" each other. Where you find one, you will almost always find the others. They are like metastasized cells of the same colony of cancer. Just as cancer cells live at the expense of everything else around them, so excuses and their relatives live at the expense of other life-giving qualities in an organization. *Your diagnosis must attempt to isolate **every** cell, or recurrence of the problem is inevitable.*

360 Organizational and Process Survey

Organization or Process under Audit: _____

Directions

Circle one number for each category that most applies to the organization or process being surveyed. (Read each item as if it were preceded by whichever of the following words is most appropriate: **"encourages," "allows," or "forces"**):

Acceptance of blame	4	3	2	1	Projection of blame
Non-entitlement attitudes	4	3	2	1	Entitlement attitudes
Proactive thinking	4	3	2	1	Reactive thinking
Can-do attitudes	4	3	2	1	Can't-do attitudes
Effective teamwork	4	3	2	1	Ineffective teamwork
Optimism	4	3	2	1	Pessimism
Taking risks	4	3	2	1	Not taking risks
Competence	4	3	2	1	Incompetence
Respectfulness	4	3	2	1	Disrespectfulness
Confronting of issues	4	3	2	1	Avoidance of issues
Being focused	4	3	2	1	Being unfocused
Empowerment	4	3	2	1	Helplessness
Being realistic with self	4	3	2	1	Being self-deceitful
Do-it-now attitudes	4	3	2	1	Procrastination
Results orientation	4	3	2	1	Excuse orientation
Creativeness	4	3	2	1	Non-creativeness
Stretching (to meet commitments)	4	3	2	1	Not stretching (to meet commitments)
Trust	4	3	2	1	Distrust
Harmonious relationships	4	3	2	1	Conflictual relationships
Courage to fail	4	3	2	1	Fear of failure
Accountability	4	3	2	1	Non-accountability
Leading	4	3	2	1	Following
Personal power to make change happen	4	3	2	1	Victimization
Acceptance of responsibility	4	3	2	1	Denial of responsibility
Long-term focus	4	3	2	1	Short-term focus

Figure 10

Application of the 360 Survey

This particular audit has a broad application. It can be used to survey any part of the organization, from its entirety down to any division, satellite, branch, or department. It can also be used to audit any process within the company: the planning process, the hiring process, the evaluation and promotion process, the sales and marketing process, the process of setting individual goals, and so on.

To repeat: It can also be used to survey individuals if and when the time is right to do that. *It is never the right time to survey individuals in the early stages of the diagnostic process.* It is far more important to diagnose the organizational structure and the processes first so as to eliminate the *reasons* that people make excuses. Many excuses will begin to go away when the reasons that people make excuses are eliminated.

Scoring the Surveys

There are 25 items on this representative list. A perfect score (which would indicate the most excuse-free environment) on each survey would be 100—4 points on each item times 25 items. The worst score possible (which would indicate the presence of the most number of excuses) would be 25—1 point on each item times 25 items.

Remember, however, that the final rating will be a composite score based on the averages of all people involved in the exercise *within a certain category or class of people* taking it (the classes being "oneself," "leadership-management," "employees," and "outside sources"). Since each category of people participating in the survey has its own unique perspective of the problem, lumping all the scores from all the classes together could contaminate the accuracy of the diagnosis.

Interpreting the Data

There should be some cause for concern *any time* the score is less than perfect (that is, any average score of less than 100). This signals that there is the *perception* that excuses are at work somewhere in your organization or your processes, even if in a small way. *Every perception is a piece of the whole reality.* It is like the elephant fable. Any single perception of the elephant was not the "real" or "whole" elephant. But it was a *piece* of the real elephant, and, as such, it had definite merit.

The point is, where there is the *perception* that the excuse-making virus is at work in your organization or your processes, then *it is* at work to some degree. If it looks like a duck and quacks like a duck, it probably is a duck. It must therefore be given immediate attention. It would be the equivalent of diagnosing and treating cancer in its earliest stages. This will greatly reduce the chance that the disease of excuse-making will spread.

The Rule for Interpreting Your Surveys

The lower the score, the bigger the problem. Anything less than a perfect score indicates that the excuse-making virus is at work in your company. The lower the score, the more of a hold the virus has on your organization. The higher the score, the less of a hold it has.

The concept of "being number one again" means that companies must strive toward the goal of being 100 percent excuse-free. Remember the starting point of this book: **Where there are excuses, there will be less than the desired results. Conversely, where there are the desired results, there will not be excuses. It is a contradiction of terms to have any excuses operating in your corporation and still be functioning at 100 percent effectiveness. Whether it is people, teams, companies, or countries: those who are number one have no room and no time for excuses. They are totally invested in getting results.**

What Is an "Acceptable" Score?

What level of performance are you satisfied with? Are you content to lead a company that is below average, average, above average—or are you driven to become (and remain) number one? There is one thing you can count on: *Winners strive to become number one. A score of 100 is number one. And when you're number one, you can't help but win!*

The End Result of the Diagnosis

As a result of the 360 surveys, you have determined to what degree your organization or your processes are infected with excuse-making. Your next job is to intervene in such a way that you will reverse the tendency in your company to unknowingly encourage, tolerate, or in some cases, even "force" people to make excuses. Doing this will help tremendously to overcome the excuse-making syndrome in your company, and to put you well on the road to recovery.

14

The Intervention Step:
Lead or Get Out of
the Way

Once the diagnoses of your organization and your processes are completed, you will know whether intervention is needed and, if so, where. Intervention is needed wherever there is the perception that excuses exist. This is because, by intervening in the excuse-making process, you are at the same time intervening in the destructive work of the many relatives of excuses as well: reactive thinking, projection of blame, pessimism, can't-do-attitudes, denial of responsibility, and so on. And with the elimination of these negatives comes a happier, more efficient place to work;

pride of achievement; cooperative relationships where everyone pulls their own weight; competitive products and services; and higher profits.

Intervention Begins with Leaders

You will recall from the chapter on leadership (Chapter 8) that *it is the responsibility of leaders to furnish the impetus necessary to establish and maintain an excuse-free culture.* So any discussion about intervening to turn around the excuse-making process must start with an evaluation of your leaders. This is the essential difference between the diagnostic step and the intervention step: the focus now turns from organization and processes to people—specifically, to the leaders.

The question now becomes: Are the leaders of the unit in question capable of making the change of taking the people from excuse-making to excuse-free behavior? It is not to be automatically assumed that present leaders have the necessary qualities. They may or they may not.

Remember, it takes specific leadership qualities to lead others into excuse-free behavior. It cannot be taken for granted that the people who are now in positions of management are up to the task. Leadership and management are two different concepts. It is a huge mistake to equate them. Leadership *"leads change,"* and management *"manages policy,"* i.e., *the status quo.* Are the people in the targeted department—those who will be called on to make the changes—leaders, or are they managers only?

The Point

You are looking for highly specific leadership qualities that are necessary for the task of achieving an excuse-free culture. If the unit targeted for intervention is the entire company, the people at the top levels must be assessed to determine whether or not they have these qualities. If the unit in question is a department or a division of the company, then the people in charge must be evaluated.

The purpose is not to chastise individuals, nor to set them up for embarrassment. It is to identify where the shortcomings are in your leaders so the problems can be corrected. You will recall that two of the qualities you need in your leaders are to be mentally tough and emotionally stable. True leaders are strong enough to look at the truth about themselves. They welcome the feedback about any behavior that is excuse-related so they can eliminate it. As Harry Truman said, "If you can't stand the heat, get out of the kitchen." If your "leaders" can't deal with the results of being evaluated for excuse-making, maybe that's a big clue that they aren't the type of leader you need.

Again, **if you want an excuse-free culture, leadership is where it all begins.** This is the cornerstone of the entire excuse-free concept.

Getting Started

There are two central questions to ask in the intervention step:

• Do the people in charge of the targeted unit have the qualities necessary to lead the unit into an excuse-free culture?

• If the answer is "no," what can be done to remedy the situation?

Are Your Leaders Qualified?

The first way to determine the qualifications of your leaders is through your own observation. You need to begin to look at your leaders in a new way: through the filter of the leadership qualities that are required to lead others into excuse-free behaviors. These qualities are listed for you in figure 11 (p. 198).

Observe the leaders of each unit that needs intervention (as determined in the diagnostic step). Start by observing them in meetings. Instead of leading the meeting yourself, just sit in on it. Don't say anything, but rather look, listen, and learn. Use figure 11 as a checklist of behaviors. Observe each of your executives, managers, supervisors, or whomever you expect to be in positions of leadership in that unit. See in what ways these individuals do, or do not, manifest the qualities necessary to lead excuse-free behaviors in others.

You should, of course, observe them in settings other than just meetings—in the hallways, in one-on-one and small-group discussions, over the telephone, and so on. But the meeting room is an excellent place to begin because it allows you the quiet opportunity to focus on your leaders in a new way. It will make you better able to spot certain qualities and behaviors outside the meeting room.

A Helpful Hint

One thing to keep in mind during your observations: If you want to know what the true leadership qualities of an individual are, don't just listen to what he says. Focus on what he does. For example, the person in question may *say* he has a guiding vision, but you want to know whether or not he really has one, and the way to find out is to look for evidence *in his behavior*. Does he make others aware of what his vision is? Does he maintain a steady course in the achievement of a vision? Is his behavior consistent with his vision? These are the types of questions you must ask yourself about his behavior.

If a picture is worth a thousand words, one's behavior is worth ten thousand words, or more.

Using the 360 Survey Again

The second way to get at the question "Do our leaders have the necessary qualities?" is through the use of the 360 survey. Many times in our consulting practices we have seen examples of individuals who thought they were doing well, while the people around them had a very different opinion. The 360 survey is an effective, non-threatening tool for discovering such differences, because the subject is observed from several points of view.

It is often true in the workplace that the perception of a person or situation is more important than the reality about that person or situation. For example, suppose the reality is that a person is not involved in excuse-making behavior. But the perception by others is that the person

195

is indeed guilty of such behavior. Something is out of sync here. At the very least, there is a problem with the extent or style of communication. The point is, *while perception may not always accurately identify the nature of a problem, it always reflects the reality that **there is** a problem.*

Anonymously and confidentially, you will want to ask people at various levels about their perceptions of the leader or leaders in question. Remember that you want to multiply the angles of perception to insure greater accuracy of your results. The greater the number of perceptions, the closer you get to the reality of the qualities of your "leaders."

Again, perceptual differences are differences that need to be resolved. It doesn't matter who's right or who's wrong, but rather what the differences are in perception. In other words, if person A thinks he's a good leader, and person B disagrees, it doesn't matter if person A is right or if person B is right. It only matters that something be done to ensure that both, or neither, come to see person A as a good leader. *If there is a perceived problem, there is a problem. Positive results come from aligned perceptions. Otherwise, resistance to all attempts to move forward is inevitable.*

Who Should Be Given the 360?

You need to involve four different groups of people in the 360 surveys:

• the leaders in the unit or units where intervention is necessary

• all executives who rank above that level of leadership in the organization, if any

• employees within the unit

• other leaders within the company who rank laterally with the leaders in question

True Leaders Get Rid of Excuses

Keep in mind here that your single focus is to evaluate leadership in terms of those characteristics that either *encourage and breed excuses* in the workplace or *discourage and eliminate excuses*. Nothing more. It's that simple. When excuses go, results happen. So you need to find out whether or not you have those players in leadership positions who can get rid of excuses.

The Leadership 360

The leadership qualities listed in this survey are the exact ones that were spelled out in Chapter 8. Figure 11 is a rating form that you can use to determine whether or not an individual meets the requirements to lead his unit into excuse-free behavior.

360 Leadership Survey

Unit or person being surveyed:_____

Directions: Circle the most appropriate number for each category where 4 = outstanding, 3 = good, 2 = fair, 1 = poor.

Has a guiding vision	**4**	**3**	**2**	**1**
Respects a higher authority	**4**	**3**	**2**	**1**
Is self-confident	**4**	**3**	**2**	**1**
Is enthusiastic	**4**	**3**	**2**	**1**
Has a high energy level	**4**	**3**	**2**	**1**
Focuses on the big picture	**4**	**3**	**2**	**1**
Is intuitive & makes decisions inductively	**4**	**3**	**2**	**1**
Expects success from self and others	**4**	**3**	**2**	**1**
Is self-disciplined	**4**	**3**	**2**	**1**
Is willing to take risks	**4**	**3**	**2**	**1**
Is mentally tough & emotionally stable	**4**	**3**	**2**	**1**
Submits to the need for additional knowledge	**4**	**3**	**2**	**1**
Is a good listener	**4**	**3**	**2**	**1**
Is "lucky"	**4**	**3**	**2**	**1**
Is introspective	**4**	**3**	**2**	**1**
Has personal integrity	**4**	**3**	**2**	**1**
Has control	**4**	**3**	**2**	**1**
Is decisive	**4**	**3**	**2**	**1**
Is a good communicator	**4**	**3**	**2**	**1**
Is sensitive to others' feelings and sense of dignity	**4**	**3**	**2**	**1**

Figure 11

The score on each survey is calculated by adding the circled numbers. There are 20 items with a possible score of 4 on each item. The highest score possible, therefore, would be 80, and the lowest would be 20.

Interpreting the Data

The goal is to bring all of your leaders to 100 percent leadership capabilities (that is, a score of 80 on the 360 survey). Our experience is that some people are more demanding than others, and some are more lenient, in the way they assess their leaders. So it is difficult to say exactly what score separates leaders from non-leaders.

A useful way to handle this difficulty is to start with the individuals who have the lowest scores, regardless of what those scores happen to be. Clearly, these people represent your biggest challenge in terms of developing an excuse-free culture. Your job is to make an important decision about each of them. Do you:

- develop the necessary leadership qualities in these individuals through specific training programs?

- reposition people within your company to ensure that you have individuals with higher scores in the leadership positions in that unit?

- let individuals with the lowest scores go and hire new people who have the necessary qualities?

Developing the Necessary Qualities

You may have noticed that some of the leadership qualities lend themselves to development more than others. For example, it is probably easier for a person to improve his communication skills than to enhance his personal integrity. This is not to say that one's integrity can't be developed, but rather that the task may be more difficult. It depends partly on the person in question.

The point is, to help you decide whether or not to begin developing the necessary leadership qualities in a particular person, you will need to look at *which* qualities need improving, and contrast this against the personality of the individual. There are many variables involved, so it is difficult to furnish a handy checklist to accomplish this. In the end, whether or not to work with your people to help them develop leadership qualities is a judgment call. One way you can come up with a clearer answer is to go ahead with training and then determine which individuals have improved and to what degree.

The Importance of Measuring the Results of Training Your Leaders

If you decide to proceed with training, *you must make sure that you measure the results of the training* to see whether you are, in fact, developing the necessary characteristics required of your leaders. If they make progress as a result of the training, then you know that you made the right decision to keep them. If not, then you may need to reconsider.

One of the failings of training programs in general is the absence of effective methods to measure the results. It's like training a distance runner without ever having access to a stopwatch. How would you know if the athlete is improving his performance? Likewise, how would you know whether or not the training programs you are using are bringing you the desired results?

Typically what happens with training and development is that somebody first recognizes there is a problem. Then they bring in a specialist to work on that problem, with no predetermined measurement at the beginning and no measurement at the conclusion. Often the training, and the results of the training, are disappointing.

This frustration and waste of resources (or perceived waste of resources) can be greatly mitigated by doing pre- and post-measurements. *No training program is worthwhile unless the results can be measured against some standard of success.*

This is why the 360 is such a tremendous tool. Its periodic use helps to determine whether or not progress has been made against predetermined weaknesses. This is how you can know in the long run whether to keep someone in a position of leadership, reposition him, or let him go. Your decision in the beginning doesn't have to be the perfect decision; it only has to be the right decision in the end.

Repositioning Your Leaders

It is quite possible that you have certain leaders in your company who do an outstanding job of demanding no-option, excuse-free behavior. They may just not be used to calling it that. In some cases, it may make sense to move one or more such individuals to the key leadership positions where help is needed. Remember from the last chapter that the purpose of the diagnostic step is to identify where and to what degree your organization or your processes are infected. The results of your diagnosis would indicate where you might want to move some of your stronger leaders.

For the persons being replaced, you will need to determine if they can be moved to other positions. Remember, **a person can be a very effective manager without necessarily being an effective leader.** To transplant someone from one position to another so that a stronger leader can take his place is not to say that he isn't a strong manager. This should have no more stigma than moving a tight end to tackle to make sure you have the right people in the right positions on your team. Tackles and tight ends are both valuable and indispensible, but the skills required of the players at each position vary considerably.

Hiring New Leaders

Letting people go and hiring others to replace them is one of the more unpleasant tasks of corporate life. Still, it is sometimes necessary. To *get results, not excuses,* you cannot compromise ensuring that you have the right people in leadership positions.

When you find it necessary to get rid of someone in a leadership position because of his inability or unwillingness to practice excuse-free behavior and demand it of others, you yourself are being a leader. You are a prime example of practicing what you preach: Your **guiding vision** (to rid your company of excuse-making) is an act of

respecting a higher authority (the authority of your values statement). It is part of **staying focused on the big picture** and not letting obstacles (i.e., the wrong person in a position of leadership) get in the way. It is an expression of **expecting success from self and others** in that success is defined as becoming excuse-free. It is an act of **mental toughness and emotional stability** to let someone go who is not suited for the assignment. It also means that you are **in control** and **decisive.** *The leadership qualities that you model when you let a person go and hire another to replace him are the very leadership qualities you expect from others.*

As for actually hiring new people into leadership positions, it will of course be absolutely necessary to hire individuals who have the characteristics of leadership as listed in figure 11 and as discussed in Chapter 8. It will do little good to fire certain individuals, only to replace them with people who are no more capable of leading than those whom you let go. The specific skills and tools required to hire leaders who can lead others into excuse-free behavior is a topic too large to cover at this time. It will, however, be explored in detail in a future work.

In Conclusion

Ridding your company (or department or unit) of excuses is your primary task. That process begins and ends in leadership. It cannot be accomplished without the right players. Your leaders must be individuals who can lead in the direction of an excuse-free culture. If that means intervention is necessary to train, reposition, or replace certain persons, then that's what must be done. You are not looking to run a popularity contest, or to be seen by everyone as Mr. Nice Guy. Your job is to *get results, not excuses* in order to become number one again. Nothing short of that should matter.

If you want to get results, not excuses, you must find the right people for the leadership positions in your company. This is your number-one priority in the intervention step.

15

The Integration Step: Developing a Unified System

One of Total Quality Management's most fundamental principles is the importance of integrating the vision
and mission statements with the personal goals of everyone
in the company. Few would argue that the TQM approach
is valid. Those companies that have applied it have
realized that a high level of commitment is necessary to
reap its benefits.

The TQM approach is not far removed from what
we mean by the concept of integration. The difference is
that TQM integrates the **vision** and **mission** statements into
everyone's personal goals with the single focus being

quality. Our system of management integrates the **values** statement into everyone's personal goals with the single focus being *excuse-free behavior.* These two approaches— or for that matter, ours and *any* other management approach—are not to be seen in contest with each other. TQM, as with other management theories, emphasizes tasks—*things to do*; our system emphasizes behaviors—*ways to do those things.*

In this sense, we look at our management system as "beyond" TQM. We don't mean by this "better than," but rather, that excuse-free behavior *enhances* the quest for quality. *When you have the proper behavior, everything else you're striving to accomplish improves,* including quality.

How Does a Company "Integrate" an Excuse-Free Culture?

Your values statement *is* your desired culture. It must become part of everything you do. Your primary values statement, remember, is *to become excuse-free.* So the question that must be asked of all behavior in your company is, "Is this consistent with our goal to eliminate excuses from the workplace?"

The point is that virtually everything you do must be filtered through the asking—and the answering—of this question. In other words, when we set up our organizational structure, when we develop our processes, when we deal with our people—are we doing this in a way that supports excuse-free behavior?

Let's look at a few examples of what it means to integrate each of these elements—organization, processes, and people.

Integration of Your Organization

One company we worked with was a two-part company: a multi-location retail operation and a single-location wholesale operation. The company made an attempt at vertical integration by having the wholesale part of their company be the sole supplier for their retail operations.

What happened is that the retailers began to complain that they couldn't make any money because wholesale was charging them too much. Wholesale claimed that they were charging that much because retail wouldn't let them sell outside of their organization. This was artificially keeping their sales level low, so they had to charge more. Naturally, this projection of blame onto each other led to a good deal of infighting because—structurally speaking—this represented a major organizational problem. Since the rewards of both parts of the company were based on sales, the company was set up organizationally to cause dissention, projection of blame, denial of responsibillity, externalization, and therefore necessarily, excuses.

This is a fairly common example of how the structure of the organization is not integrated with a values statement to have an excuse-free culture. Any time this is the case, one of two things is true: either there is *no* values statement to become excuse-free; or the values statement to become excuse-free *is* in place, but the organization won't allow for that value to be integrated.

In this particular case, the second was true. That is, the company had a values statement in place to become excuse-free, and they believed in it. But the company was blocked in its effort to achieve its goal until the structure of their organization was repaired. They needed to decide what business they were in, wholesale or retail. And when they did, excuse-making went away and the desired results began to happen.

****

The thrust of the integration step is (1) to adopt the values statement to become excuse-free, and (2) to make certain that it can be applied, and that no blocks exist or are allowed in the effort to implement it.

Integration of Your Processes

There are many examples that could be used here because companies typically have multiple processes. Some examples include:

- the human resource process
- the process of developing individual goals
- the sales process
- the marketing process
- the invoicing process
- the financial statement process
- the product development process
- the purchasing process
- the customer service process
- the problem-solving process

We will use only the first example—the human resource process—to look at integration. Specifically, let's look at the hiring, training, evaluation, and promotion portions of the human resource process.

1. When hiring: Are people screened against the backdrop of excuse-making? Are they asked questions that relate to their own personal values to see if they are consistent or inconsistent with being excuse-free? Do you know what questions to ask to find out if their personal values are excuse-free? Is there a company policy about expectations of results-oriented rather than excuse-oriented behavior? Is this communicated clearly to them? Are there clear penalties for excuse-making in your company, and are the interviewees told what those penalties are?

2. Concerning training: Are your training programs geared toward the elimination of excuses? Are periodic measurements and accountabilities built into the training process? Are those people who are discovered through employee evaluations to be making excuses specifically taught how to reverse their behavior? Are training programs in place that explain why people make excuses? Are there programs to help people deal more effectively with those who make excuses? Are training programs that contradict the excuse-free effort eliminated or modified? Are leaders taught how to lead others into excuse-free behavior?

3. Regarding evaluations and incentives: Are employee evaluations tailored to assess one's performance based on excuse-free standards? Are employees' incentives—whether recognition, pay raise, or promotion—based on their excuse-free behavior? Are promotions given on the basis of survival and seniority, or are they the consequence of clear and accurate measurement of results due to the absence of excuses in one's work-related behavior? Remember, where there are no excuses, there will be results.

Integration of Your People

This relates directly to the leadership issue. We've talked about how instrumental your leaders are to the development of an excuse-free culture. They alone furnish the impetus to turn around the behaviors in an excuse-infected company.

So the question needs to be asked: "Do the people you have in leadership positions have the qualities necessary to lead your company into excuse-free behavior?" This, you will recall, was the primary focus of the intervention step. If your "leaders" are excuse-makers themselves or are not focused on leading others into an excuse-free environment, then you have not yet properly integrated your people.

In addition, *everyone* must have some of the same qualities that your leaders have, even if they are not in direct leadership positions. For example, all employees must respect a higher authority, be self-disciplined, be good listeners, and have personal integrity. Your values statement to become excuse-free can't be fully integrated into your people until all your employees have developed the leadership skills that apply individually to themselves.

The Integration Step: Developing a Unified System

The Company That Pulls Together Wins Together

Every company, large or small, works on various ways of improving its organization, its processes, and its people. Most companies have a vision statement and/or mission statement and/or values statement. *But very few companies work to integrate all of these into a unified system. To do so is the point of the integration step.*

A company whose values statement to become excuse-free is not integrated into its organization, processes, and people, as well as into its vision and mission statements, is like one team in a tug-of-war match in which each person on the team is tugging in a different direction. The team isn't pulling together. Any competitor with a more coordinated effort will almost surely win.

In contrast, the company that integrates the goal to become excuse-free into its entire system will work as a unit and overpower any company that pays little attention to this issue. A company with an integrated excuse-free system is a streamlined company. It is a company destined to win.

Notes and Quotes

And oftentimes excusing of a fault doth make the fault worse by the excuse.

Shakespeare: King John

16

The Implementation Step:
All Aboard!

Definition

Im-ple-ment, v. 1. To carry into effect; to fulfill, accomplish. 2. To provide the means for carrying into effect or fulfilling; to give practical effect to.

****

The implementation step involves getting your people to actually achieve excuse-free behavior. In the end, this is what getting results is all about. All of the understanding you've gained, and the best of your diagnostic and interventional efforts, amount to very little until the behavior is fully owned by your employees. They are the soldiers who must fight the corporate war.

Implementation is usually one of the toughest jobs when it comes to changing corporate behavior. Most leaders do a credible job of developing the concepts and understanding what needs to be done. Often they get excited about the anticipated changes. But by the time it gets to actual implementation, the whole thing falls flat. One reason for this is our mistaken belief that new behavior is something we do once or twice, and then it's learned. But human behavior doesn't change that quickly. Implementation is a never-ending process if it is to be effective.

The Five Stages of Implementation

There are five key stages to the implementation step of developing an excuse-free culture:

- motivation (or buy-in)
- establishment of accountabilities and key indicators
- benchmarking
- coaching
- reward and recognition

The Distinction Between Power and Authority

Before we address each of these five stages, it is

helpful to look at the distinction between power and authority. The terms are often mistakenly used interchangeably. But they differ in an important way.

Authority is the aggregate of the rights vested in, or granted to, individuals by an organization. **Power** is the ability or capacity to act on, or enforce, that authority. Usually those who have authority also have the power to enforce their authority. But not always. *Any time there is resistance to authority and the resistance succeeds, at that moment the power shifts from the authority base to the person or persons who are resisting.*

An Example

Jerry is the sales manager for an international company that distributes commercial building products. He oversees the work of 12 regional managers, each of whom supervises 6 district managers. Jerry has been granted the authority by the company to establish policy for all 72 of the people who answer to him.

Jerry established new reporting policies and regulations that took effect on January 1, 1993. Specifically, each district manager was to submit a bi-monthly written report to his regional manager, who in turn would submit a report to Jerry. Prior to that, reports had been required monthly.

All 72 individuals resented the new policy, feeling they were too busy as it was. The reports took an average of four hours to complete, and they saw it as a waste of time to do that twice a month rather than once. So they didn't do the second report each month.

Perturbed at the lack of response, Jerry restated the new policy several times throughout the year, but nothing ever changed. Whereas Jerry has the authority to fire all 72 people and start over, from a realistic point of view he can't do that. He would be without a sales force; it would be difficult to hire qualified people who were knowledgeable about the business; sales would drop drastically; and so on. The headaches would be immense. *In this situation, (1) the power has shifted from Jerry to his managers, even though Jerry still has the authority; and (2) his managers have exercised their power by not implementing his new policy.*

So What Should This Mean As It Concerns the Implementation Step?

The key to the implementation step is buy-in by employees. The key to buy-in is motivation.

****

Times have changed regarding motivating people in the workplace. It used to be that you could motivate people to change through the use of authority *and* power. This is no longer true. Management still has the authority to make recommendations, set policy, and decide on various matters. But the power-wielding has changed drastically from, say, 20 years ago. Management has lost much of its power to enforce policy, to hire and fire people, and to "run the show" in ways that were commonplace in the past.

Why Is This the Case?

At the dawn of the industrial age, those in authority held all the power. The collective oppression of the working people eventually caused labor to organize in reaction to the abuse of power. As a result, some of the power began shifting to the rank and file of the union. This was the first step in the movement of power away from those in positions of authority.

Even so, the power gained by the working class stayed mostly in the hands of the union leaders. People in the workplace did not have personal power to change their working situations. Until about twenty years ago, the average employee worked for one company for the better part of his or her productive years. It was not uncommon for people to stay with the company that first employed them until they retired. Rarely did people jump from one company to another. And the concept of "career change" was almost unheard of.

In fact, until fairly recently there was a social and professional stigma against changing jobs. If somebody changed jobs four or five times, it was a black mark on their resume. They were considered "job hoppers." Now as you look at a resume you might wonder if someone stayed employed with a company for *too* long. There is almost a stigma against job longevity. One tends to suspect that a person who stuck to one place must have been too comfortable there, doesn't like challenge, doesn't stretch himself, may not be ambitious, probably doesn't have much diversity of experience, and so on.

The point is that in the past it was not usually in the best interests of an individual to change jobs or careers. After being with a company for X-number of years, the cut in pay that one would have to take to move to another job, including the loss of perks and benefits, prevented much movement.

But Times Have Changed

Starting with legislation in the mid-seventies—which mandated equal opportunity for all employees in a company to participate in the same retirement plan—it became more and more difficult for companies to have retirement plans for their workers. As a result, many companies dropped them. Retirement plans were an effective method for keeping employees with the company, even if they weren't entirely happy with their jobs. With the loss of retirement plans came the loss of the golden handcuffs that held many such people in their jobs. In addition, tax laws have moved steadily in the direction of taxing all benefits, which makes the accrual of benefits to an employee less and less appealing.

Also, as companies become more sophisticated, they are moving away from seniority raises and are basing promotions and raises on merit and results. Just staying with a company does not assure promotions or additional monies as had been true in the past.

In Other Words

The social and business conditions have changed so much that there is little resemblance to what was happening

20 years ago. Middle-class America has become fairly comfortable.

It is now common practice for people to leave their jobs after four or five years. In addition, the average person changes careers three or four times in his lifetime. There is no longer sufficient financial reason for people to stay put. Most people can change jobs, or careers, with little or no loss of income and benefits.

The result is that the power base has shifted away from management toward the employees. People no longer have to stay in one job, so the threat of losing one's job has lost its power. People can usually go elsewhere to find equal or greater financial opportunity, and thus incentives have lost much of their once-magical appeal. The point is that companies can no longer motivate people to change through the traditional use of reward and punishment.

Stage One: Motivation

Motivating people in the workplace today is a new ball game. It is getting people to buy-in to change by helping them see what value the change has for them as individuals.

It is joked that the most widely listened-to radio station in our society today—one that plays non-stop at the unconscious level—is station **WII-FM: What's In It-For Me!** This frame of mind spills over into our companies in a big way. In the past, when management asked for change in behavior, the average worker was inclined to reply, "What good will this do for the company?" Today the first question is usually "What will this do for me personally?"

The point is that to motivate people in the workplace

nowadays, it is important to *find out what motivates each person individually.* That is, what are the personal reasons that make changing his behavior worth his while?

Rules for the Motivation Stage

Rule #1: You can't motivate groups, only individuals.

The traditional approach to motivating people in the workplace is in the group setting. Managers stand up in front of the group and say that such and such is going to help make the company more profitable. But this approach isn't effective anymore because people aren't all that interested in what such and such will do for the company. Since your people change for *their* reasons, not yours and not the company's, it follows that they must be worked with individually. How to do this will be covered in stage four of this chapter under "coaching."

Rule #2: Each person is motivated by different things.

We can no longer assume that everyone is motivated by the traditional incentives: job security, pay raise, and so on. Since, as we said, middle-class America is a fairly comfortable place to be today, more and more people are looking for different things from their jobs. Some people, for example, are motivated by a job that doesn't cause a lot of stress, others by never having to work more than 40 hours per week, and still others by jobs that never make demands on their time outside of normal working hours.

We can all think of countless examples of salespeople who—if they stretched themselves and moved out of their comfort zones—could make considerably more money for themselves and for their companies. But they are content with the amount of money they are presently making, which leads us to rule #3.

Rule #3: Money in itself is not a motivation for anyone.

At least not directly. What motivates many people is what money can do. For some people money provides security; for others, freedom; for others, it's a scorecard used to meter their success; for others, it enables them to purchase "toys"; and for others it relieves the pressure of debt.

The irony is that most corporations assume that what motivates their employees is money alone. They start putting all sorts of financial incentives on the table. Most motivational programs in companies are financially based. The result is that you are only appealing to the people who are motivated by the particular form in which you are granting the money. That's one reason that the same people usually win cash-prize contests. This leaves little room for others to be motivated.

One of the most successful motivation and incentive programs we've done is to put a budget out and let each employee know what that budget was. Then we gave each of them a choice about what to do with the money if they reached their goals. The choices included cash in combination with a trophy or plaque, specific "toys" to choose from, a shopping spree, an investment plan, etc. This allowed each employee to take the money and use it in the way that was most meaningful to him.

Then again, it's important to keep in mind that money is rarely as valuable a motivator as recognition and challenge. It is important to ascertain what type of recognition

221

specific individuals want. Some employees are very satis-fied with a nice note or letter, or just a pat on the back with private congratulations. Others want their name in lights for everyone else in the company to see.

Increasingly, research is showing us that "challenge" is becoming more and more of a personal motivator for people. Which brings up an interesting irony: Typically a company will hire people based on what they have done, not on what they may be able to do if challenged to stretch and grow. This hiring approach destines people to be unchallenged in their new jobs. Yet challenge is one of the highest motivators that we know of.

Rule #4: You must determine "who" motivates each individual.

The day is gone when we can assume that "the boss" can, or must, motivate his workers. Not everyone is motivated by supervision. Management's responsibility to-day is to find out *whom* each individual depends on for his or her motivation, and then to work with those factors.

Many times we have seen people highly motivated by their spouses, so a statement like "Won't your spouse be proud of you when you accomplish such and such?" can be very effective. Sometimes people are motivated by their parents and children. We have seen many cases where people want to succeed to show their parents that they can make it on their own. In one case, we worked with a woman who was highly motivated by the fact that she wanted her eight-year-old daughter to see that she could be successful in the business world, and that business success was not just for men.

Rule #5: Stay cognizant of the fact that everything has the potential to motivate someone.

You've heard the sayings "One man's meat is another man's poison" and "Different strokes for different folks." The application of these statements here is that you never know what truly motivates each individual until you take the time to find out. For one person it may be the size of the desk, for another the location of their work station, for another the uniform they wear. It helps to refrain from imposing one's own values on what should motivate other people, and to stay open to what they prefer.

Rule #6: Whatever motivates people tends to change.

Once a person reaches his motivational objective, he will likely become motivated by whatever will help him reach his next goal. Motivation is a moving target, and managers must stay continually updated about how it is changing for each employee.

Rule #7: Motivation takes time.

Many readers will relate to what often surfaces in management seminars as the single biggest area of frustration: *How can I motivate my people?* One of the reasons for this is that motivation takes much more time than most managers ever think of expending. When you get right down to the details of how to motivate people, it requires a large investment of time spent individually with employees, trying to figure out what makes them tick, and what the right buttons are to push to keep them moving. The point of this entire section on motivation is that motivation in the workplace from now on is at the *individual* level.

The Solution to the Problem

That is where the corporate power base now lies.

Stage Two: Establishment of Accountabilities and Key Indicators

---

Companies are starting to recognize and give attention to the importance of accountabilities and key indicators. We applaud this as a first step, yet more must be done in applying these concepts.

Key indicators are indicators of performance and predictors of the future. Generally, people are starting to understand the importance of defining three to five key indicators for each company. By monitoring their key indicators, an organization is in effect continually taking its own pulse. What hasn't yet been accomplished, however, is applying the same concept to each employee. The goal is to have three to five key indicators for each person that serve as his or her accountabilities.

Traditionally, accountabilities have been tied directly into the vision and mission statements, and have therefore been task-based. Emphasis has been on attaining sales quotas, getting reports in on time, achieving less than five percent error in processing paperwork, and so on.

Most companies today are still following this same pattern of building accountabilities around the vision and mission statements. This approach will not work if the goal is to become excuse-free. Corporations must begin to place more emphasis on their values statement than on their vision and mission statements. The fast-changing conditions of the marketplace require that it is more important to have the right behavior than the right mission. People with the right behavior will automatically develop the right mission.

By the same token, companies that begin to tie their employees' accountabilities and key indicators into employee behavior will discover two distinct benefits. First, they will be changing and enhancing employee behavior, which is the goal of accountabilities in the first place. Second, they will not limit employee performance by putting a ceiling on whatever the task at hand is, as tends to happen when accountabilities are measured by task accomplishment. Instead, workers will have the flexibility to adapt as needed, as long as the emphasis is on their excuse-free behavior. The point is that behavior-based accountabilities keep employees more attuned to changing with a fast-changing market.

We're saying that accountabilities and key indicators must be tied into the values statement—specifically, into the values statement to become excuse-free. This values statement is behavior-based rather than task-based, and therefore builds in more latitude and more flexibility for responding to market conditions.

The role of accountabilities in the development of an excuse-free culture is such an enormous topic that we can barely mention it here. Future books and newsletters will devote considerable time to this critical element of the success formula. For now, your task is to look at the accountabilities and key indicators that you have and see if they are behavior-based or task-based. Once this is determined, we'll help you move forward from there.

Stage Three: Benchmarking

Benchmarking is about the need for measurement. If you want to improve something, you must measure it.

What benchmarking does is set a starting point and a methodology for measuring the progress of any change effort you wish to undertake.

The tool we recommend for benchmarking is the same one used for the diagnosis, namely, the 360 survey. Whereas the questions will be different, what will be the same is that they will be qualitative rather than quantitative, since what must be measured is behavior, not task completion. Benchmarking is helpful for this because it allows the accumulation of a number of opinions from different perspectives. As you do the benchmarking, you are also looking to make sure that the weaknesses and difficulties that show up are tied into the accountabilities and key indicators. The two processes go hand in hand.

This is similar to what we mentioned in Chapter 14 about training and development programs. The practice of training people without pre- and post-measurements often amounts to a waste of resources because there is no way to know for certain whether or not any change occurred. So with accountabilities: In order to know whether or not the factors for which a person is held accountable have been achieved, those factors must be periodically measured. Otherwise, too much is left to subjective interpretation. And this becomes a breeding ground for conflict, passing of responsibilities, projection of blame, and all the other excuse-related behaviors.

Stage Four: Coaching

Coaching is for individuals, not teams. This relates back to rule #1 under the motivation stage: You can't motivate groups, only individuals.

226

Yet this is precisely what makes the coaching step undoubtably the most difficult of all. Finding the time to properly coach individuals is a very difficult challenge for managers and leaders today, given the flattening of management structures and an increase in the ratio of employees to managers. Part of the reason for the difficulty, however, is that coaching sessions are too often based on "telling" rather than on facilitation.

The point of coaching is not to have a two-hour sit-down session every week so that the manager can tell the employee what to do. It is, rather, a process whereby an employee learns how to coach himself to reach his own answers, solutions, and directions under the mentorship of his manager. Again, this could take volumes to cover in detail, which we promise to do in other books and newsletters. There are a few elements, however, that can be stressed here:

• Coaching sessions must be regularly planned and executed, preferably no less often than twice a month, and ideally once a week.

• Coaching sessions should always have a predetermined agenda, with no surprises.

• The manager should be asking questions, and the employee should be doing most of the talking.

• The focus of the coaching session should be on behavior, not tasks.

• Coaching sessions should be limited to a certain length of time. Twenty to thirty minutes is a good average. In the first coaching session, employee and employer will struggle to hold the time to that limit. However, by insisting that the time be held to a specific limit, eventually both will become more focused and better prepared, and you will find that it takes less time than at first. This awareness is critical because our experience indicates that managers get away from coaching their people mainly because of time constraints. Yet the issue of time constraints doesn't need to be a major concern. A manager with eight employees reporting directly to him surely should be able to find four hours a week to properly coach his people. What tends to happen, however, is that the four hours expand to ten, and neither employee nor employer sees a lot of value in the process because there is too much "telling" and not enough questioning and development.

Stage Five: Reward and Recognition

When a company is successful in implementing excuse-free behavior, a celebration is clearly in order. Keeping in mind that the celebration may have to be individually tailored, let's not forget that implementation without some type of reward and recognition is like winning an Olympic marathon and not getting a gold medal. The reward is necessary to complete the task of helping people reach their goal of "what's in it for me," which is the motivation that began the entire process of change.

And Last

In the end, the power to implement excuse-free

behavior rests with the employees and not with management. We repeatedly hear employees crying out for help to become more empowered. This management system—*Let's Get Results, Not Excuses*—and, in particular, this implementation step, is empowerment in the fullest sense of the word. The goal of everyone in any organization should be to empower the employees in that organization. That goal can finally be reached through excuse-free behavior.

The implementation step is virtually impossible without successful high-level communications. All five steps are critically tied to the concept of good communication. Again, however, to spell out the details of a communication style that will best accomplish these various steps would far exceed the space limitations of this book. Yet committed as we are to the cause of giving you a total, airtight package for eliminating excuses from your workplace, we will soon publish other needed information.

Notes and Quotes

Where the heart is willing, it will find a thousand ways: but where the heart is weak, it will find a thousand excuses.

Anonymous

17

In Conclusion

We said in the Preface that the subject of excuse-making is far too big a topic to cover in a single work, and that this book would be at most an introduction to the problems that result from excuses in the workplace. As promised, much more information will follow on this new management approach.

Nevertheless, we are faced at this point with the question "How do we end a book about a subject that we have just begun to explore?" Obviously, it wouldn't be practical, nor does space allow, for a review of every point made throughout the book. Still, there are certain signposts that do mark the trail of where this book has taken you.

The Solution to the Problem

Our hope is that a review of these will help solidify the basics of how excuses operate in our organizations, and the danger they pose.

1. People Make Excuses to Protect Themselves

There is nothing inherently devious or immoral about excuse-making. Everybody does it on occasion. As the eye blinks reflexively when an object moves suddenly toward it, excuse-making is an instinctive, unconscious, automatic response to protect oneself in the face of real or perceived criticism, blame, or failure.

Lies, white lies, rationalizations, and excuses are distinct from each other in certain ways. Most notably, excuses are pervasive and generalized. They become a socially acceptable way of defending ourselves, and thus are considered a fact of life more than a character flaw. Excuse-making is a low-grade social ailment—excusitis—that most people are well-practiced at by the age of four. In corporate America, this four-year-old behavior resurfaces often and expresses itself extensively. This is because of the many situations in our organizations and processes that tend to invite, allow, encourage, and even "force" self-protection.

2. Excuses, Explanations, and Reasons Are Closely Related Concepts

The difference between excuses and explanations or reasons is whether or not an individual is willing to accept

232

the responsibility for a wrongdoing, and whether or not he is willing to do whatever is necessary to correct any problem that may have resulted from that wrongdoing.

For example, if a person who is late for work claims that he was late because the traffic was unusually heavy (thereby implying that he couldn't help it—the problem is *outside* of himself), that is an excuse. If, on the other hand, he says that he was late because he didn't anticipate heavy traffic and therefore didn't allow enough time to make up for it—and he states expressly that he wants to make up for whatever was not done as a result of being late—that is an explanation or reason.

Partly because excuses are often passed off as explanations or reasons, and partly because excuse-making is a pervasive, socially acceptable phenomenon, it can be fairly difficult to recognize exactly what constitutes an excuse and what does not. Yet it is very important to learn to identify *all* excuses in the workplace because:

3. Excuses Are Dangerous to Our Companies; They Never Exist Alone

Wherever there are excuses, there are also many other problems infecting corporate America. *Excuses and other corporate problems always appear together.* The symptoms include: reactive thinking, denial of responsibility, projection of blame, victimization, pessimism, procrastination, helplessness, can't-do attitudes, entitlement, incompetence, fearfulness, complacency, lack of pride in workmanship, externalization, conflict, poor teamwork, avoidance of issues, and self-deceit. Excuse-making "goes-with" every one of these problems. Their relationship is systemic in that the chronic problems facing our organizations and excuse-making are mutually co-existent—one cannot exist without the other.

4. *When You Get Rid of Excuses, All the Other Problems Go Away*

This is what makes our approach to management truly revolutionary. Excuse-making is the one common denominator of every management problem. *Get rid of excuses and you get rid of all the other problems. That's why, if you want results, you must get rid of excuses!*

This is in striking contrast to other, more traditional approaches to corporate problem solving. Typically the person in charge has a list of organizational problems. Perhaps those problems are obvious, or maybe they turned up in a traditional audit. Either way, the next step is to go out and hire one consulting or training firm to address one problem, another firm to address the next problem, and so on, one problem at a time.

Usually each consulting and training project is totally independent of the others. As a result, there is little if any harmony of purpose; little if any regard for sequence and timing; little if any measurement to determine what is and isn't working. This is not to mention the fact that the problem being addressed may be more of a symptom than the real, underlying problem. None of this is true about developing an excuse-free culture. *One stone kills all the birds at the same time.*

Harmony of purpose, sequence and timing, measurement and adjustment, and addressing the real problem— these are all givens when you work to create an excuse-free culture. **When you get rid of excuses, all the other problems go away.**

5. *The Best Way to Get Rid of Excuses Is to Create an Extraordinary Organization with Extraordinary Processes*

In order to get people to stop making excuses in the workplace, you must first get rid of the reasons that people make excuses. You do this by creating an extraordinary organization with extraordinary processes. The consequence is that you then get extraordinary performance out of ordinary people. *In other words, you get results, not excuses!*

6. *Step One in Creating an Extraordinary Organization with Extraordinary Processes Is to Make Sure That You Have the Right People in Leadership Positions*

Leaders, managers, and administrators don't perform the same functions. Administrators administer past policy; managers manage current conditions; leaders lead by showing the way, introducing, and going first. Leadership is, by definition, proactive, creative, empowered, optimistic—in short, excuse-free.

The leadership that your company needs in the quest to become number one does not happen by chance. It is the result of an aggressively pursued course of action where effective leaders are sought out, hired, promoted, rewarded, developed, and trained. Whether they come from the ranks of management or non-management, whether from inside the company or outside, whether they are experienced or not, the point is that you must have the right leaders in order to develop an excuse-free culture and, consequently, to get the results that you really want.

7. It Gets Easier from There

Ours is a management system based on the impor-tance of changing **behavior**. That is a unique approach. It moves the focus from *what* people do to *how* they do it—to the standards of conduct. In other words, it moves the focus from vision and mission statements to values state-ments—in particular, to the values statement of becoming and remaining excuse-free.

Once you are committed to the values statement of having an excuse-free culture, then you diagnose where the excuse-making virus is at work in your company. Next you intervene by getting your leaders in place to lead your people into excuse-free behavior. This enables you to inte-grate your vision, mission, and values statements in order to create an extraordinary organization with extraordinary processes. It's smooth sailing the rest of the way. Imple-menting the system—benchmarking, establishing account-abilities and key indicators, measuring behaviors by use of 360-degree audits, motivating, coaching, rewarding—is a relatively straightforward process once you understand that the key to corporate success is excuse-free behavior in your people.

****

A Final Note

In spite of all the recent negativity about American business, the time has come when some credit is due. Though for years our status in the world marketplace fell steadily, we are coming back. The message of the doomsayers who continue to beat the drum that American business is losing the race is beginning to sound old. The sky is not falling, and it is not time to run for the hills.

But we still have our share of problems. One of those problems—in fact, *the biggest single problem facing our companies today*—is the problem of excuse-making in the workplace. The problem is not that we've ignored it or denied it or pretended that it wasn't there. *The problem is that we haven't before recognized excuse-making as the huge problem that it is.*

But now we do recognize it. And because we do, the qualities of the American people that made this country and its companies number one before will make us number one again. *The enemy is known, and that enemy is excuse-making. When excuses go, results happen. And getting results is what being number one is all about!*

Notes and Quotes

Ten of the most commonly used excuses in the workplace:
1. That's the way we've always done it.
2. I didn't know you were in a hurry for it.
3. That's not in my department.
4. No one told me to go ahead.
5. I'm waiting for an okay.
6. I didn't think it would make any difference.
7. That's his job, not mine.
8. Wait till the boss comes back and ask him.
9. I'm so busy. I forgot.
10. I just work here: I'm not paid to make decisions.

Unknown

Bibliography

Bardwick, Judith M. *Danger in the Comfort Zone.* New York, NY: AMACOM, a division of American Management Association, 1991.

Bennis, Warren. *On Becoming a Leader.* Reading, MA: Addison-Wesley Publishing Company, 1989.

Bliss, Edwin C. *Doing It Now: A Twelve-Step Program for Curing Procrastination and Achieving Your Goals.* New York, NY: Scribner, 1983.

Burke, Jane B. *Procrastination: Why You Do It, What to Do About It.* Reading, MA: Addison-Wesley Publishing Company, 1983.

Caldwell, John. *Excuses, Excuses: How to Get Out of Practically Everything.* New York, NY: Crowell, 1981.

Bibliography

Colson, Chuck, and Jack Eckerd. *Why America Doesn't Work.* Dallas, TX: Word Publishing, 1991.

Connors, Roger. *The Oz Principle.* Englewood Cliffs, NJ: Prentice-Hall, 1993.

Covey, Stephen R. *The 7 Habits of Highly Effective People.* New York, NY: Simon and Schuster, 1989.

Iacocca, Lee. *Iacocca: An Autobiography.* With William Novak. New York, NY: Bantam Books, Inc., 1984.

Johnson, Linda Carlson. *Responsibility.* New York, NY: Rosen Publishing Group, 1990.

Mead, Lawrence M. *Beyond Entitlement: The Social Obligations of Citizenship.* New York, NY: Free Press, 1986.

Monks, Robert. *Power and Accountability.* New York, NY: Harper Business, 1991.

O'Toole, James. *Making America Work: Productivity and Responsibility.* New York, NY: Continuum, 1981.

Rodgers, T.J., William Taylor, and Rick Foreman. *No Excuses Management.* New York, NY: Doubleday, 1992.

Ryan, Kathleen D., and Daniel K. Oestreich. *Driving Fear Out of the Workplace.* San Francisco: Jossey-Bass Publishers, 1991.

Scherkenbach, William W. *The Deming Route to Quality and Productivity*. Wasington, DC: CEEPress Books, 1992.

Stevenson, Burton Ebert. *The Home Book of Verse*. New York-Chicago-San Francisco: Holt, Reinhart, Winston, 1953.

Wahlroos, Sven. *Excuses*. New York, NY: MacMillan Publishing Company, Inc., 1981.

Walton, Mary. *The Deming Management Method*. New York, NY: Perigee Books, 1986.

James M. Bleech

Jim is the Chairman of the Board of the Leadership Development Center. He is a Certified Professional Consultant to Management, and a former CPA. In his 25 years of private industry experience, Jim has held positions as Chief Operating Officer of a large multi-national construction firm and Chief Executive Officer of a high-profile business in the service sector. Currently he consults with numerous individuals ranging from entrepreneurs of small companies to Fortune 500 senior executives. He is a highly sought-after public speaker and seminar leader. His expertise has been primarily in the areas of sales and marketing growth, and personal leadership skill development for CEO's.

David G. Mutchler

David is the President of the Leadership Development Center. He is a Certified Professional Consultant to Management and a member of the National Bureau of Professional Management Consultants. David's background is in education and psychology. In years past, he was widely recognized as a highly successful teacher and coach. He holds college degrees in education, psychology, philosophy, and social work. In more recent years David has worked as a trainer and consultant to the business community both nationally and internationally. His areas of expertise are in communication training, organizational development, and leadership training for managers and corporate executives.

Notes

Notes

Notes

Forthcoming Topics Related to Excuse-Free Behavior

Excuse-Free Leadership

Self-Esteem and Excuse-Making

Skills and Tools for Hiring Excuse-Free Leaders

Coaching People into Excuse-Free Behavior

Empowerment Is Becoming Excuse-Free

Excuse-Free Accountabilities and Key Indicators

Diagnosis of Your Culture, A-Z

Management and Leadership Differences

Excuse-Free Career Advancements

Corporate Planning and Excuses

Teamwork and Excuses

No-Excuse Risk-Taking

Self-Motivation and Results

Putting an End to Procrastination

Developing Excuse-Free Customers

Presently available, the

"Let's Get Results"

newsletter!

<u>*The*</u> on-going tool to help you create an excuse-free workplace!

Every month the authors of **Let's Get Results, Not Excuses!** bring you the latest techniques in every important area of your business, including:

• Interviewing

• Developing performance evaluation criteria

• How to look at departmental organizations

• Differences between management and Leadership

• Measuring and rewarding excuse-free behavior

• How to improve your corporate processes

"Excuse-making is the default position for people in organizations unless clear corrective measures are taken to keep that from happening."

Make your company an

Excuse-Free Company

through the programs developed by the authors of

Let's Get Results, Not Excuses!

Products and Services Currently Available to You and Your Company Include:

- Newsletters
- On-Site Seminars
- Off-Site Seminars
- Leadership Development Retreats

(see next page for descriptions)

The "Let's Get Results" Newsletter

You know how important continuing education is for both personal growth and the success of your company. With continuing education comes continuous improvement. This is an informative monthly publication that delivers to you on-going amplification of the step-by-step process to help you rid your company of the excuse-making virus.

The "Let's Get Results" Half-Day Seminar

Perfect for annual meetings, conventions, and planning sessions. An overview of how excuses infect the corporate environment and how damaging they can be. You will also learn the steps necessary to start the process of eliminating excuses from your workplace.

The "Let's Get Results" One-Day and Three-Day Seminars

Gets to the specifics regarding excuses in your company. Helps you with the first steps of diagnosis, an essential aspect of creating a no-excuse organization, as well as how to proceed from there. Three-day seminars help you customize the diagnosis, and provides help on techniques for intervention, hiring, training, coaching, etc.

Advanced Excuse-Free Leadership Retreat

For CEO's and top management ONLY. A comprehensive five-day retreat that covers what you need to know to implement excuse-free leadership in your company from the top down.

For information please contact:

Leadership Development Center
6620 Southpoint Drive South
Suite 240
Jacksonville, Florida 32216
(800) 659-1720
Fax (904) 279-1726

my Book

Grade 2

Modules 1-3

Authors and Advisors

Alma Flor Ada • Kylene Beers • F. Isabel Campoy

Joyce Armstrong Carroll • Nathan Clemens

Anne Cunningham • Martha C. Hougen • Tyrone C. Howard

Elena Izquierdo • Carol Jago • Erik Palmer

Robert E. Probst • Shane Templeton • Julie Washington

Contributing Consultants

David Dockterman • Jill Eggleton

Meet in the Middle

Be a Super Citizen

"You've got to give more than you take."

—Christopher Reeve

How can being a
good citizen make a
difference to others?

Get Curious Video

3

Words About Citizenship

Complete the Vocabulary Network to show what you know
about the words.

citizen

Meaning: A **citizen** is a member of a community, state, or country.

Synonyms and Antonyms	Drawing

difference

Meaning: When people make a **difference**, they do something that helps others.

Synonyms and Antonyms	Drawing

kind

Meaning: Someone who is **kind** is nice, caring, or gentle.

Synonyms and Antonyms	Drawing

We Are ★ ★
SUPER CITIZENS

My dog Bailey is the best! When we learned about good citizens in school, my teacher asked us to think of ways we could be good citizens. I thought about Bailey. She's friendly and gentle. I just knew she could be a good therapy dog.

First, I found a dog club near where I live. My mom and I took Bailey there. Bailey took a test to see how she behaved. She was calm and acted well with strangers. She listened to commands.

After some training classes, we became a therapy dog team. Now my mom and I take Bailey to visit people. Bailey gives them comfort and love.

I like raising a therapy dog. We are good citizens together. Bailey makes a difference in the lives of the people we visit. She helps make their lives better.

FAST FACT

Therapy dogs are not the same as service dogs. Service dogs are trained to provide a certain kind of help for a person with special needs.

7

Prepare to Read

GENRE STUDY **Fantasies** are stories with made-up events that could not really happen. As you read *Clark the Shark,* look for:

- animal characters who talk and act like people
- the beginning, middle, and end of the story
- how pictures and words help you understand what happens

SET A PURPOSE **Ask questions** before, during, and after you read to help you get information or understand the text. Look for evidence in the text and pictures to answer your questions.

POWER WORDS
munch
bellowed
rough
handle
cool
bounce
grinned
might

Meet Bruce Hale.

CLARK THE SHARK

by Bruce Hale

illustrated by Guy Francis

In all the wide blue seas, in all the wide blue world,
the top school for fish was Theodore Roosterfish Elementary.
And of all the fish at Theodore Roosterfish, the biggest and
the strongest was Clark the Shark.

10

Clark loved school, and he loved his teacher, Mrs. Inkydink. He loved to play upsy-downsy and spinna-ma-jig with his friends. Clark *loved* his life.

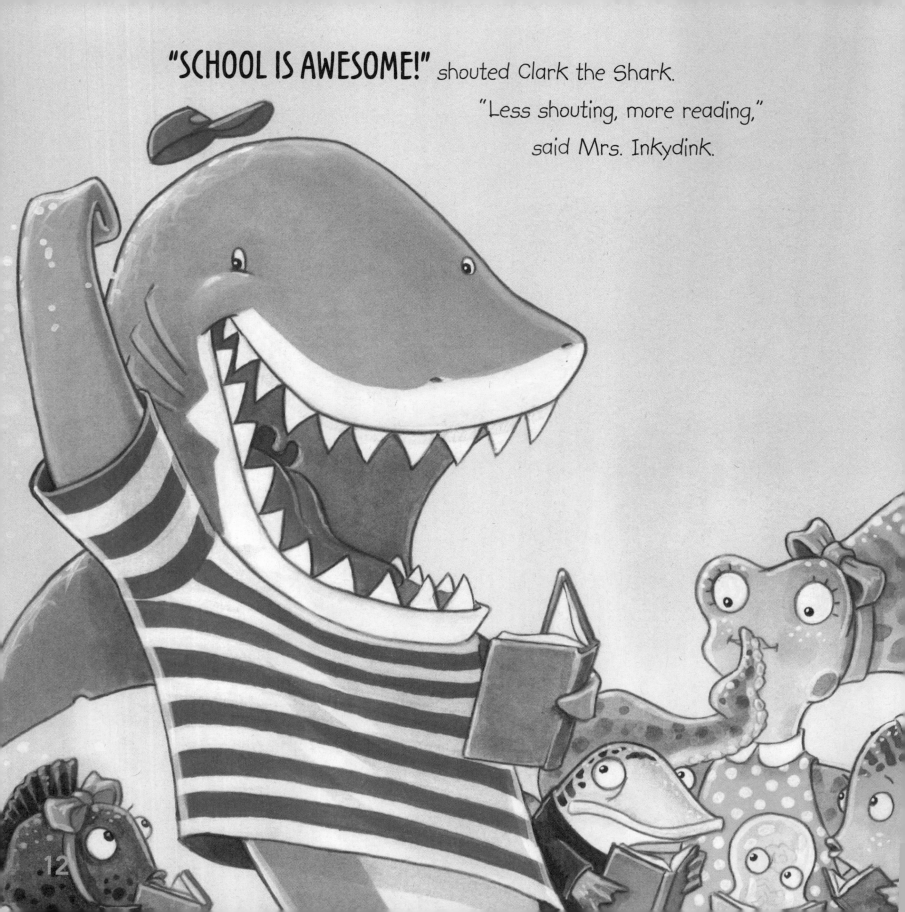

"SCHOOL IS AWESOME!" shouted Clark the Shark.

"Less shouting, more reading," said Mrs. Inkydink.

12

"LUNCHTIME IS SWEEEEET!"

yelled Clark the Shark.

"Munch your *own* lunch," said his best friend, Joey Mackerel.

"RECESS ROCKS!" bellowed Clark the Shark.

"You are playing rough, Clark!"

13

Yes, Clark loved his life with all of his sharky heart. But he loved everything *way* too much.

He was too loud.

He was too wild.

He was just too much shark for the other fish to handle.

After a while, no one would play with Clark. No one ate lunch with him. No one sat with him at circle time. Even his best friend, Joey Mackerel, said, "Cool your jets, Clark! You're making me crazy!"

One day, Clark asked Mrs. Inkydink, "What's *wrong* with everyone?"

Mrs. Inkydink patted his fin. "Clark, sometimes you play too hard, you munch too hard, and—gosh—you even help too hard."

"But life is SO exciting!" said Clark.

"There's a time and a place for everything," said Mrs. Inkydink. "And sometimes the rule is *stay cool*."

STAY COOL!

At recess, Clark tried to stay cool, but he pushed the swing with too much zing! "Sorry," said Clark. "I forgot."
"Yikes!" cried Joey Mackerel.

At lunch, Clark tried to stay cool, but everything smelled so good that he munched a bunch of lunches.
"Sorry," said Clark. "I forgot."
"We're STARVING!" said his friends.

16

In class, Clark tried to stay cool, but a good book got him all shook up.

"Now, Clark!" said Mrs. Inkydink. "This isn't the time or the place. Tell me, what's the rule?"

"Stay cool," said Clark.

"Hey, that rhymes!" he cried.

Then Clark got a big idea in his sharky head. *Maybe if I make a rhyme, I'll remember every time!* he thought. The next day, he put his plan to work.

In class, when lessons got exciting, Clark wanted to bounce up out of his seat.

Instead, he told himself: "When teacher's talking, don't go walking."

And what do you know? It worked!

"Attaboy, Clark!" said Mrs. Inkydink.

Clark smiled. "Lessons are fun!"

At lunch, everything smelled *sooo* yummy. When Clark wanted to eat and eat and never stop, he told himself: "Only munch your own lunch." And it worked again!

"Way to go, Clark!" said his friends.

Clark grinned. "Lunch is fun."

At playtime, Clark told himself: "Easy does
it, that's the way.

"Then my friends will let me play."

And playtime was fun. Once more, Clark
loved his life.

20

But then a shadow fell across the playground—a *gi-normous* shadow with tentacles galore. "It's a new kid, and he looks scary!" cried Joey Mackerel. "Swim for your lives!"

The squid squashed the slide, and it snapped off the swings.

"Oops. My bad," said the new kid.

"Wait," said Clark. "He just wants to play. Let's find a way!"

And he swam at the new kid with all his might. Clark played harder than he ever had before—upsy-downsy and spinna-ma-jig.

Why, he even made up a new game: tail-whump-a-lumpus!

22

"Wow, that was fun," said the new kid breathlessly, and he settled down.
"If you want to come to school, you've got to stay cool," said Clark.

"That's right, Clark," said Mrs. Inkydink. "And thanks for taking care of our new classmate, Sid the Squid."

"Hooray for Clark the Shark!" everyone cheered.

That night Clark's mother asked, "What did you learn at school, dear?"
"There's a time and a place for everything," Clark said. "Sometimes you stay cool."

"But sometimes a shark's gotta do what a shark's gotta do."

Turn and Talk

Use details from *Clark the Shark* to answer these questions with a partner.

1. **Ask and Answer Questions** What questions did you ask yourself about Clark before, during, and after reading? How did your questions help you understand the story?

2. Why do Clark's friends stop playing with him? How do you think that makes him feel? Use details in the text and pictures to explain your ideas.

3. Choose one of Clark's rhyming rules. Explain how it helps him to be a good citizen.

Talking Tip

Your ideas are important! Be sure to speak loudly and clearly as you share them.

Write a Description

PROMPT How do you know that Clark wants to do the right thing? Use details from the words and pictures to explain your ideas.

PLAN First, think about the story. Then draw a scene that shows Clark trying to do the right thing.

WRITE Now, write sentences to describe a time when Clark tries to do the right thing. Remember to:

- Find details in the story that explain your idea.

- Use describing words to tell what Clark does or tries to do.

_____

_____

_____

_____

_____

_____

_____

_____

_____

_____

Prepare to Read

GENRE STUDY **Fantasies** are stories with made-up events that could not really happen. As you read *The Great Puppy Invasion*, look for:

- details about the setting that you would not see in real life
- events that are too silly to happen in the real world
- a lesson the characters learn

SET A PURPOSE As you read, stop and think if you don't understand something. Reread, ask yourself questions, use what you already know, and look for visual clues to help you understand the text.

POWER WORDS

panicked

ridiculous

prohibited

cautiously

Meet Alastair Heim.

THE GREAT PUPPY INVASION

by Alastair Heim

illustrated by Kim Smith

One day, a puppy showed up in little Teddy's town.

Then two.

Then **hundreds**.

The locals panicked. They had never seen **puppies** before.

Little Teddy's town had a long history of ridiculous rules.

Fun was forbidden.
Play was prohibited.
Cuteness was downright criminal.
And *today* was quickly becoming a colossally . . . **cute** . . . **catastrophe**.

The mayor held an emergency meeting in the town hall.
"We must get rid of these adorable creatures," she declared.

The townspeople tried everything they could
to rid themselves of the puppies.

They threw sticks at them.

But the puppies brought the
sticks right back.

They tried chasing the
puppies away.

But the puppies grew even
more delightful.

"Let's try feeding them," someone suggested. "THEN maybe they'll leave."

And *that's* when their tails started wagging . . .

37

People ran for their lives!
The puppies trotted along after them.

They barked.

They yip-yipped.

They ruff-ruff-ruffed.

38

39

One by one, doors began to slam, **slam, slam . . .**

. . . until everyone was safely inside.

But, as little Teddy reached his front porch,
he heard a *teeny* whimper . . .
coming from the *tiniest* puppy of all.

And he wondered how something so sweet and so playful and so adorably sad could possibly be scary.

Just then, the puppy stepped forward, sat down on little Teddy's lawn, and lifted its fuzzy front paw.

Little Teddy approached. The puppy's enormous eyes grew even larger.

He crept closer and closer as the townspeople looked on in horror . . .

43

One by one, the townspeople emerged from their homes. The rest of the puppies sat down and lifted their front paws, too.

The townspeople cautiously stepped forward, then carefully crouched down to kindly shake paws with the cute, countless canines . . .

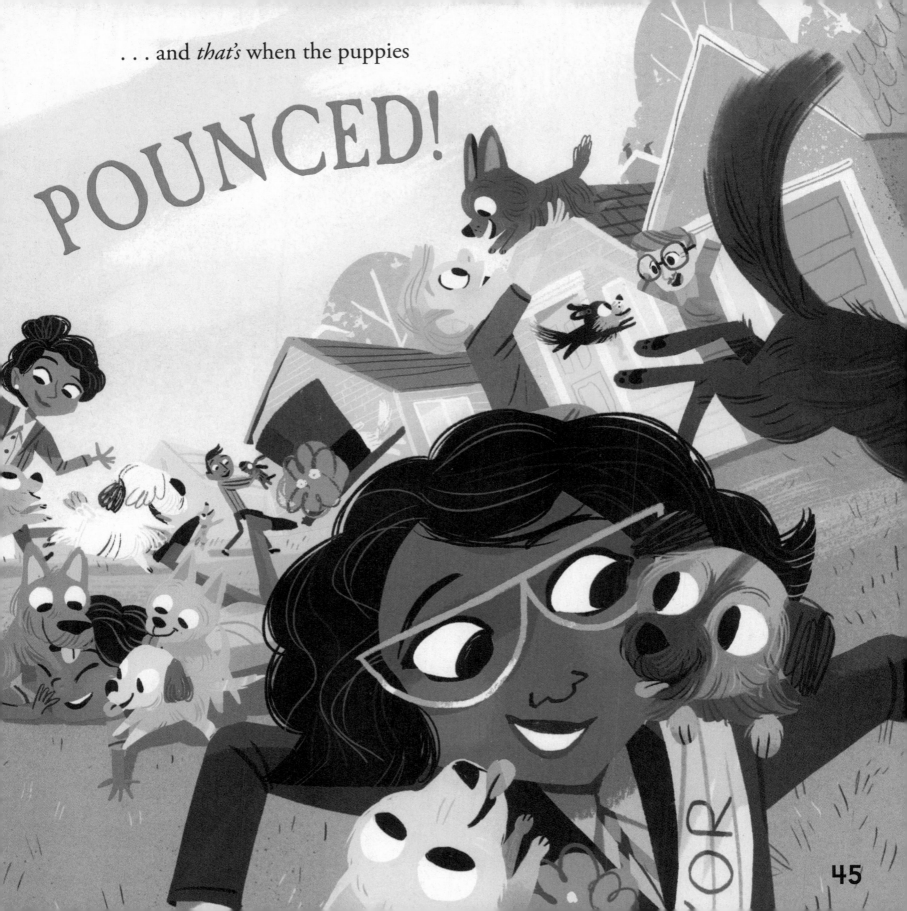

. . . and *that's* when the puppies

POUNCED!

45

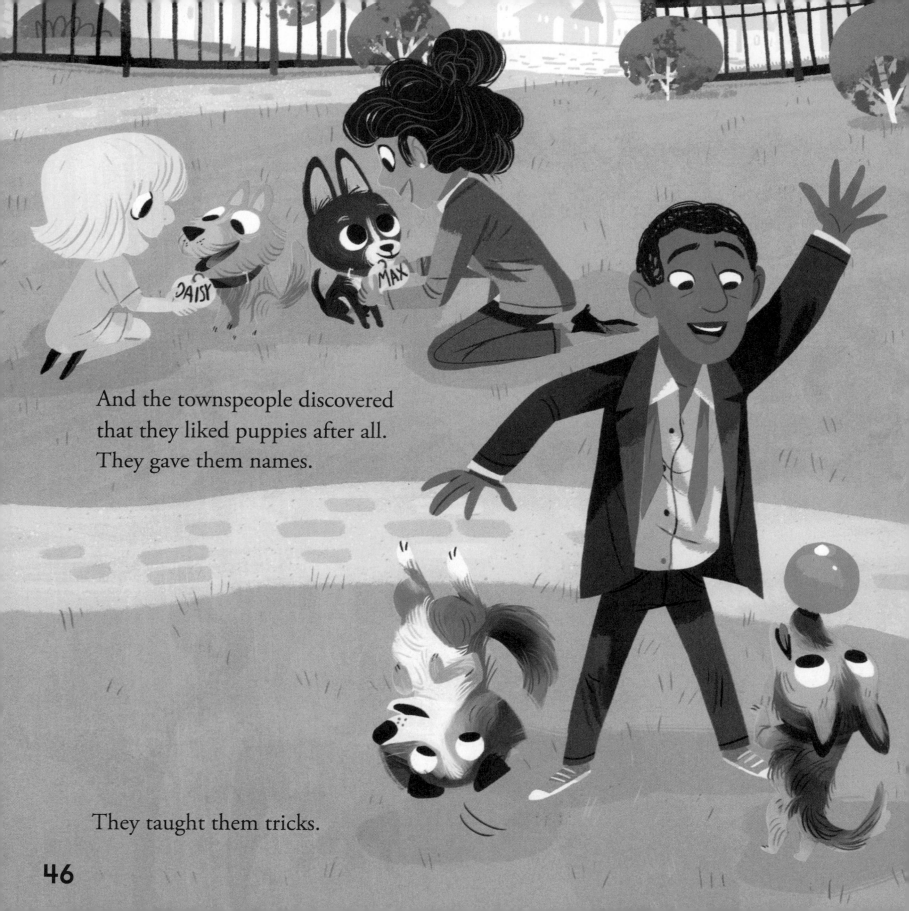

And the townspeople discovered
that they liked puppies after all.
They gave them names.

They taught them tricks.

46

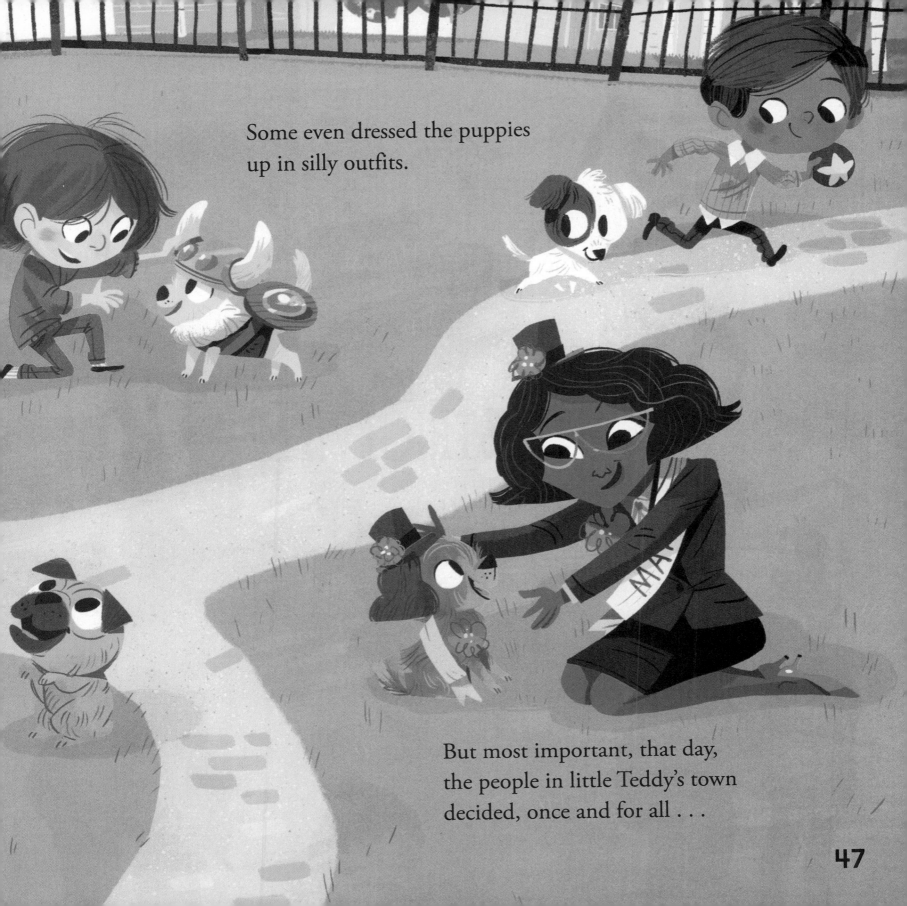

Some even dressed the puppies
up in silly outfits.

But most important, that day,
the people in little Teddy's town
decided, once and for all . . .

47

Turn and Talk

Use details from *The Great Puppy Invasion* to answer these questions with a partner.

1. Monitor and Clarify What did you do when you came to a part of the text that you didn't understand? Tell how it helped or didn't help you.

2. How do the townspeople feel when the puppies first come to town? Why do their feelings change? Use details from the text and pictures to explain your answer.

3. What lesson do you think the townspeople learn?

Listening Tip

Look at your partner as you listen. Wait until your partner finishes speaking before you talk.

Write an Opinion

PROMPT Do you think the puppies will make Strictville a better place to live? Why or why not? Use details from the words and pictures to explain your ideas.

PLAN First, write whether you think the puppies will or will not make Strictville better. Then write or draw reasons why you feel that way.

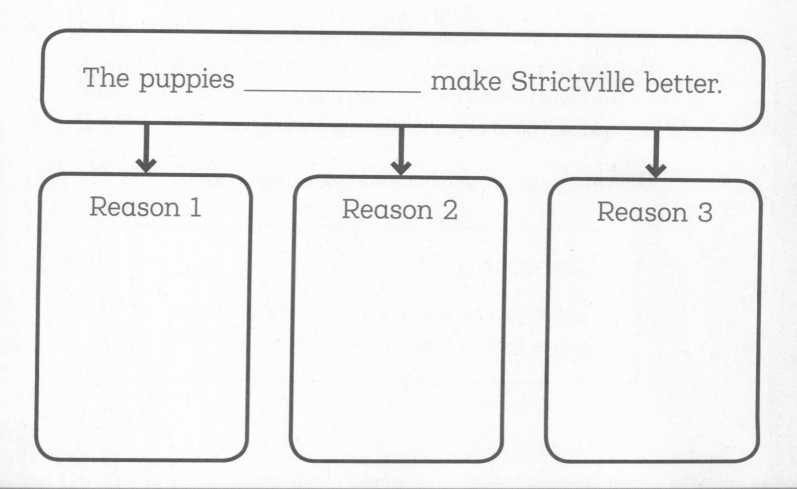

The puppies _____ make Strictville better.

| Reason 1 | Reason 2 | Reason 3 |

WRITE Now write your opinion. Tell whether you think the puppies will make Strictville a better place. Remember to:

- Support your opinion with reasons and details from the text.

- Use transition words like *also* and *as well* to tell about the next reason.

- Write a conclusion sentence.

_____

_____

_____

_____

_____

_____

_____

_____

Prepare to Read

GENRE STUDY **Informational text** is one kind of nonfiction. It gives facts about a topic. As you read *Being a Good Citizen*, look for:

- main topic and details
- photographs
- facts about events

SET A PURPOSE As you read, **summarize** the text. Use your own words to retell the central idea and the relevant details in an order that makes sense.

POWER WORDS

elected

local

mock

compliment

Build Background: Ways to Help Your Community

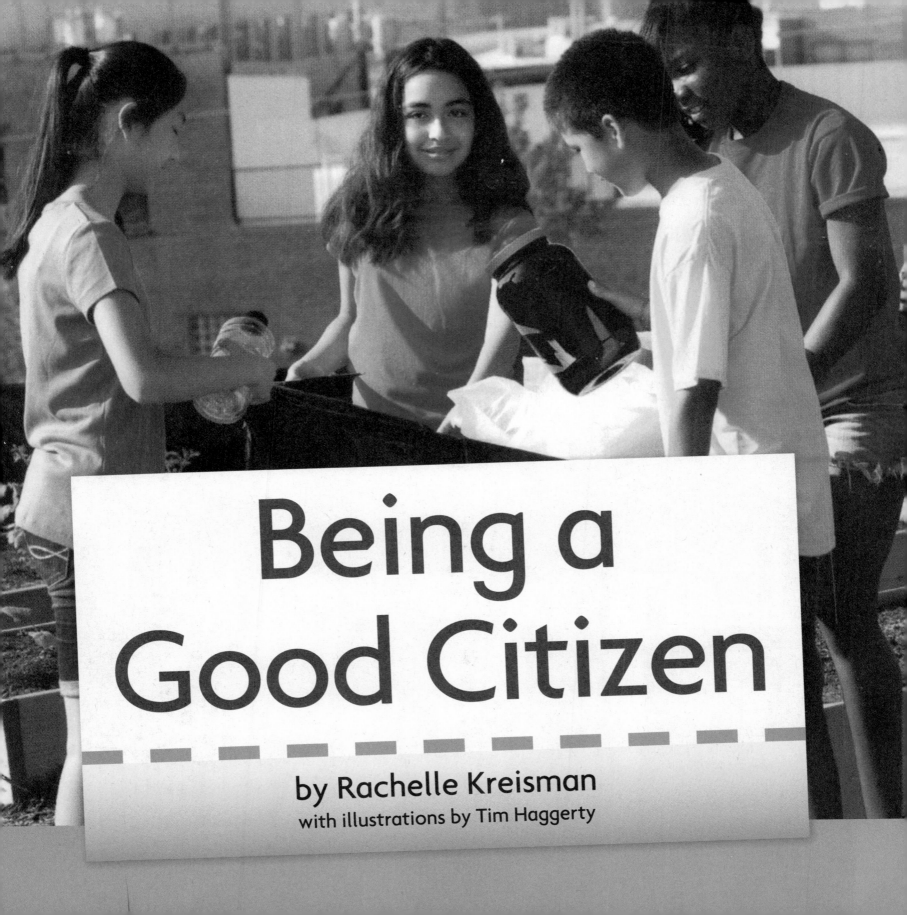

Being a Good Citizen

by Rachelle Kreisman

with illustrations by Tim Haggerty

Community Living

Everyone is part of a community. A community is a place where people live, work, and play. Each community is made up of neighborhoods. Those neighborhoods are made up of people. You are one of those people! So you are part of a community.

Good citizens make the community a better place. A citizen is a person who lives in a certain place. It can be a town or city, state, or country.

How can you be a good citizen? Make a difference in your community! Learn about your elected officials and follow rules. Get involved in community activities. Be a good neighbor and help others. Do you want to learn more? Of course, you do! Keep reading to find out more about how you can be a good citizen.

JUST JOKING!

Q: How did the ocean greet its neighbor?

A: It waved!

55

Get Involved

Good citizens are involved in the community. They get to know their neighbors and other citizens. They work to make their community a better place to live.

What can you do to get involved? Start by taking part in after-school activities. Join a community center or youth group. They have programs and activities just for kids. You can have fun and make new friends.

JUST JOKING!

Q: Did you hear the joke about the community center's roof?

A: Never mind—it's over your head!

After-school activities can be a good way to try new things.

Another way to get involved is to follow local news. That will let you know what is going on in your community. For example, you might learn that your police department is teaching a free bike safety class. Maybe you will want to take the class.

How can you follow the news? Read school and local newspapers. Watch the local news with a parent. Then talk about what you learned. Ask family members their opinions and share your own.

Being a good citizen includes voting. Citizens can vote in local, state, and national elections. You must be 18 years old to vote in most states.

Every four years, citizens elect the president of the United States. Kids can vote too! How? Many schools invite kids to take part in a mock election. It helps students learn about the election process.

DID YOU KNOW?
People in the United States vote on Election Day. It is always the Tuesday after the first Monday in November.

How else can you get involved? Learn about your community history. Visit museums and town landmarks. Go with a parent to take a tour of your city hall. Meet some of your elected officials. Attend a school board meeting.

Some schools have a student council. They organize special activities and help make school decisions. If you have a student council, you can vote to elect officers. You may also want to serve on the council!

Most museums welcome students.

Help Others

Good citizens are active in community service. They volunteer their time to help others. They also donate items and money to people in need. That can make a big difference in people's lives.

Helping others can make a difference in your life too. It can bring you a lot of joy! Doing good deeds can inspire others to do the same.

FUN FACT
Doing a kind act can make you just as happy as receiving one. Both affect your brain in the same way. They make your brain give off feel-good chemicals, say scientists.

What can you do to help others? Start by doing random acts of kindness. Those acts are small, kind gestures. For example, draw a picture for a friend or family member. Say a friendly "hello" to a neighbor. Give flowers to a teacher. Hold the door open for the next person. Read a book to a younger child. Give someone a compliment.

You can do random acts of kindness every day. See how many kind acts you can do for others.

Being a good citizen helps make your community a better place. It also makes you feel good about yourself. Are you ready?

Use details from *Being a Good Citizen* to answer these questions with a partner.

1. Summarize What have you learned about good citizens from this text? Use your own words to retell the central idea and the important details in an order that makes sense.

2. Find three questions the author asks readers. Why do you think she asks questions instead of just telling the facts?

3. Use details from the text to tell how helping in the community can also help you.

Talking Tip

Use details from the text to explain your ideas. Complete the sentence below.

I think _____ because _____.

Write Directions

PROMPT If someone asked you for directions about how to be a good citizen, what would you tell him or her? Use details from the words and pictures to explain your ideas.

PLAN First, think of three steps to follow to be a good citizen. Write or draw them below.

Step 1	Step 2	Step 3

WRITE Now write directions that tell how to be a good citizen. Be sure your directions are easy to follow. Remember to:

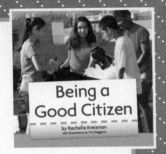

- Choose the most important details in the text.

- Use action words that tell your readers exactly what to do.

_____

_____

_____

_____

_____

_____

_____

_____

_____

Prepare to Read

GENRE STUDY **Realistic fiction** stories are made up but could happen in real life. As you read *Picture Day Perfection*, look for:

- the beginning, middle, and end of the story
- characters who act and talk like real people
- problems that real people might have
- ways pictures and words help readers understand the story

SET A PURPOSE As you read, **create mental images,** or make pictures in your mind, to help you understand details in the text.

POWER WORDS
planned
perfect
hamper
disaster
scowl
mood
queasy
fiddled

Meet Deborah Diesen.

PICTURE DAY PERFECTION

by Deborah Diesen

illustrated by Dan Santat

I'd planned for months. This was going to be the
year of the perfect school picture.

But some days, not everything goes according
to plan.

The day started with the worst case of bedhead *ever*.

EXHIBIT A: FRONT VIEW

EXHIBIT C: BACK VIEW

EXHIBIT B: SIDE VIEW

EXHIBIT D: THE LOOK ON MY BROTHER'S FACE WHEN HE SAW MY HAIR.

Then it took me *quite* some time to unearth my favorite
shirt. I finally found it at the *very* bottom of the hamper.

You might call it "stained."
You might call it "wrinkled."
You might even call it "smelly."
You wouldn't be wrong.

Breakfast was "Picture Day Pancakes," a family tradition.
This year's festivities involved a small syrup disaster.

71

More accurately described as a *large* syrup disaster.
And it occurred exactly as the bus pulled up.
I had a feeling we'd be getting a new family tradition.

72

On the bus, I got into a small bit of trouble.

Make that a *large* bit of trouble. The bus driver made me sit in the seat *right behind him* for the rest of the ride.

By the time I got into school, my picture day face was fixed in a scowl.

In class, Mrs. Smith collected our photo order forms. Do you think my mom checked "Emerald Green" for my photo background? Or "Peacock Blue?" Or "Pizzazzy Purple"?

No. Once again, of all the backgrounds in the world, Mom checked snoring-boring "Traditional Gray."

No one gets "Traditional Gray."

BACKGROUND COLOR
CHOOSE ONE:

Except for me.

And it just so happens to be the only color in
the world that makes my favorite shirt disappear.
All but the stains and the wrinkles.

After that, the teacher had us all stand up and practice our Picture Day smiles. Personally, I thought we needed a little something to get us in the Picture Day mood.

Whoops!
Got myself in trouble.

Again.

Luckily, I got to rejoin the class in time for Art.
Art involved quite a lot of paint.
Or at least it did for *me*.

77

Finally, it was time to line up for our photos.

Ned, just in front of me, got the *last* complimentary plastic comb.

I watched as classmate after classmate smiled for the camera. I got queasy listening to everyone say "Cheese."

I can't *stand* cheese.

The mere thought of it turns me green! *Deeply* green. And just as my face reached its most *awful* pea-green shade, it was . . . *my turn*.

I stepped forward.
I sat down on the stool.
It was hard as a rock, and cold as an iceberg.

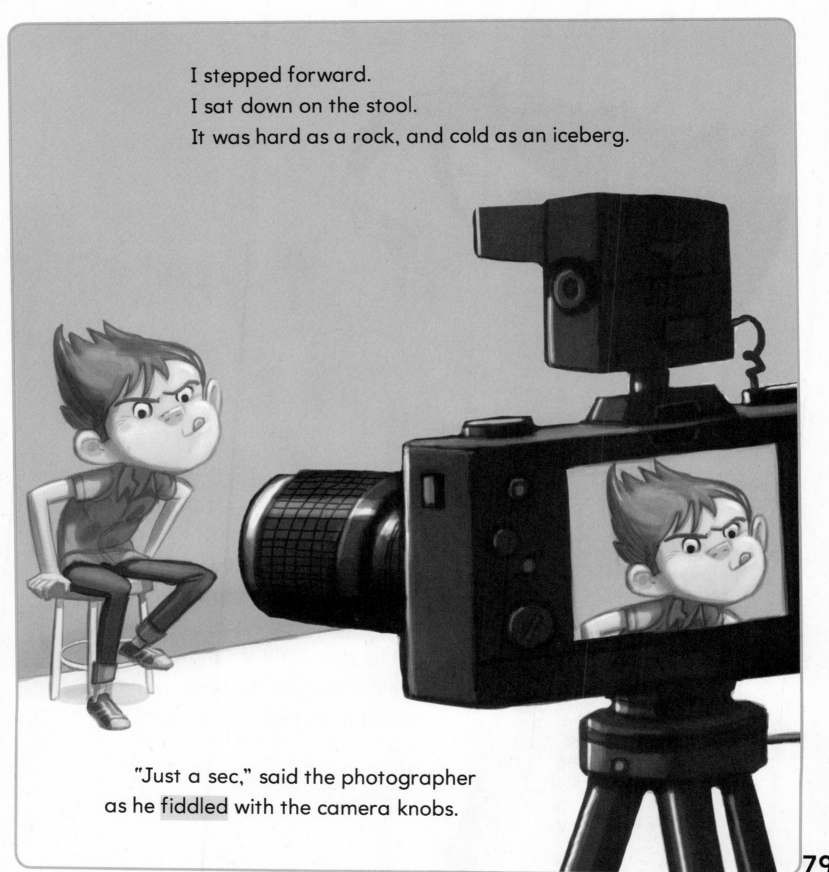

"Just a sec," said the photographer
as he fiddled with the camera knobs.

As I sat and waited, everything that had happened rushed through my mind. The monstrous messes. The muddles and the mix-ups. The whole day, from the moment I'd rolled out of bed, had gone . . .

PERFECTLY!

Even better than planned!
This year, I was finally going to
have *the perfect school picture.*

And that's when I heard a

CLICK!

In a flash, all my hard work—

my perfectly tangled hair,
my perfectly rumpled shirt,
my perfectly sticky face,
my perfectly composed scowl,
that perfect boring background,
those perfect paint splatters,
that perfect sickly pallor—

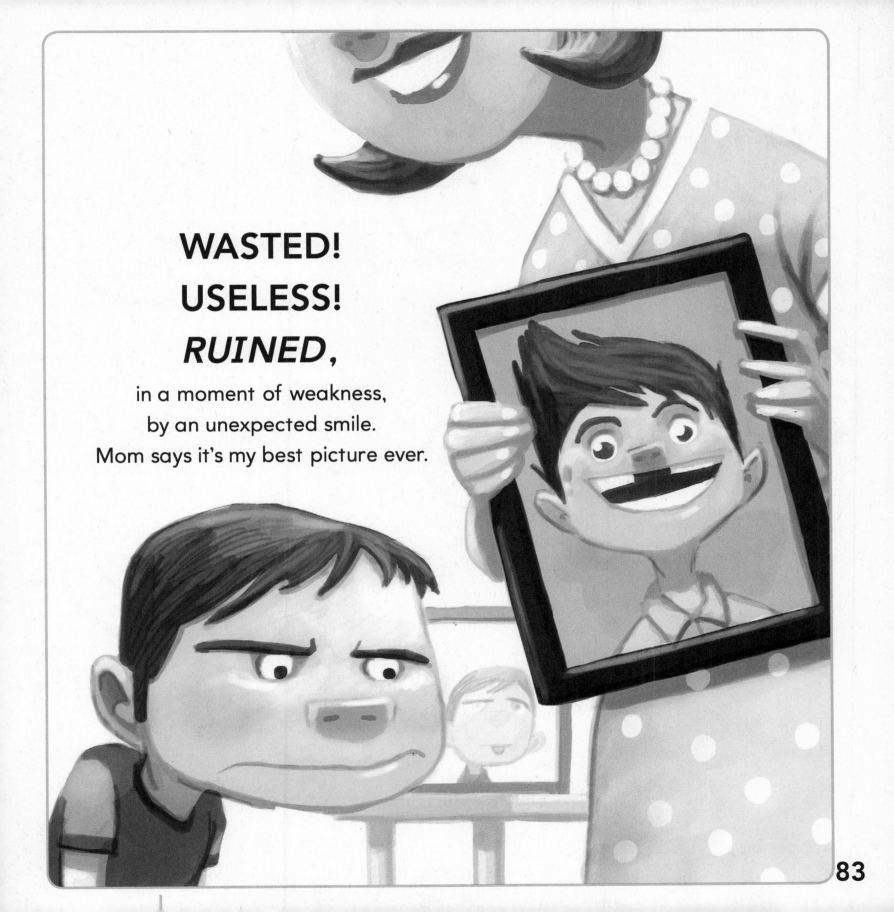

WASTED!
USELESS!
RUINED,
in a moment of weakness,
by an unexpected smile.
Mom says it's my best picture ever.

83

But just *wait* till she sees *next* year's.

Use details from *Picture Day Perfection* to answer these questions with a partner.

1. **Create Mental Images** What does the boy want his school photo to look like? Use details in the text to help you picture it in your mind. Then describe your picture to a partner.

2. What was the author's purpose for writing this story? Why do you think she called it *Picture Day Perfection?*

3. How is the boy different from characters you've read about recently? Explain whether you think he learns a lesson.

Talking Tip

Complete the sentence to ask your partner for more information about an answer.

Tell me more about _____.

Write a Sequel

PROMPT Use what you know about the boy in *Picture Day Perfection* to write sentences about what he might do on next year's picture day. Look for details in the words and pictures to help you think of ideas.

PLAN First, draw a picture of one thing the boy might try next year. Add a caption to describe what the boy is doing.

WRITE Now write your sequel! Explain what you think the boy's plan will be for next year's picture day. Remember to:

- Look for details in the story that give clues about what the boy might do next year.

- Write details that describe what the boy is thinking, feeling, and hoping.

_____

_____

_____

_____

_____

_____

_____

_____

_____

Prepare to View

GENRE STUDY **Videos** are short movies that give you information or something for you to watch for enjoyment. As you watch *Get Involved: Be Awesome!*, notice:

- how pictures, sounds, and words work together
- what the video is about
- how the video makes you feel
- what the video is trying to persuade you to do

SET A PURPOSE Think about the video's **central idea.** Can you figure out its message? Think about how that message helps you understand what it means to be a good citizen.

Build Background: Making a Difference

Get Involved:
BE AWESOME!

As You View Are you ready to make your mark? Listen for details about how to become involved in your community. How do the ideas in the video help you understand what it means to be a super citizen?

Use details from *Get Involved: Be Awesome!* to answer these questions with a partner.

1. **Central Idea** What message does the video share? What does the girl try to persuade you to do?

2. What does the girl mean when she says "make your mark"?

3. The girl says to keep trying when things get tough. Do you think that is good advice? Explain why or why not.

Listening Tip

Be sure to wait until your partner has finished speaking before asking a question or adding new information.

Let's Wrap Up!

? **Essential Question**

How can being a good citizen make a difference to others?

Pick one of these activities to show what you have learned about the topic.

1. The Award Goes to...

You have read about what it means to be a good citizen. Think about someone you know who has made a difference to others. Compare the person to one of the characters you read about. Create a Super Citizen Certificate for that person. Tell a partner whom you chose and why.

2. A Letter to Me

We can all make a difference in our own special way. How will YOU be a good citizen this year? Write a letter to yourself to explain your plan. Think about what you are good at and what you like to do. Look back at the texts for ideas about how to be a good citizen.

Word Challenge

Can you use the word difference in your letter?

My Notes

Look Around and Explore!

"Isn't it splendid to think of all the things there are to find out about?"

—L. M. Montgomery

How does exploring
help us understand
the world around us?

Get Curious Video

95

Words About Discovering Our World

Complete the Vocabulary Network to show what you know about the words.

examine

Meaning: When you **examine** something, you look at it carefully.

Synonyms and Antonyms	Drawing

identify

Meaning: When you **identify** something, you say what it is.

Synonyms and Antonyms	Drawing

record

Meaning: When you **record** notes, you write them down.

Synonyms and Antonyms	Drawing

What's the Matter?

Everything around you is made up of matter. There are three kinds of matter: **solid**, **liquid**, and **gas**.

Look around for different kinds of matter right in your classroom. Use the **Kinds of Matter** section to figure out what kind of matter each thing is. Can you find all three kinds of matter?

Which kind of matter did you find the most of?

Kinds of Matter

SOLID
A solid's shape does not change.

Examples of Solids

apple

bike

bat

LIQUID
A liquid becomes the shape of its container.

Examples of Liquids

juice

water

soup

GAS
A gas does not have a shape. It fits all the space in its container.

Examples of Gases

air

The ball is filled with air.

steam

your breath

Your breath is a gas, too.

99

Prepare to Read

GENRE STUDY **Informational text** is nonfiction. It gives facts about a topic. As you read *Many Kinds of Matter*, look for:

- captions with art or photos
- photographs
- how visuals and words work together to help you understand the text

SET A PURPOSE Read to make smart guesses, or **inferences,** about things the author does not say. Use clues in the text and photos to help you.

POWER WORDS

amount

material

space

example

easily

forms

planet

tasty

Build Background: Solids, Liquids, and Gases

MANY KINDS OF MATTER

by Jennifer Boothroyd

MATTER

Matter is everywhere. Matter is anything that has mass and volume. Mass is the amount of material in an object. Volume is the amount of space an object takes up.

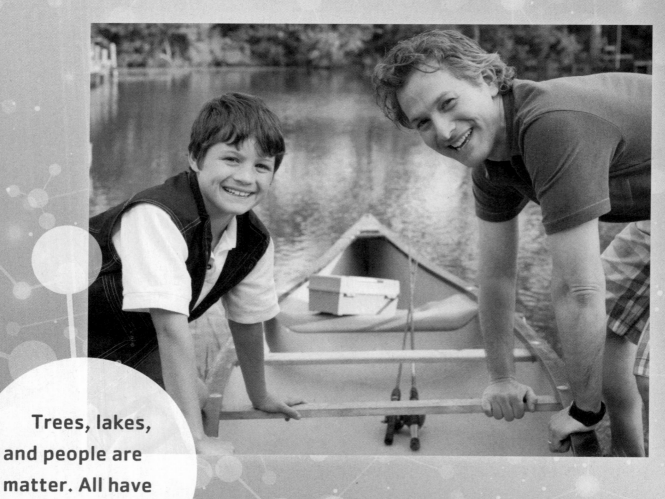

Trees, lakes, and people are matter. All have mass and volume.

There are three kinds of matter.

The three kinds of matter are solids, liquids, and gases.

103

SOLIDS

Books, rocks, and toys are solids.

Solid matter holds its own shape. Solids do not take the shape of their container. Marbles fill a jar. But the marbles are still round.

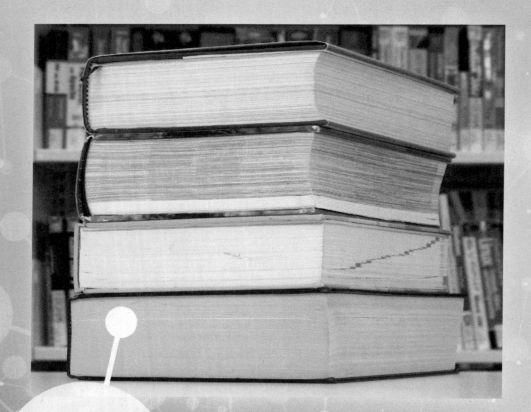

Books are one **example** of a solid.

The shape of solids does not change when you put them in a container.

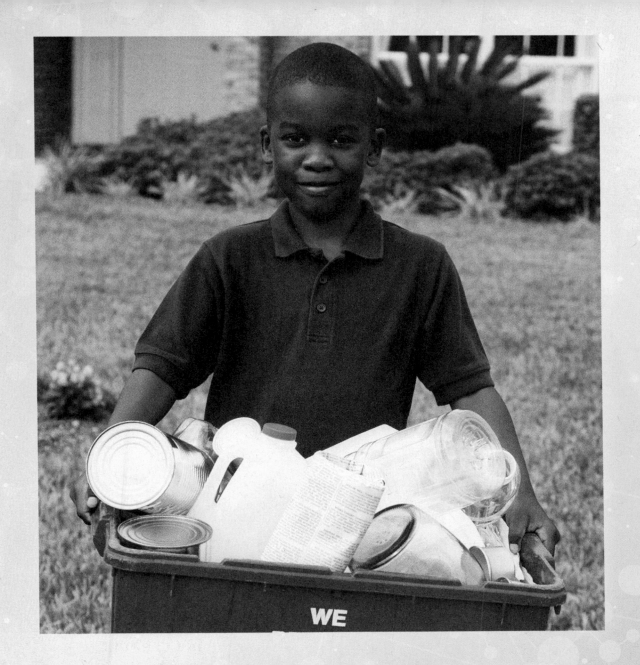

Solids are not easy to compress. *Compress* means to squeeze something into a tight space. Bottles and cans are solids. It's not easy to squeeze them into this recycling bin!

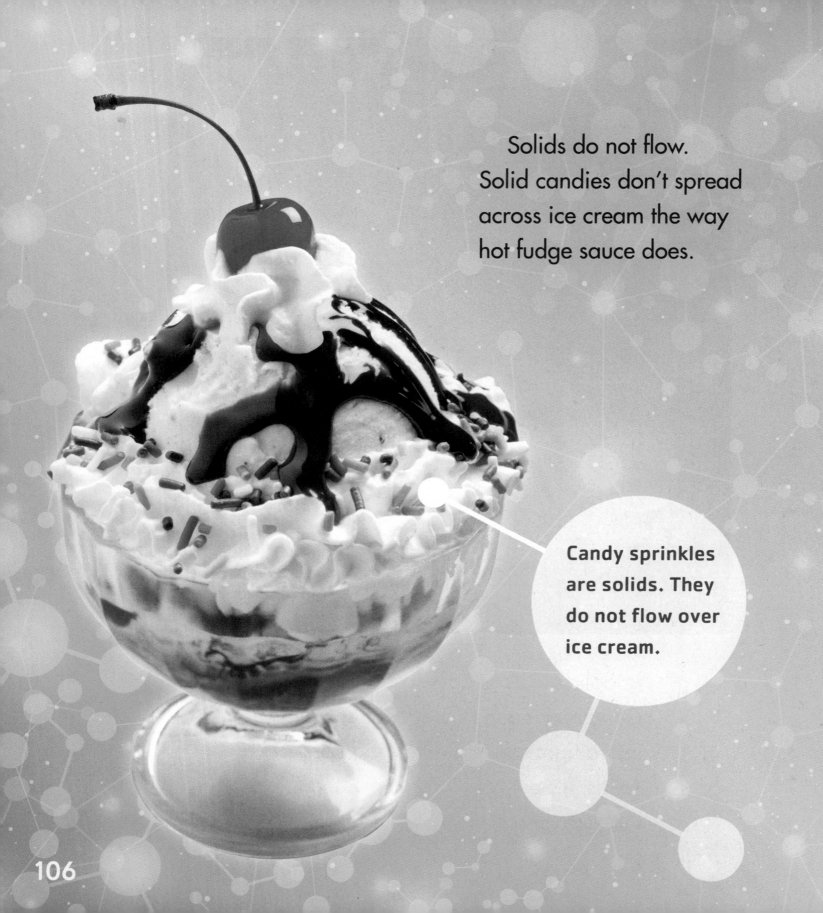

Solids do not flow.
Solid candies don't spread
across ice cream the way
hot fudge sauce does.

Candy sprinkles
are solids. They
do not flow over
ice cream.

106

LIQUIDS

Oil, syrup, and water are liquids.

Liquid matter does not hold its own shape. Liquids take the shape of their container. Water inside a swimming pool takes on the shape of the pool.

Oil is one example of a liquid.

Water in a square pool takes on a square shape.

Liquids are not easy to compress. Milk is a liquid. You couldn't fit the milk in the jug into the little carton.

Liquids flow. Liquid syrup spreads across pancakes.

GASES

Air, steam, and your breath are gases.

Your breath is one example of a gas.

Gas matter does not hold its own shape. Gases take the shape of their container. The air inside a hot air balloon takes on the shape of the balloon.

Gases are easy to compress. Carbon dioxide is a gas. It's inside soda cans. It's squeezed into the cans to give the soda bubbles.

Carbon dioxide rushes out of soda cans when you open them.

Gases flow. The air inside a bubble spreads to fill the space inside the bubble.

MATTER AND CHANGES

Matter can change from one kind to another.

Some solids can change to liquids. Some liquids can change to gases. Water is a special kind of matter. You know that water is a liquid. But it can easily be found in all three forms on our planet.

The liquid in this cup is changing to a gas.

Water becomes a solid if it is cooled.

It turns into ice.

Water turns into ice when it freezes. Water freezes when it reaches a temperature of 32°F (0°C).

Water becomes a gas if it is heated.

It turns into steam.

Water turns into steam when it boils. Water boils when it reaches a temperature of 212°F (100°C).

Water at any temperature can change
into water vapor. Water vapor is a gas.

This change is called evaporation.

Some people use
a drying rack after
washing their dishes.
The dishes dry
after the water
evaporates.

Water vapor changes back into liquid water when it cools in the air.

This change is called condensation.

You can see condensation after a hot shower. The water vapor touches the shower door and turns back into a liquid.

Have you ever seen condensation on a shower door?

Other matter can change forms, too. Cheese is a solid. It melts when it gets hot. It changes to a liquid.

Bread dipped in melted cheese is a **tasty** treat.

Juice is a liquid. It freezes when it gets cold. It changes to a solid.

Ice pops can be made by freezing juice.

We use solids, liquids, and gases every day.

They are an important part
of our lives and our planet.

Use details from *Many Kinds of Matter* to answer these questions with a partner.

1. **Make Inferences** Look at the cup on page 112. What is causing the liquid in that cup to change to a gas? How do you know?

2. Compare the three kinds of matter. How are solids, liquids, and gases the same? How are they different?

3. What examples does the text give for each kind of matter? What other examples can you name?

Listening Tip

Listen politely to your partner, and wait until it is your turn to speak.

Write a Description

PROMPT How does a snowman change as it melts? Use details from the words and pictures in *Many Kinds of Matter* to explain your ideas.

PLAN First, picture a snowman in your mind and write words that describe it. Then, picture a melted snowman and write words that describe it.

Snowman	Melted Snowman

WRITE Now, write sentences to describe how a snowman changes as it melts. Remember to:

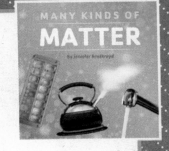

- Find details in the text and pictures that tell about how matter can change.

- Use describing words.

_____

_____

_____

_____

_____

_____

_____

_____

Prepare to Read

GENRE STUDY **Fantasies** are stories with made-up events that could not really happen. As you read *The Great Fuzz Frenzy*, look for:

- animal characters that talk and act like people
- the beginning, middle, and ending of the story
- setting, or where the story takes place

SET A PURPOSE As you read, **make connections** by finding ways that this text is like things in your life and other texts you have read. This will help you understand and remember the text.

POWER WORDS
gasped
frenzy
battleground
feud

Meet Janet Stevens and Susan Stevens Crummel.

by Janet Stevens and Susan Stevens Crummel
illustrated by Janet Stevens

THE GREAT FUZZ FRENZY

"Violet! No!"

"Violet! Where's the ball?"

"WOOF!"

124

Down it went.

BOINK!
BOINK!

"Run for your life!"

"Watch out below!"

THUMP!
THUMP!

RUMBLE!
RUMBLE!

"HELP! HELP!"
"HEEELLLP!"

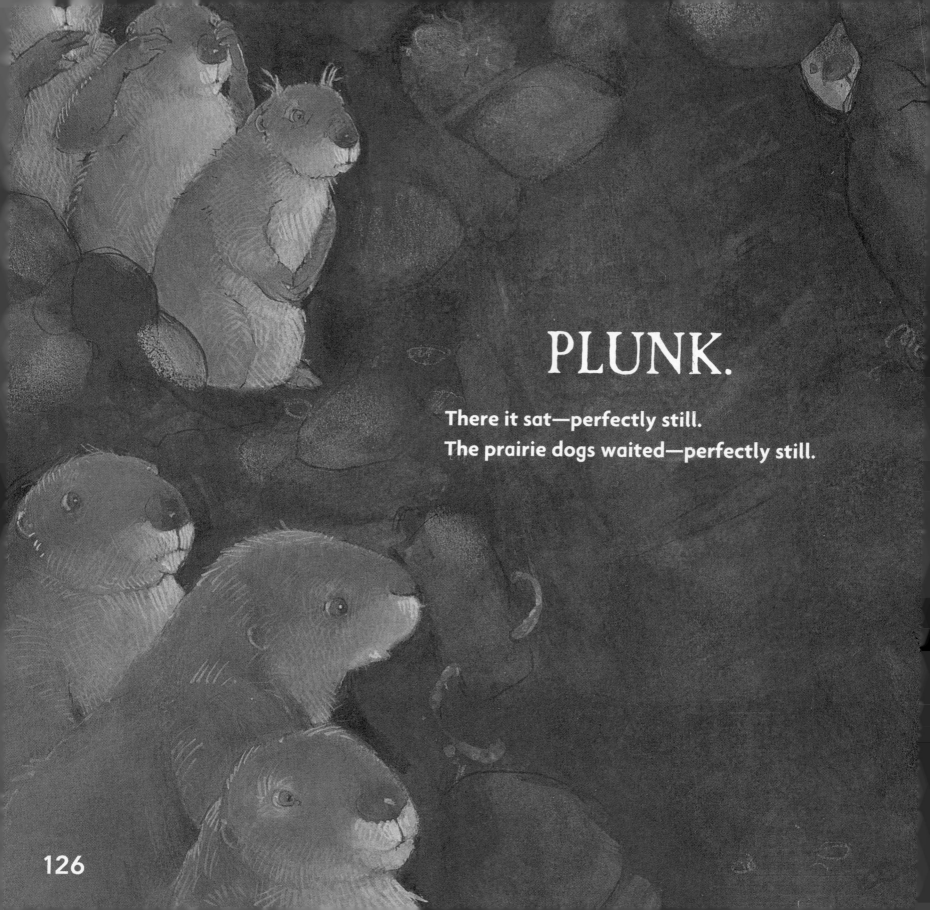

PLUNK.

There it sat—perfectly still.
The prairie dogs waited—perfectly still.

Slowly they crept out.

Inch by inch. Dog by dog.

"What is it?"

"A thing."

"A good thing or a bad thing?"

128

129

"Stand back!" boomed a voice. "You act like gutless groundhogs—afraid of your own shadow!"

"Oh no, it's Big Bark!"

"Big *Mouth* is more like it."

"He's the meanest dog around."

"I thought he left town."

"Well, I'm back," growled Big Bark. "So out of my way. Let me have a look."

But before anyone could move, little Pip Squeak raced past
Big Bark, reached out, and poked the big round thing.
"Noooooo!" the crowd yelled.
"It's fuzzy!" said Pip.
"Oooooooh!" the crowd gasped.

A tiny piece of fuzz was caught in Pip's claw.
She looked at it. Turned it. Sniffed it. Then she
put it on her head. "Look at me!"
"Ahhhhhh!" the crowd sighed.
"Quit hammin' it up, you half-pint hamster!"
snarled Big Bark. *"I'm* in charge."

131

But those prairie dogs didn't listen. They had to have fuzz.

"I like it."
"Me, too."
"I want some."
"Do you?"

"Oh yes!"
"So do I!"
"So do we!"
"So do they!"

"Big Bark, move over!"
"Get out of our way!"

They charged past him
and grabbed at the fuzz.

133

The prairie dogs pulled it. Puffed it.
Stretched it. Fluffed it.
Tugged it. Twirled it.
Spiked it. Swirled it.
They fuzzed their ears, their heads, their noses.
They fuzzed their feet, their tails, their toeses.

134

Big Bark was beside himself. "Listen to me, you ridiculous rodents! Stop this fuzzy foolishness!"

135

But those prairie dogs didn't listen.
They were busy being hot dogs and silly dogs.
Corny dogs and frilly dogs.
Top dogs. Funny dogs.
Superdogs. Bunny dogs.

"You're all nuts, you
squirrelly fuzz freaks!"
yelled Big Bark, storming off.

News of the fuzz spread from hole to hole. Burrow to burrow. Town to town.

Soon prairie dogs from everywhere were coming to see that fuzz.

They came, they saw, they picked.

They twisted it. Braided it. Danced, and paraded it.
It was a fuzz frenzy.
A fuzz fiesta.
A fuzz fandangle.
The whole prairie was abuzz about fuzz.

They picked and pruned and pulled and pinched.
They pinched and pulled and pruned and picked.

Until . . .
the fuzz ran out.

That big round thing was fuzzless. Naked as a plucked chicken.

Some prairie dogs got a lot of fuzz.
Some got a little. Some got no fuzz
at all—and they were mad.

"Give me that fuzz!"
"Why?"

"Because."
"It's my fuzz."
"Well, it *was*!"

"Get that fuzz!"

"GET THAT
FUZZ!"

141

Pulling, grabbing, swiping, nabbing, poking, jabbing—it was war! War between the fuzzes and the fuzz-nots. Their peaceful town was a battleground.

It was a fuzz fight.

A fuzz feud.

A fuzz fiasco.

"I started this," moaned Pip Squeak. "I have to do something. Everyone! Stop! Stop fighting!"

But those prairie dogs didn't listen. The battle raged
on—friend against friend, cousin against cousin, dog against
dog—until no one was left standing.
They were pooped. Fuzzled out. Fast asleep.

143

Hours later the prairie dogs began to stir.
"Uh-oh!"
"Where's the fuzz?"
"I don't know!"
"Where did it go?"
"SOMEONE HAS STOLEN OUR FUZZ!"
cried Pip Squeak.

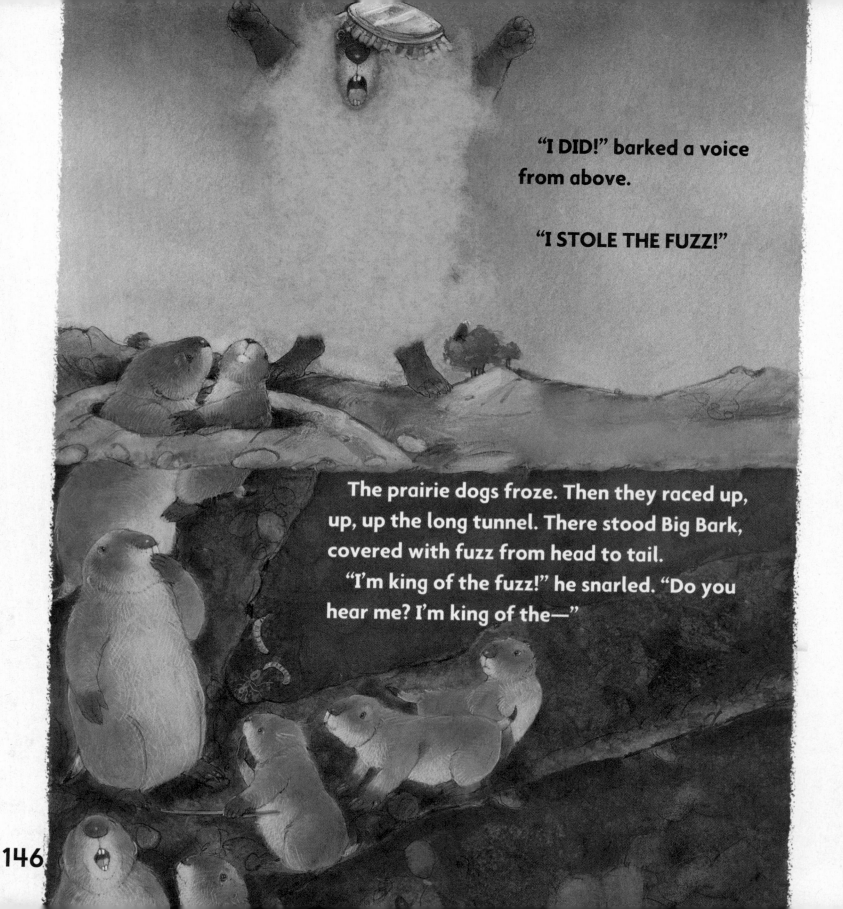

"I DID!" barked a voice from above.

"I STOLE THE FUZZ!"

The prairie dogs froze. Then they raced up, up, up the long tunnel. There stood Big Bark, covered with fuzz from head to tail.

"I'm king of the fuzz!" he snarled. "Do you hear me? I'm king of the—"

146

SWOOP!

The sky went black.

147

"What happened?"

"Where's Big Bark?"

"Look!"

There he was, high above their heads, dangling from the talons of an eagle.

"No more Big Bark!" the crowd cheered. "Yaaaaaay!"

"Don't *yaaaaaay*! He's one of *us*!" yelled Pip. "We have to save him! How would *you* like to be Eagle's lunch?"

"Noooooo!" the crowd yelled.

148

"Big Bark, wiggle free!" the prairie dogs shouted.

"Shake loose!"

"Hurry!"

"We"ll catch you!"

Big Bark twisted and turned, wormed and squirmed. At last he was free of the fuzz!

"Yaaaaaay!" the crowd cheered.

149

Big Bark fell faster and faster.
"Noooooo!" Prairie dogs scattered.

"Get back here!" yelled Pip. "Quick!
Make a circle! Hold out your paws!"
They ran left, then right, then left.

PLOP!

"You saved me!" Big Bark cried. "But I stole your fuzz! Now it's gone forever."

"Good," said Pip Squeak. "Fuzz is *trouble*. Right?"

"Yaaaaaay!" the crowd cheered. Friend hugged friend. Cousin hugged cousin. Dog hugged dog.

"We don't need fuzz," said Pip. "But with Eagle around, we do need a watchdog with a big—"

152

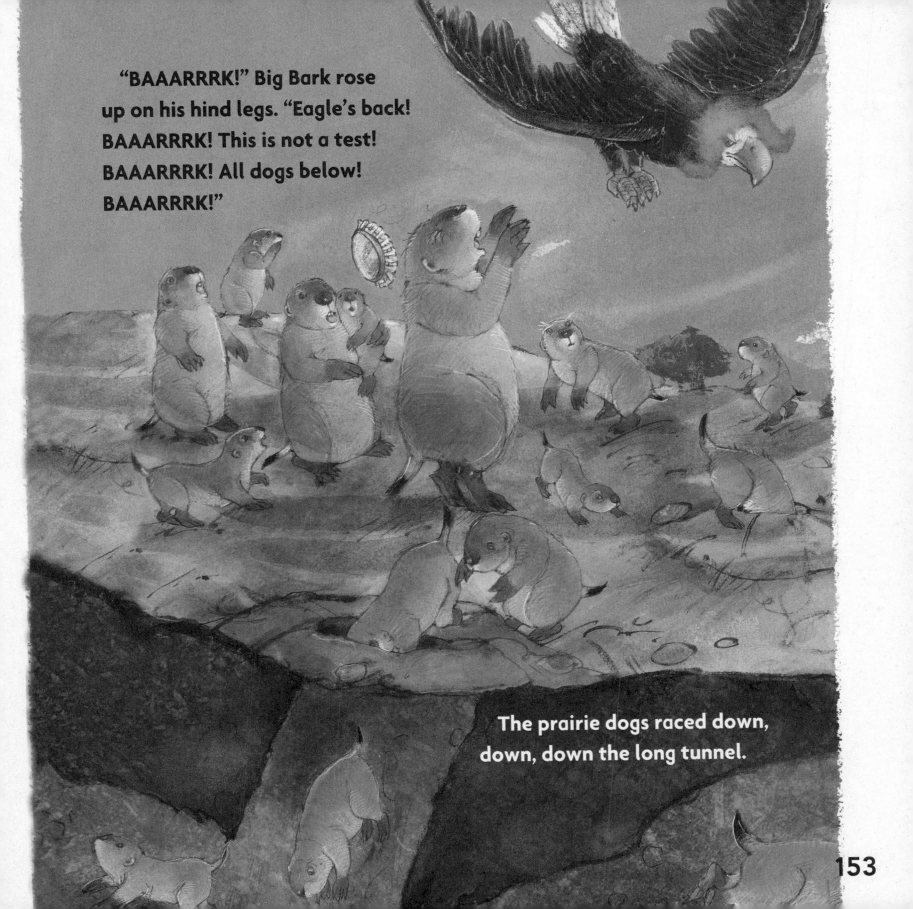

"BAAARRRK!" Big Bark rose
up on his hind legs. "Eagle's back!
BAAARRRK! This is not a test!
BAAARRRK! All dogs below!
BAAARRRK!"

The prairie dogs raced down,
down, down the long tunnel.

153

"Whew! We made it!"

"That was close!"

"Three cheers for Big Bark, the best watchdog ever!"

"YIP, YIP, YAAAAAAY! YIP, YIP, YAAAAAAY! YIP, YIP, YAAAAAAY!"

"Just doing my job!" Big Bark smiled.

"Are we ever getting tangled up with fuzz again?" cried Pip Squeak.

"Noooooo!" the crowd yelled. "No more fuzz! No more fuzz!"

And from that day forward, the prairie dogs lived happily—and fuzzlessly—ever after.

Use details from *The Great Fuzz Frenzy* to answer these questions with a partner.

1. **Make Connections** Think about a time when it was hard for you to share. How does that help you understand what happens when the prairie dogs find the fuzz?

2. Why do the prairie dogs cheer when Eagle takes Big Bark? Why do their feelings change?

3. Find places in the story where the authors repeat words and sounds. How does this make the story fun to read?

Talking Tip

Ask to learn more about one of your partner's ideas. Complete the sentence below.

Tell me more about _____.

Write an Invitation

PROMPT The prairie dogs have a celebration after they find the tennis ball. What could they say to persuade other prairie dogs to join in the fun? Use details from the words and pictures to explain your ideas.

PLAN First, think of reasons why other prairie dogs would want to join the celebration. Write or draw them below.

Reason 1	Reason 2	Reason 3

Come to the fuzz fiesta!

WRITE Now, write sentences to invite the prairie dogs to the fuzz fiesta. Remember to:

- Look for details in the story that show how the prairie dogs feel about fuzz.

- Describe the celebration in a way that will make other prairie dogs excited about going.

_____

_____

_____

_____

_____

_____

_____

_____

_____

Prepare to Read

GENRE STUDY **Poetry** uses images, sounds, and rhythm to express feelings. As you read *Water Rolls, Water Rises*, look for:

- alliteration, or a pattern of words with the same first sound (like *can* and *cats*)
- the line breaks in each stanza
- repetition of sounds, words, or lines
- words that appeal to the senses

SET A PURPOSE As you read, use the poet's words to **create mental images,** or make pictures in your mind. How do the pictures help you understand what the poet is describing?

POWER WORDS
strokes
tumbling
plumes
wisps

Meet Pat Mora.

Water Rolls, Water Rises

by Pat Mora   illustrated by Meilo So

*W*ater rolls
onto the shore
under the sun, under the moon.

160

Water rises
into soft fog,
weaves down the street, strokes an old cat.

162

Blown by the wind,
water sails high.
Tumbling cloud plumes curl through the air.

163

*S*low into rivers,
water slithers and snakes
through silent canyons at twilight and dawn.

164

*D*own smooth canals,
water streams, water slides,
gliding up roots of tulips and corn.

165

Filling deep wells,
water hums in the dark,
sloshes in buckets, quenches our thirst.

167

*S*wirling in wisps,
water twists then it twirls,
frosts scattered dry leaves, rubs lonely, bare trees.

169

In storms, water plunges
in thunder's brash roar,
races through branches from lightning's white flash.

170

Then water rests,
drowsy in reservoirs,
its glistening silence shimmers like stars.

*I*n the murmur of marsh wind,
water slumbers on moss,
whispers soft songs far under frog feet.

172

*W*ater burbles in springs,
gurgles and turns
down streams and rivers seeking the sea.

173

Skidding and slipping,
swooping round bends,
spinning on tree roots, careening down cliffs.

174

Looping and leaping,
rushing to dive
into glimmering sea waves, spangle and splash.

175

Around our round world,
water rolls, water rises
under gold sun, under white moon.

176

Use details from *Water Rolls, Water Rises* to answer these
questions with a partner.

1. **Create Mental Images** Close your eyes and picture one of the
settings in the text. Describe what you see, hear, and smell.
Which of the author's words help you create the picture?

2. Why do you think the author wrote this text? What does she
want readers to know?

3. Why do you think this text uses illustrations instead of
photographs to picture the author's words?

Talking Tip

Ask to learn more about one of your partner's
ideas. Complete the sentence below.

Please explain _____.

Write a Poem

PROMPT How would you describe water in a poem? Find important details in the words and pictures from *Water Rolls, Water Rises* to help you explain your ideas.

PLAN First, make a details chart. On one side, write details about water. Then, think of interesting words that describe each detail. Write them on the other side of your chart.

Details	Words

WRITE Now write your poem using the best words from the chart. Remember to:

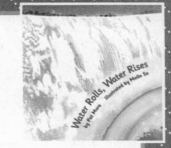

- Use words that paint a picture of your topic.

- Think about how the words in your poem sound together.

_____

_____

_____

_____

_____

_____

_____

_____

_____

_____

Prepare to Read

GENRE STUDY ▸ **Dramas** are plays that are read and performed. As you read *The Puddle Puzzle*, pay attention to:

- the cast of characters
- dialogue, or what the characters say
- setting, or where and when the story takes place
- stage directions that tell performers what to do

SET A PURPOSE ▸ **Ask questions** before, during, and after you read to help you get information or understand the text. Look for evidence in the text and pictures to **answer** your questions.

POWER WORDS

agency

business

confidently

eagerly

seeps

mystery

ace

located

Meet Ellen Weiss.

The Puddle Puzzle

by Ellen Weiss

illustrated by Joe Cepeda

Cast of Characters

TAYLOR
BRANDON
CARLOS
ADRIANA

Setting

a neighborhood on
a sunny spring day

Scene 1

TAYLOR: I am so excited! The Miller Detective Agency is open for business!

BRANDON: I am excited, too!

TAYLOR: Now we just have to wait for our first customer.

CARLOS: Is that the detective agency?

TAYLOR: Come over! We are open!

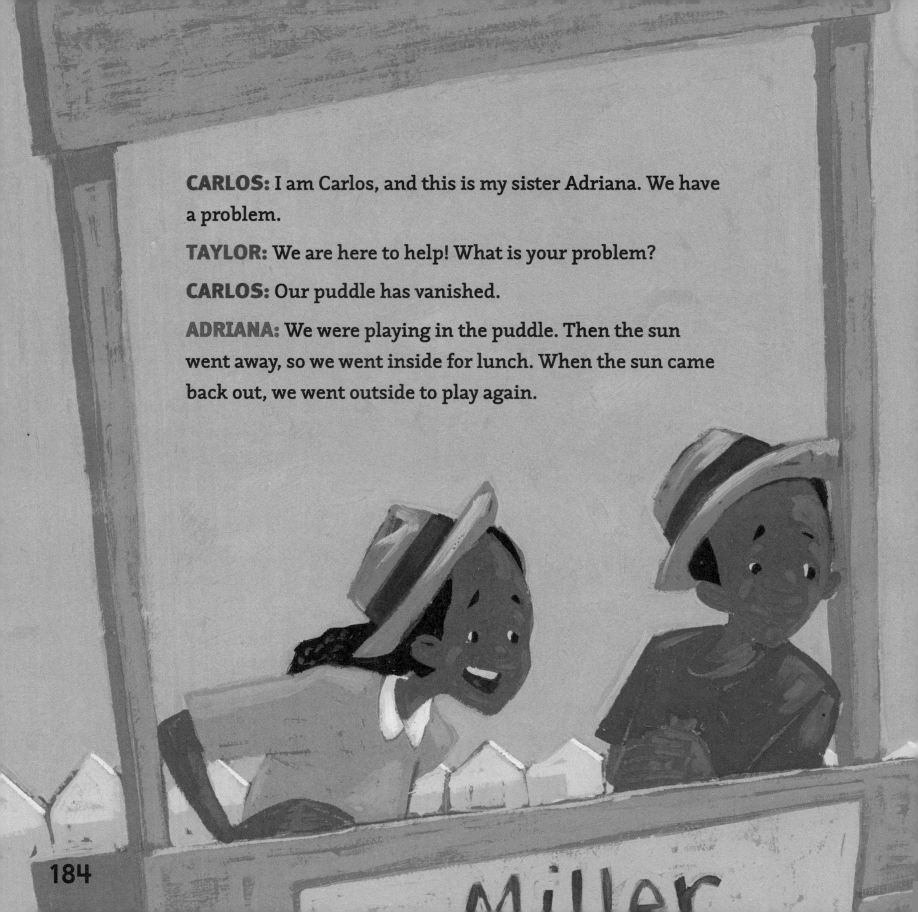

CARLOS: I am Carlos, and this is my sister Adriana. We have a problem.

TAYLOR: We are here to help! What is your problem?

CARLOS: Our puddle has vanished.

ADRIANA: We were playing in the puddle. Then the sun went away, so we went inside for lunch. When the sun came back out, we went outside to play again.

CARLOS: But our puddle was gone! Can you help us find it?

TAYLOR: This is a very hard case. We will do our best to solve it for you.

BRANDON: *(smiling confidently)* I know the answer! I know!

TAYLOR: Shhh, Brandon. I am the oldest, so I am in charge. We need to go and look for clues.

TAYLOR: This is where your puddle was located?

CARLOS: Yes, it was right here.

TAYLOR: *(taking out her notebook and writing)* One puddle, missing. *(She looks around.)* Maybe somebody stole it. Was anyone around here?

CARLOS: Nobody!

TAYLOR: Maybe it is hiding. I will look behind this bush. Nope! It is not here.

BRANDON: *(eagerly)* I know what happened!

TAYLOR: Shhh, Brandon!

BRANDON: But I know what happened!

TAYLOR: Now I am looking for footprints.

ADRIANA: Maybe we should let Brandon talk.

BRANDON: Thank you! Ahem. *(He clears his throat.)* A puddle is full of water, right?

CARLOS: Right!

BRANDON: But water can have three different forms.

CARLOS: It can?

BRANDON: Yes! When we are splashing in a puddle, the water is a liquid. If you freeze water, it turns into a solid.

ADRIANA: Ice!

BRANDON: There is one more thing water can be, too. It can be a gas.

ADRIANA: A gas?

BRANDON: Yes! When we boil water, the steam that seeps out of the kettle is a gas. When the sun shines on a puddle and heats it up, the water turns into a gas, too. A gas does not have a shape or a size. Sometimes we cannot even see it!

CARLOS: So that is what happened to our puddle!

BRANDON: It went into the air, and now we cannot see it or feel it. This is called evaporation.

TAYLOR: Mystery solved!

189

TAYLOR: Brandon, I'm sorry I didn't let you talk today. You knew the answer and I was too excited about gathering clues to listen. I think we need a new sign.

BRANDON: *(smiling proudly)* That is much better.

TAYLOR: We are ace detectives!

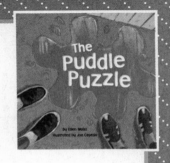

Use details from *The Puddle Puzzle* to answer these questions with a partner.

1. **Ask and Answer Questions** What questions did you ask yourself as Brandon and Taylor tried to solve the mystery? What questions did you ask at the end?

2. Which details explain what happened to the missing puddle?

3. How does the new sign make Brandon feel at the end of the drama? Why does he feel that way?

Talking Tip

Complete the sentence to add more to one of your partner's answers.

I'd like to add that _____.

Write Stage Directions

PROMPT Where would you add more stage directions to help readers perform the drama? Use details from the words and pictures to explain your answer.

PLAN First, draw a scene from the drama. Add labels that tell what the characters are doing or feeling.

WRITE Now write stage directions you would like to add to the drama. Be sure they describe what the characters are doing or feeling as they say their lines. Remember to:

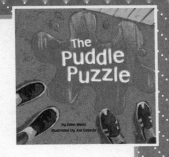

- Include words that clearly describe actions or feelings.

- Include the character's lines that the stage directions go with. Think about how you would read them.

_____

_____

_____

_____

_____

_____

_____

_____

_____

Prepare to Read

GENRE STUDY **Fine art** describes art such as paintings, drawings, music, and dance. As you read *Looking at Art*, notice:

- people or objects in the art
- how the art makes you feel
- the subject of the art
- the type of artwork

SET A PURPOSE Look at what is happening in the art. Think about how it creates a story in your mind. Compare what you see in the art to what you read in the text.

Build Background: Art Critics

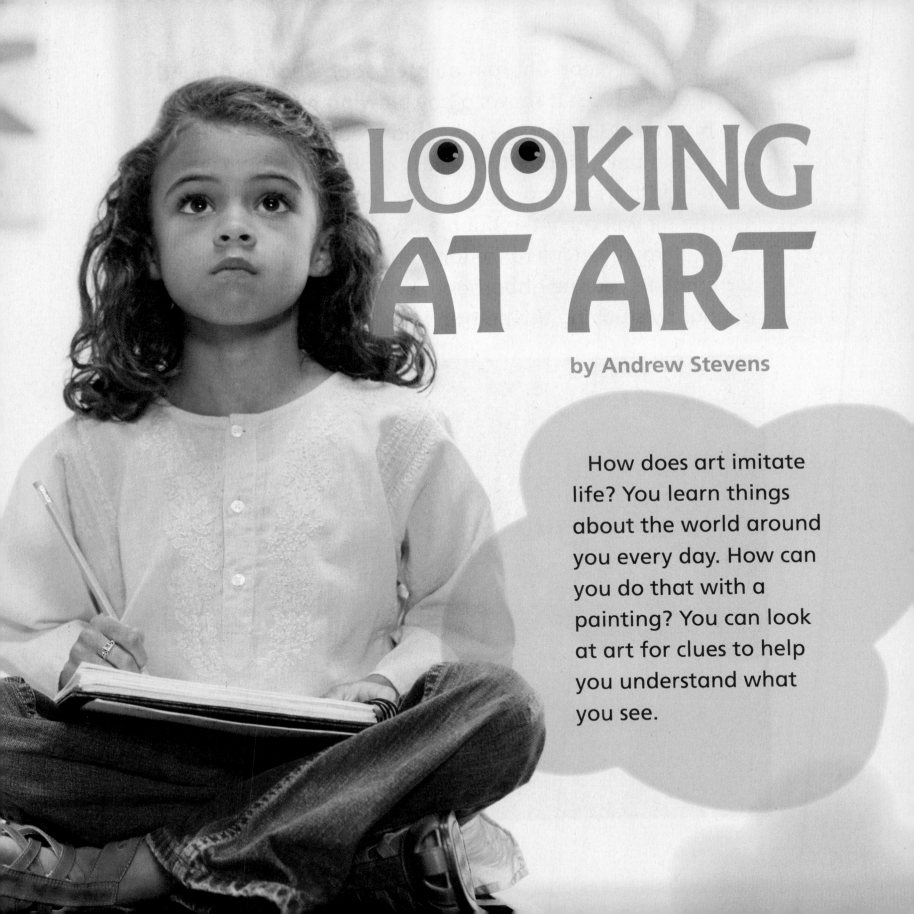

LOOKING AT ART

by Andrew Stevens

How does art imitate life? You learn things about the world around you every day. How can you do that with a painting? You can look at art for clues to help you understand what you see.

Jean Siméon Chardin painted *Soap Bubbles* around the year 1733. It shows a boy blowing a bubble. See his cheeks? If he were using big breaths, his cheeks would be puffed out. He must know the bubble will pop if it grows too quickly! The boy might be hoping the air will carry the bubble away.

If you lived in France long ago, you might see this scene in your neighborhood. What else can you figure out by studying the painting?

Jean Siméon Chardin,
Soap Bubbles
oil on canvas

Turn and Talk

Use details from *Looking at Art* and the painting *Soap Bubbles* to answer these questions with a partner.

1. **Connect Text and Visuals** What details from the image or the text tell you the painting was made a long time ago? How would it look different if the artist painted it today?

2. What are the characters doing in the painting? What do you think they will do next?

3. How does the author use words about science to tell about the painting?

Listening Tip

You learn from others by listening carefully. Think about what your partner says and what you learn.

197

Let's Wrap Up!

(?) Essential Question

How does exploring help us understand the world around us?

....

Pick one of these activities to show what you have learned about the topic.

1. Observe, Explore, Discover!

You have read about how observing can help you learn about our world. Write five tips to help someone explore and make new discoveries. Look back at the texts for ideas about places and ways to explore.

bouncy

round

2. Picture the Matter

Draw or find pictures for each of
the different kinds of matter. Then
make a collage. Add labels to describe
how the objects in your collage look, sound,
feel, smell, or taste.

My Notes

Meet in the Middle

"You must speak words that matter."

—Kate DiCamillo

? Essential Question

How can people work out disagreements?

Get Curious Video

201

Words About Solving Problems

Complete the Vocabulary Network to show what you know about the words.

compromise

Meaning: A **compromise** is when people agree to something by each giving up a little of what they want.

Synonyms and Antonyms	Drawing

decision

Meaning: When you make a **decision**, you make up your mind about something.

Synonyms and Antonyms	Drawing

disagreement

Meaning: In a **disagreement**, people have different ideas about things.

Synonyms and Antonyms	Drawing

MEET ME HALFWAY

What does it mean when people say, "Let's meet in the middle"? They are talking about **compromise**, or a way to end a disagreement.

When people compromise, they each give up a little of what they want. These comic strips show examples of compromise.

205

Prepare to Read

GENRE STUDY **Realistic fiction** stories are made up but could happen in real life. As you read *Big Red Lollipop,* look for:

- characters who act and talk like real people
- a lesson the main character learns
- problems that real people might have

SET A PURPOSE As you read, stop and think if you don't understand something. Reread, ask yourself questions, use what you already know, and look for visual clues to help you understand the text.

POWER WORDS

invited

screams

plead

musical

shove

scoots

greedy

scurries

Meet Rukhsana Khan.

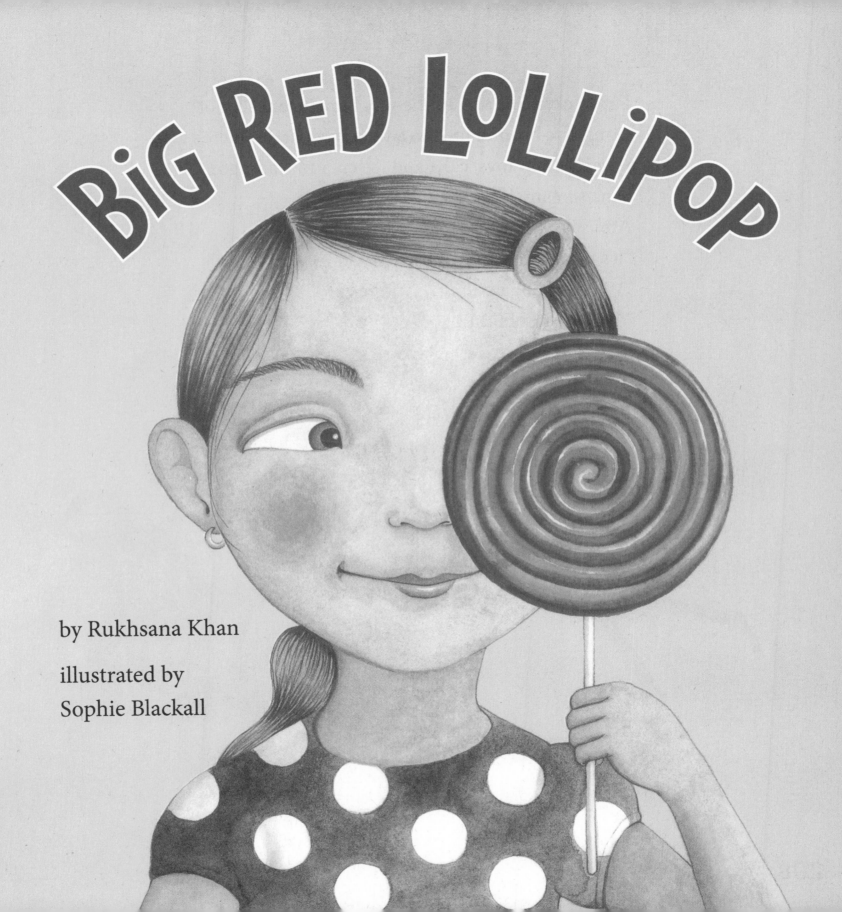

BiG RED LoLLiPoP

by Rukhsana Khan

illustrated by
Sophie Blackall

I'm so excited I run all the way home from school.

"Ami! I've been invited to a birthday party! There's going to be games and toys, cake and ice cream! Can I go?"

Sana screams, "I wanna go too!"

Ami says, "What's a birthday party?"

"It's when they celebrate the day they were born."

"Why do they do *that*?"

"They just do! Can I go?"

Sana screams, "I wanna go too!"

"I can't take *her*! She's not invited."

"Why not?" says Ami.

"They don't do that here!"

Ami says, "Well that's not fair. You call up your friend and ask if you can bring Sana, or else you can't go."

"But Ami! They'll laugh at me! They'll never invite me to another party again!"

Sana screams, "I wanna go too!"

209

I say, "Look, Sana, one day you'll
get invited to your own friends' parties.
Wouldn't you like that better?"

"No! I wanna go now!"

I beg and plead, but Ami won't listen. I have no choice.
I have to call. Sally says, "All right." But it doesn't sound all
right. I know she thinks I'm weird.

At the party, I'm the only one who brought her little sister. Sana has to win all the games, and when she falls down during musical chairs, she cries like a baby.

Before we leave the party, Sally's mom gives us little bags. Inside there are chocolates and candies, a whistle, a ruby ring, and a big red lollipop! Sana eats her big red lollipop on the way home in the car. I save mine for later.

Sana doesn't know how to make things last. By bedtime, her candies are all gone, her whistle is broken, and the ruby in her ring is missing. I put my big red lollipop on the top shelf of the fridge to have in the morning.

All night I dream about how good it will taste.

213

In the morning, I get up early to have it. Sana's already up. When she sees me, she runs away.

I open the fridge door. All that's left of my lollipop is a triangle stuck to a stick.

"SANA!"

I hear a sound in the front hall closet. I should have known. That's where she always hides.

I shove aside the coats and boots. "I'm going to *get* you!"

Quick as a rat, she scoots through my legs and runs around and around the living room, the dining room, the kitchen, yelling, "Ami! Ami! Help! Help!"

Ami comes out, rubbing her eyes. Sana runs behind Ami, where I can't get her.

"What's going on out here?" says Ami.

Sana says, "Rubina's trying to get me!"

Ami puts her hands on her hips. "Are you trying to get your little sister again?"

"She ate my *lollipop*! The greedy thing! She ate it!"

Ami says, "For shame! It's just a lollipop! Can't you *share* with your little sister?"

I want to cry, but I don't.

Sana runs to the fridge and brings back the triangle stuck to the stick. "Look! I didn't eat *all* of your lollipop! I left the triangle for you!"

"See?" says Ami. "She didn't eat *all* of it. She's sharing with you! Go ahead. Take the triangle."

So I have to take it.

"Go ahead. *Eat* the triangle."

But I don't. With all my might, I throw it across the room. It skitters under the sofa.

Sana scurries after it and eats that too.

The worst thing is that all the girls at school know if they invite me to their birthday parties, I have to bring Sana.

I don't get any invitations for a really long time.

Then one day Sana comes home waving an invitation.

"Ami! I've been invited to a birthday party! There's going to be games and toys and cake and ice cream! Can I go?"

Our little sister Maryam screams, "I wanna go too!"

Sana says, "No! I can't take *her*! She's not invited!"

Ami says, "Well . . . it's only fair. You went to Rubina's friend's party, now Rubina and Maryam can go to your friend's party." I say, "Leave me out of it."

Ami says, "Fine then, you have to take Maryam."

Now it's Sana's turn to beg and plead. Ami won't listen.
Sana's begging so hard she's crying, but still Ami won't listen.

I *could* just watch her have to take Maryam. I *could* just let her make a fool of herself at that party. I *could* just let her not be invited to any more parties, but something makes me tap Ami on the shoulder.

"What?"

"Don't make Sana take Maryam to the party."

"No?" says Ami.

"No," I say.

Ami thinks for a moment, then says, "Okay."

So Sana gets to go by herself.

After the party, I hear a knock on my door.

"What do *you* want?" I ask Sana.

"Here." She hands me a big green lollipop. "This is for you."

"Thanks," I say.

After that we're friends.

Use details from *Big Red Lollipop* to answer these questions with a partner.

1. **Monitor and Clarify** How did using what you know about birthday parties help you understand the events in the story?

2. How did the other girls at the party feel about Rubina bringing Sana? Use details from the text and pictures to explain your answer.

3. Why do you think Rubina tells Ami to let Sana go to the party without Maryam? What does that tell you about Rubina?

Listening Tip

Look at your partner as you listen. Wait until your partner finishes speaking before you talk.

Write a Journal Entry

PROMPT How would the story be different if Sana were telling it? Think about the story events as you explain your ideas.

PLAN First, choose one event in the story to write about. Fill in the chart with what Sana does, says, and feels during that event.

Actions	Words	Feelings

WRITE Now write a journal entry from Sana's point of view that describes the event. Remember to:

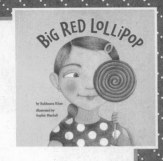

- Include details that show what Sana does, says, and feels.

- Use the words *I* and *me* to tell the story as Sana would.

_____

_____

_____

_____

_____

_____

_____

_____

_____

_____

Prepare to Read

GENRE STUDY **Informational text** is nonfiction. It gives facts about a topic. As you read *Working with Others,* look for:

- the main topic and details
- headings that stand out
- photographs

SET A PURPOSE You know that informational texts include facts. Make a **prediction,** or good guess, about the information you will read about in this text. Read to see if your prediction is right. If not, make a new prediction.

POWER WORDS

blamed

argue

respectful

practice

Build Background: Teamwork and Cooperation

WORKING WITH OTHERS

by Robin Nelson

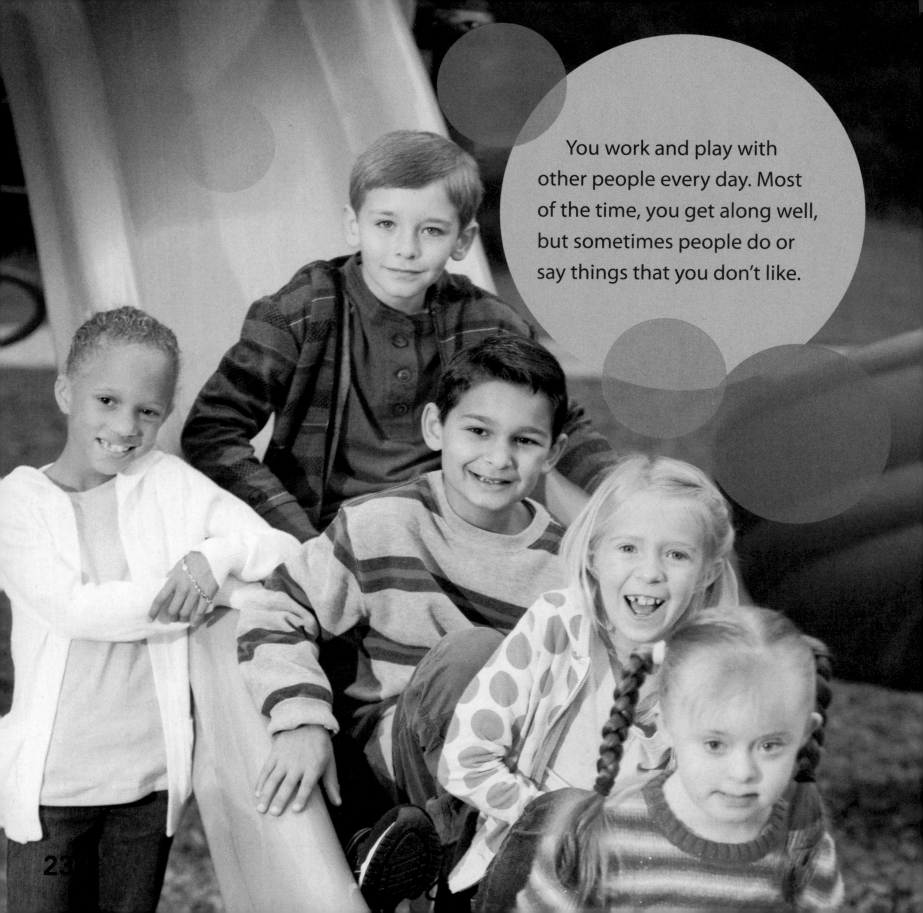

You work and play with other people every day. Most of the time, you get along well, but sometimes people do or say things that you don't like.

23

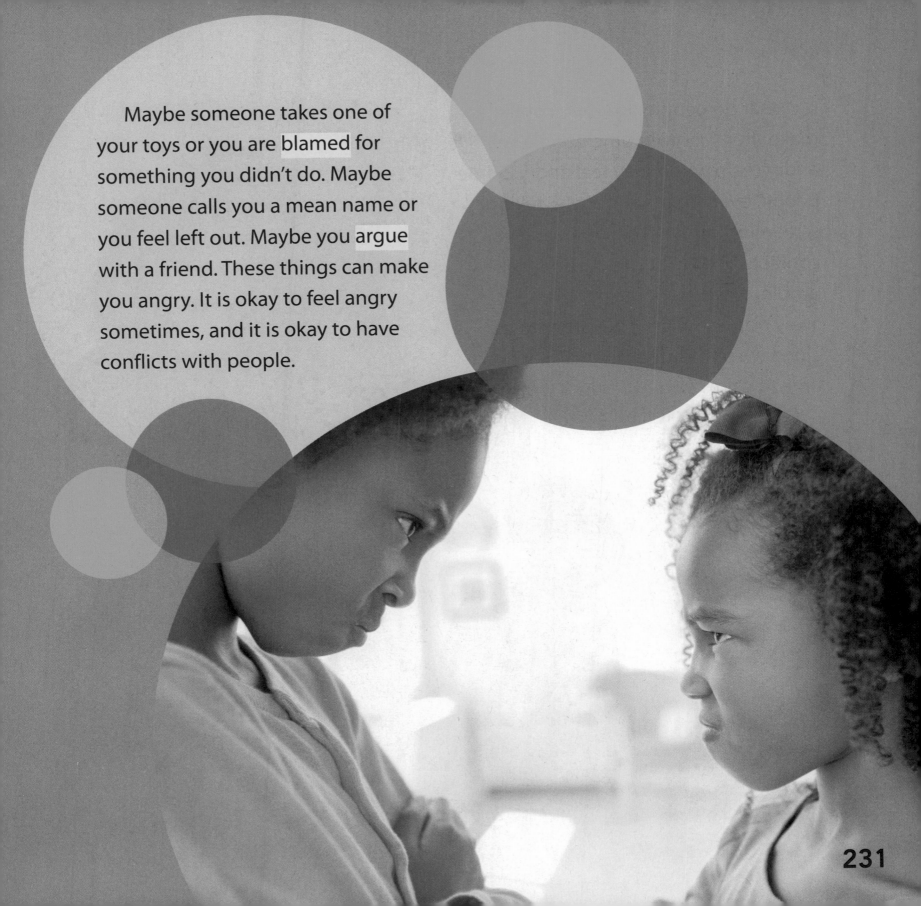

Maybe someone takes one of your toys or you are blamed for something you didn't do. Maybe someone calls you a mean name or you feel left out. Maybe you argue with a friend. These things can make you angry. It is okay to feel angry sometimes, and it is okay to have conflicts with people.

231

What do people do when conflicts make them angry? Some people yell and scream when they feel angry. Some people even hit other people. Yelling, screaming, and hitting do not solve conflicts. They hurt people and make problems worse. Some people walk away from conflicts. They want to be alone when they feel angry. They need time to calm down.

232

Walking away is okay at first. But it won't solve anything. People need to work things out with each other. People should talk about their feelings. Talking can solve conflicts. Talking can make everyone feel better.

We can solve conflicts without arguing. Take turns talking to let everyone share his or her opinion. Sometimes you will not agree with a person's opinion. Listen to what the other person is saying and ask questions.

Use respectful words. Don't call each other names. Apologize when you are wrong. Make sure everyone has a chance to speak. Then you can solve conflicts together. Think of ideas to solve the conflicts. Decide which ideas will work best.

234

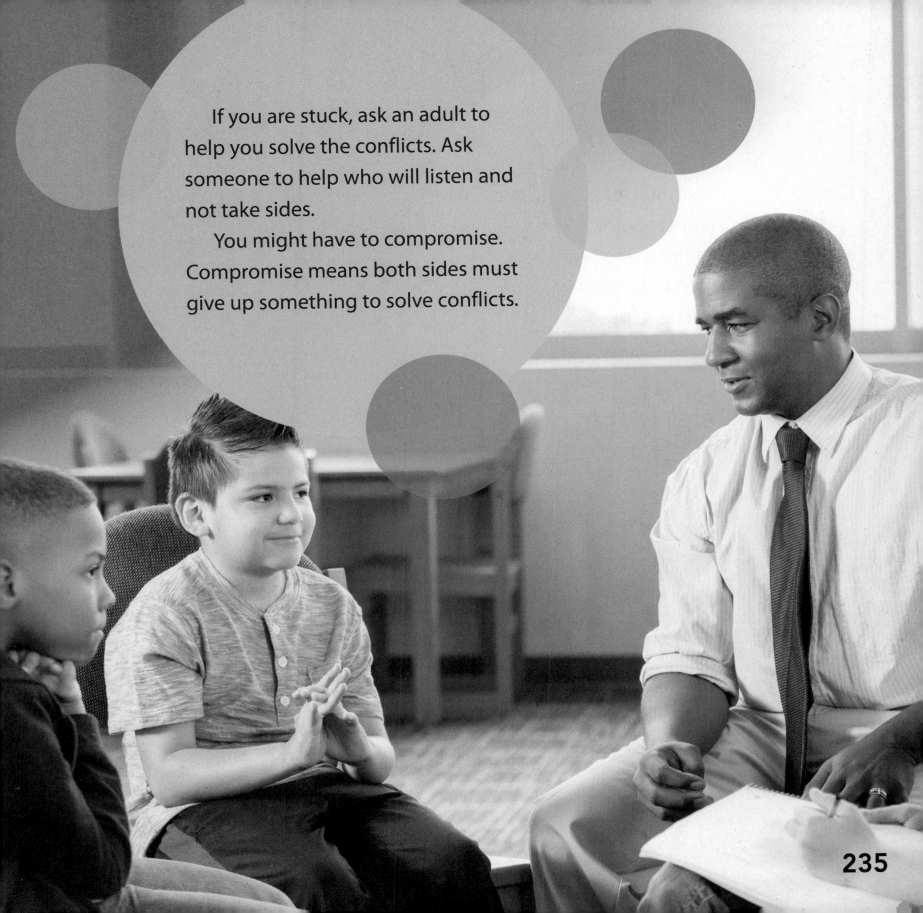

If you are stuck, ask an adult to help you solve the conflicts. Ask someone to help who will listen and not take sides.

You might have to compromise. Compromise means both sides must give up something to solve conflicts.

235

Solving conflicts peacefully takes practice. Work together! Solve conflicts as a team. Talk them out, and everyone will be happy!

236

Dealing with Anger

What do you do when you feel angry? You might feel too angry to talk about how you feel. Here are some ways for you to calm down and get the anger out.

- Take deep breaths and count slowly.

- Write down what happened and how you feel about it.

- Draw a picture.

- Listen to calm music.

- Read a book.

- Take a walk or do some other kind of exercise.

- Pound on a pillow.

- Stomp your feet.

Talking Things Out

When you feel a little better, it is time to talk. Here are some things to remember when talking things out.

- Tell the other person how you feel and why you feel that way. Be honest. Ask that person how he or she feels.

- Remember that your body also tells a person how you are feeling. Show that you care about what he or she is saying. Don't cross your arms or make faces.

- Look at the person you are speaking to. Do the same thing when the other person is speaking to you.

- Listen carefully to what the other person has to say.

- Wait for your turn to speak.

- Apologize when you are wrong or if you hurt someone's feelings.

- Try to find a way to do things differently next time.

Turn and Talk

Use details from *Working with Others* to answer these questions with a partner.

1. **Make and Confirm Predictions** What predictions did you make about the facts you would read in this text? What were you right about? What was different?

2. Use information from the text to describe things that can cause a conflict.

3. Why is it a good idea to make sure that everyone has a chance to speak when solving conflicts?

Talking Tip

Ask to learn more about one of your partner's ideas. Complete the sentence below.

Please explain _____.

Write an Explanation

PROMPT How do you solve a conflict with someone? Use details from the words and photos to explain your answer.

PLAN First, make notes about steps you can follow when you are having a conflict.

WRITE Now write an explanation that tells someone what to do to solve a conflict. Remember to:

- Look for details in the text that are good examples of how to solve a conflict.

- Use action words that tell your reader exactly what to do.

_____

_____

_____

_____

_____

_____

_____

_____

_____

_____

Prepare to Read

GENRE STUDY **Biographies** tell about real people's lives. As you read *Gingerbread for Liberty!,* look for:

- information about why this person is important
- the place where the person lived, worked, or traveled
- ways the person has made a difference

SET A PURPOSE Read to find out the most important ideas in each part. Then **synthesize,** or put together these ideas in your mind, to find out what the text really means to you.

POWER WORDS
booming
skill
threatening
persuade

Meet Mara Rockliff.

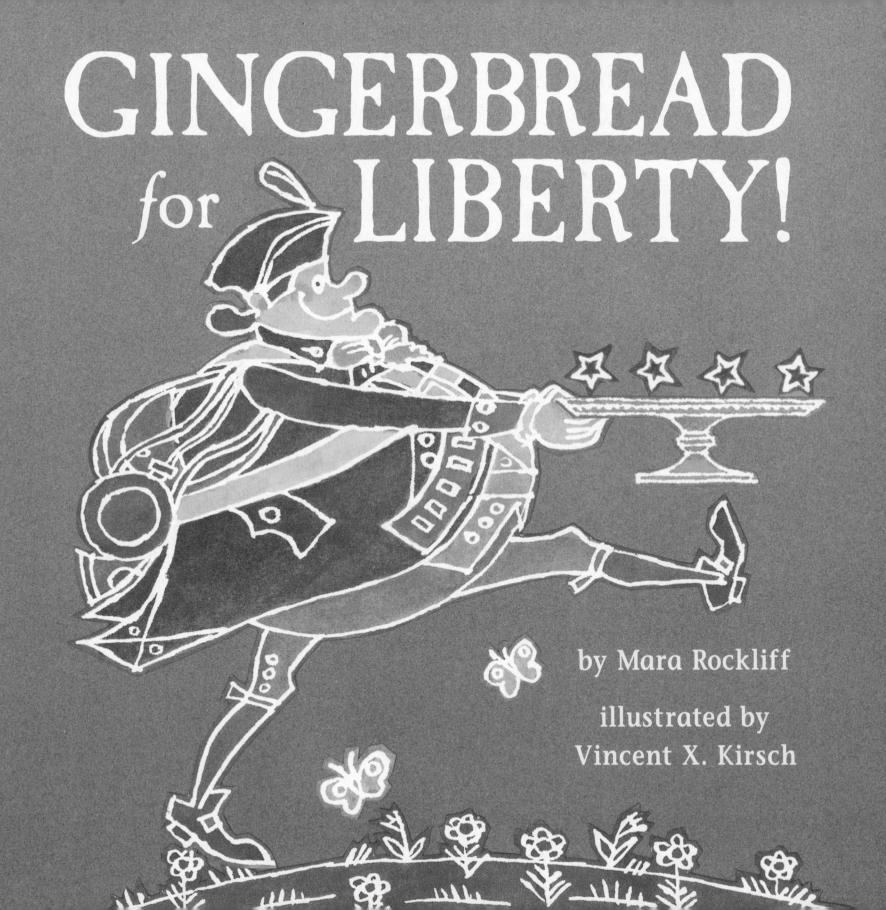

GINGERBREAD
for LIBERTY!

by Mara Rockliff

illustrated by
Vincent X. Kirsch

Everyone in Philadelphia knew the gingerbread baker.
His honest face . . . his booming laugh . . .

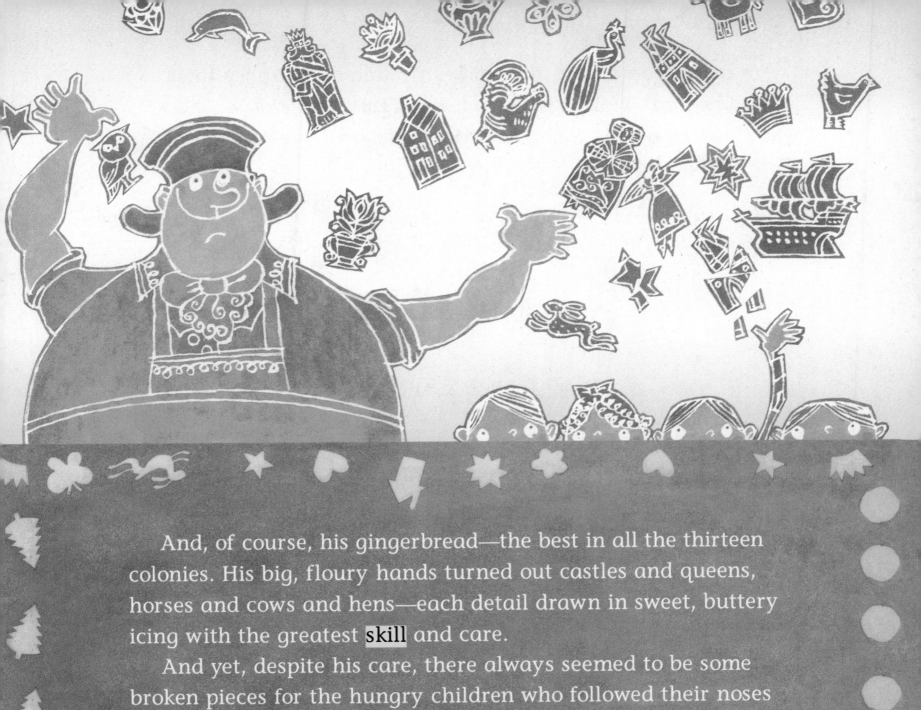

And, of course, his gingerbread—the best in all the thirteen colonies. His big, floury hands turned out castles and queens, horses and cows and hens—each detail drawn in sweet, buttery icing with the greatest skill and care.

And yet, despite his care, there always seemed to be some broken pieces for the hungry children who followed their noses to the spicy-smelling shop.

"No empty bellies here!" the baker bellowed. "Not in *my* America!"

245

For once upon a time, he had been young and hungry too.
And he had followed his own nose to this New World, where
a hard-working young man could open his own bakery and
always have enough to eat.

But now, something was in the air (besides the smell
of baking gingerbread).
Newspapers shouted

REVOLUTION!   INDEPENDENCE!   LIBERTY!

Boys rolled up blankets, shouldered guns, and kissed mothers
goodbye.
The baker hung his apron up. He dusted flour off his hands.
"Where are you going?" asked his wife.
"To fight for my America!" he said. "I was a soldier once."
"That was long ago and far away," she said. "You are a baker now,
and you are old and fat."

The baker knew his wife was right.
But he knew also that he loved his country.
Somehow, he had to find a way to help.

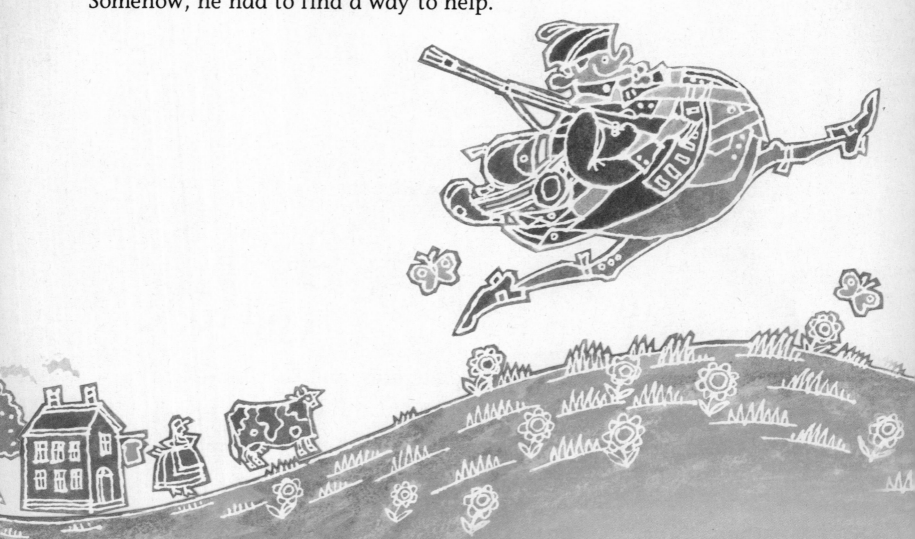

He packed his bags and went to join General Washington.

General Washington did not say the baker was
old and fat. General Washington was too polite.
Anyway, he had other troubles on his mind.

The baker rolled up his sleeves.
"No empty bellies here," he told General Washington.
"Not in *my* America!"
But bigger trouble was on the way.

Across the ocean. . .

The king of England wrote to other rulers and hired THEIR armies to help him squash the revolution.

251

When the ships sailed into sight, even General Washington turned pale. Who had ever seen such an army?

253

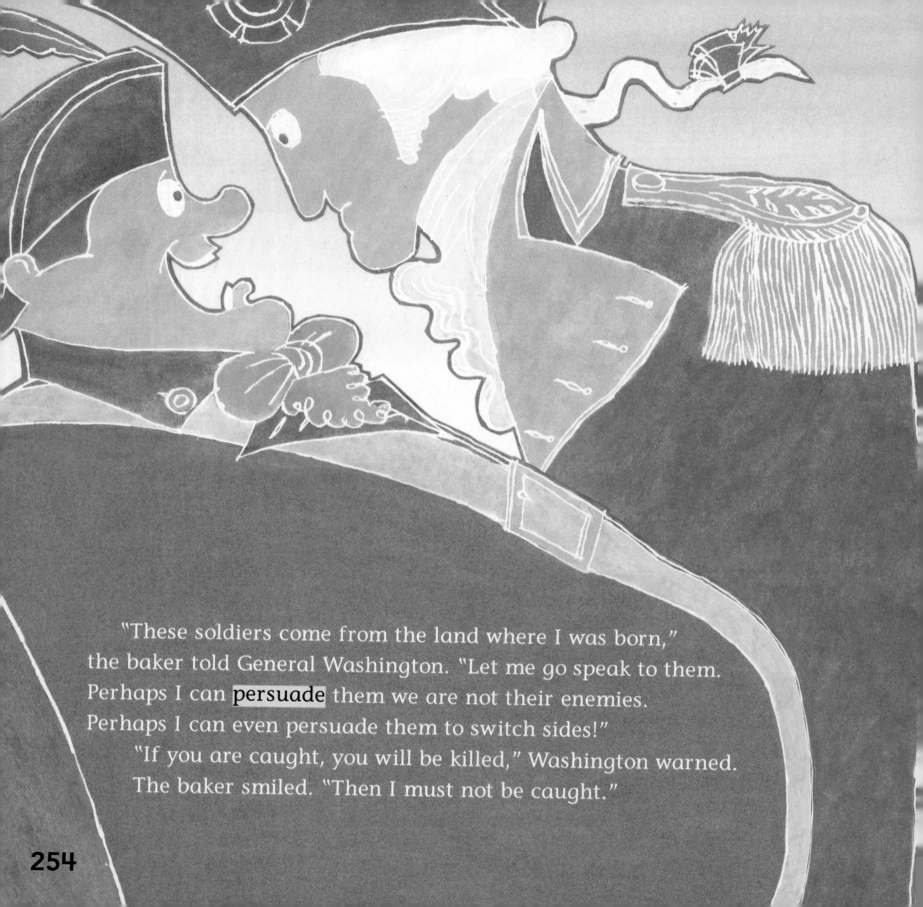

"These soldiers come from the land where I was born,"
the baker told General Washington. "Let me go speak to them.
Perhaps I can persuade them we are not their enemies.
Perhaps I can even persuade them to switch sides!"
"If you are caught, you will be killed," Washington warned.
The baker smiled. "Then I must not be caught."

254

In the darkest hour of the night, he rowed across the bay. With each dip of his oars, he thought of words to win the soldiers over to the American cause.

REVOLUTION! (splash)
Befreiung!

INDEPENDENCE! (splash)
Unabhängigkeit!

LIBERTY! (splash, splash)
Freiheit!

But when he looked into their hungry faces, all his fine words slipped away.

What could he say?

"I have a bakeshop . . ." he began.

As the baker spoke, the soldiers seemed to see the fragrant steam rising from his ovens. They could almost smell the spicy gingerbread, and taste the sweet, buttery icing on their tongues.

256

"And you always have enough to eat?"
the soldiers asked.
   "No empty bellies here," the baker told them.
"Not in *my* America!"

Across the ocean. . .

257

Many, many loaves—and battles!—later . . .

THE BRITISH HAVE SURRENDERED!
THE REVOLUTION IS OVER!
WE WON!

"My work is done!" the baker cried.

Washington said, "Not quite."

Did he bake the British soldiers gingerbread for their dessert?

We'll never know . . .

A gift from General Washington

and his baker

They didn't leave a crumb.

Use details from *Gingerbread for Liberty!* to answer these questions with a partner.

1. Synthesize Why did the baker want to join General Washington? How did that decision change history?

2. What does the author want to describe? What does the illustrator want to show?

3. How did General Washington's feelings about the baker change? What do you think Washington learned from this experience?

Listening Tip

Look at your partner as you listen. Nod your head to show you are interested.

Write a Conversation

PROMPT How do you think General Washington reacted when the baker explained what happened with the hired soldiers? Use details from the text and pictures to explain your ideas.

PLAN First, draw a picture of the baker talking to General Washington. Show how each character feels. Add speech balloons to show what they are saying.

WRITE Now write a conversation between the baker and General Washington. Have the baker explain how he talked the hired soldiers out of fighting. Remember to:

- Look for details in the text that give clues about how General Washington might react.

- Include feeling words such as *amazed, proud, scared,* and *thrilled* to help the characters express how they feel.

_____

_____

_____

_____

_____

_____

_____

_____

_____

Prepare to Read

 GENRE STUDY **Realistic fiction** stories are made up but could happen in real life. As you read *Pepita and the Bully,* look for:

- characters who act and talk like real people
- events that could really happen
- setting in modern time in a place that could be real

SET A PURPOSE As you read, **retell** the story. Use your own words to tell what happened in the beginning, middle, and end of the story.

POWER WORDS

wrinkled

frown

yanked

dragged

mumbled

nearby

excuses

hesitant

Meet Ofelia Dumas Lachtman.

Pepita and Bully
and the

by Ofelia Dumas Lachtman

illustrated by Alex Pardo DeLange

Pepita waved goodbye to the bus driver. She raced down Pepper Street, her black braids bouncing behind her. She was in a hurry to get home and talk to Mamá. She wanted to tell her that three days in her new school were enough. She did not want to go there again.

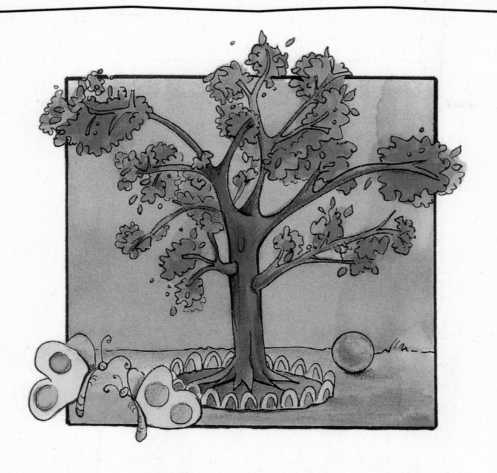

Pepita's face wrinkled up into a big frown. She was sorry because she really liked Miss Chu, her teacher. Miss Chu had black eyes and a soft, sunny smile. Pepita also liked her classroom with bright bulletin boards and cut-out, red letters that said, "Welcome to a New School Year." She especially liked the playground with its tall shady tree and benches. But she did not like Babette. She had brown hair, blue eyes, and skin that looked like peach ice cream, but she was not nice.

Pepita's frown grew bigger when she remembered her first day of school. She had gone up to Babette and said, "Hello, my name's Pepita. What's yours?"

"Pepita, yuck," Babette said. "That's not a name. That's nothing but a noise."

Pepita felt her face grow hot. She was angry. "It is so a name," she said, "and it's mine!"

Babette just turned and walked away.

On the second day, Miss Chu asked her students to talk about their favorite things. Pepita told them her dog Lobo could understand Spanish.

At recess, Babette said, "I'll bet your dog has fleas."

Pepita felt her face grow hot. She was angry. "He does not!" she cried.

Babette just turned and walked away.

And today was even worse. Babette yanked her braids and said, "Your braids look like two raggedy ropes. You should cut them off."

Pepita felt her face grow hot. She was really angry. "They are *not* ropes," she cried. "They're braids! And if you pull them again, I'll tell Miss Chu!"

Babette yelled, "Tattletale, tattletale," and turned and walked away.

Pepita was glad when the school day was over. *Yes*, she thought as she raced home, *three days are enough. I don't want to go to that school again.*

In the middle of the block, Pepita saw Mrs. Green digging in her garden.

"Hello, Mrs. Green," she said, "Can I ask you something? Do you think my name is funny?"

"Why no, Pepita," Mrs. Green answered. "Your name has a very lovely sound. It reminds me of bright little flowers."

Pepita nodded and smiled. "That's nice," she said. "Thank you, Mrs. Green."

A few houses down the block, Pepita saw José, the mailman, stepping out of his truck.

"Hello, Señor José," she called. "Can I ask you something? Do you think Lobo understands Spanish?"

"Why, yes, Pepita, I do," the mailman answered. "I told him to sit. And when he did, I said, '*Buen perrito*. Good little dog,' and he wagged and wagged his tail. Of course he understands Spanish."

Pepita nodded and smiled. "I thought so, too," she said. "Thank you, Señor José."

When Pepita was near her own house, she saw Mrs. Becker standing by her easel, painting a pot of red geraniums.

"Hello, Mrs. Becker," she said. "Can I ask you something? Do you think my braids look like raggedy ropes?"

"Why, no, Pepita," Mrs. Becker answered. "Your braids are very lovely. They remind me of black satin ribbons shining in the sun."

Pepita nodded and smiled. "That's nice," she said. "Thank you, Mrs. Becker."

When Pepita got home, she found her mother in the kitchen. "Mamá," she said, "I can't go back to that school again."

"Why?" Mamá asked. "I thought you liked your new school."

"So did I," Pepita said, "until I talked to Babette."

"And who is Babette?" Mamá asked.

"Babette is a bully," Pepita said. "She's mean to me, Mamá. I'm not going back to school."

"No, no," Mamá said, "that cannot be. School is important. But let's see what Papá has to say."

At supper that night, Pepita told her family what Babette had said to her. "She says my name is nothing but noise, that Lobo has fleas, and that my braids are raggedy ropes. And she yanked them! That's why I'm not going back to school!"

"I see," Papá said, "but you have to go to school. So tomorrow if Babette yanks your braids again, you must tell your teacher. But if Babette says mean things to you, either you can answer her politely or you can walk away. But whatever you do, you must be kind."

"Kind?" Pepita asked. "Is that like *nice*?"

Papá nodded. "Yes, *nice* will do."

Pepita's brother Juan said, "Just don't fight with her. Bullies like fights."

In bed Pepita tossed and turned and tumbled until her blankets were in a tangle. She dragged her doll Dora out from under the blankets and placed her against the pillow. "Dora," she said, "tomorrow Babette will say mean things to me."

Dora's face looked sad.

Pepita sat up straight and punched the pillow. "What if she tries to hit me?!"

Dora disappeared under the blankets.

Pepita pulled her out again. "Don't worry, Dora," she said, "I'll think of something." Dora huddled close. They snuggled together and fell asleep.

In the morning, Pepita got out of bed slowly. She dressed slowly. She ate breakfast slowly. She twisted and turned and muttered and mumbled while Mamá brushed and braided her hair. But no matter what Pepita did, nothing slowed down the clock. It was time to go to school.

"Mamá," Pepita complained, "three days are enough."

But Mamá said, "School is important, and if you don't hurry, you'll be late."

So Pepita went to school. Her classroom was sunny and bright. Her teacher smiled at her. But across the room Babette wrinkled up her nose and made an ugly face. At recess Mindy asked Pepita to play hopscotch. Pepita was about to say yes, but she saw Babette standing nearby. She gave Mindy a friendly wave, went to the farthest corner of the playground and sat under the shady tree. Babette was right behind her.

"That's my bench," Babette said. "I don't like you sitting there."

Pepita stood up. "What *do* you like?" she asked, and started to walk away.

"I don't like you for sure," Babette said.

Pepita felt her face grow hot. She was angry. She stopped and turned. "Maybe you don't like anything at all," she called.

"Maybe you don't even like your name. *Maybe you don't even like yourself.* And I'll bet you don't even have a dog!"

"You aren't nice," Babette said, and a tear rolled down her cheek. "You aren't nice at all."

Pepita's mouth dropped wide open. Her brother had told her not to fight. Papá had told her to be kind. And look what she had done! Babette was crying!

"Most times I'm nice," Pepita said, "and I'm polite, too. But you say mean things. Maybe if you stop being mean, somebody would ask you to play, too."

"I wouldn't play if you were playing because I don't like your braids," Babette said.

"See? You're being mean."

"I wouldn't play if you were playing because you have a funny name," Babette said.

"You're just being mean again. Anyway, Pepita's who I am."

"But I might play," Babette said, "if . . ."

"Stop making excuses!" Pepita said. "Do you want to play or don't you?"

Babette bit her lip, sniffed and gave a hesitant little nod.

"Okay," Pepita said, "but you'd better blow your nose."

She handed Babette a tissue from her pocket. Then she swung around and raced toward the center of the yard. "Wait, Mindy! Wait for us! Babette and I want to play!"

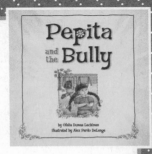

Use details from *Pepita and the Bully* to answer these questions with a partner.

1. **Retell** Take turns telling the story events in order. Use order words such as *first, next, after,* and *at the end* to help you.

2. Who is telling the story? Why do you think the author chose this point of view?

3. Papá tells Pepita to be kind. What do you think of this advice? Find details in the text and pictures that show how Pepita feels about it.

Talking Tip

Ask to learn more about one of your partner's ideas. Complete the sentence below.

Please tell me more about _____.

Write a Letter

PROMPT What should Babette say to apologize to Pepita? Look
for details in the text and pictures that tell what Babette did and
how it made Pepita feel.

PLAN First, write notes about the things Babette should
apologize for.

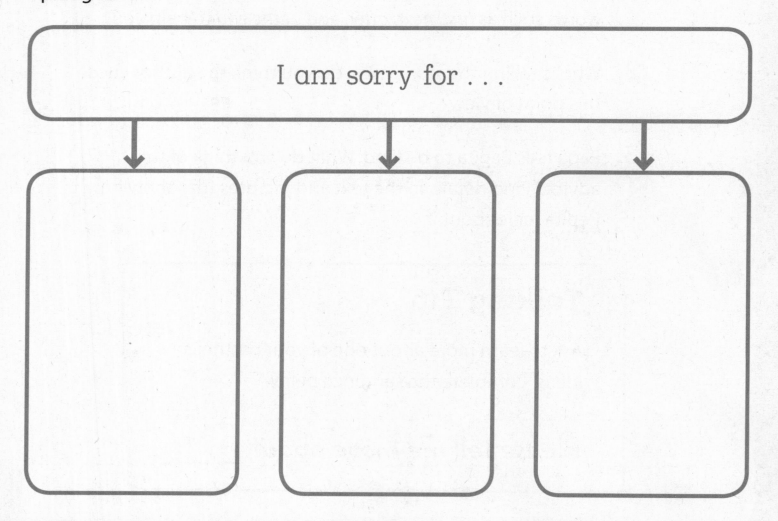

I am sorry for . . .

WRITE Now help Babette apologize! Write an apology letter from Babette to Pepita. Remember to:

- Use the word *because* to explain why Babette is sorry.

- Begin your letter with *Dear Pepita*. End the letter with *Your friend, Babette*.

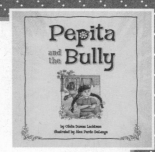

_____

_____

_____

_____

_____

_____

_____

_____

_____

_____

Prepare to Read

GENRE STUDY **Infographics** give information quickly and in a visual way. As you read *Be a Hero! Work It Out!,* notice:

- the purpose of the infographic
- how pictures, symbols, and words work together
- words or phrases that stand out
- what the author wants you to learn

SET A PURPOSE Authors have different purposes for writing. Read to find the **author's purpose** for writing this text. This will help you explain what the author wants you to know or learn from reading this text.

Build Background: Bullying

BE A HERO!
Work It Out!

by Ruben Cooley

 Identify the problem.

 Think about the problem.

 Attack the problem, not the person.

 Listen and have an open mind.

 Be respectful of feelings.

 Know that everyone makes mistakes—own up to yours.

Knock out these enemies:

Hitting	Making threats	Pushing
Name-calling		Making excuses
Not listening	Making mean faces	Bullying

Hello, citizens!

Captain Problem Solver here!

I have been told there are some problems on the streets. Some kids don't know how to solve problems. No, not *math* problems—problems with each other. I need your help spreading the word about my tips!

Let's break these down a little. When you are sharing my tips, these are three important ones to start with. When there is a problem, kids should first identify that there is a problem. People don't agree all the time. So they should think about what the problem is before doing anything. Remember to attack the problem, not the person. That would just make the problem worse!

BE A HERO!
Work It Out!
by Ruben Cooley

- Identify the problem
- Think about the problem
- Attack the problem, not the person.
  - Listen and have an open mind.
  - Be respectful of feelings.
  - Know that everyone makes mistakes—own up to yours.

Knock out these enemies: Hitting, Making threats, Pushi... Name calling, Making excus... Not listening, Making mean faces, Bullyi...

1. Identify the problem.

2. Think about the problem.

3. Attack the problem, not the person.

4. Listen and have an open mind.

5. Be respectful of feelings.

6. Know that everyone makes mistakes—own up to yours.

Kids should listen to each other. Someone else might have a different idea of what happened. It could be just a misunderstanding. Listening to each other also shows that the other person's feelings are being respected. Knowing someone cares about your feelings makes you feel better, right? It can help with problem solving, too!

Finally, owning up to mistakes is part of life. As you share my tips with other kids, make sure you know this one well. Practice it yourself! Everyone can make mistakes, and admitting you have made one can be hard. It makes you a brave citizen to admit you have made one!

Hitting

Bullying

Making threats

Name-calling

Pushing

Not listening

Making excuses

Making mean faces

These are the enemies that can stop kids from solving a problem and make the problem worse. Look for them every day and help stop them!

My work here is done. Thank you for sharing my tips about problem solving, citizens! I know with your help, we will have more citizens on the streets being problem solvers!

Be a problem solver superhero like me!

Use details from *Be a Hero! Work It Out!* to answer these questions with a partner.

1. **Author's Purpose** What is the author's purpose for writing this text? Use details from the text to explain your answer.

2. How do the numbers, symbols, and words help you understand what the hero is trying to persuade you to do?

3. The hero says that it is brave to own up to your mistakes. Think about a time you made a mistake. How does that help you understand what the hero means?

Talking Tip

Use details from the text to explain your ideas. Complete the sentence below.

I think _____ because _____.

Let's Wrap Up!

? Essential Question

How can people work out disagreements?

Pick one of these activities to show what you have learned about the topic.

1. Sing It Out

Make up a song about what to do when a problem comes along. Look back at the texts for ideas about how to resolve a conflict. Share your song with the class.

> **Word Challenge**
>
> Can you use the word compromise in your song?

2. Make a Glossary

Find words in the texts that tell about solving problems. Make a list of at least five words. Then put them in ABC order. Write the meaning of each word next to the word.

My Notes

Glossary

A

ace [ās]   Someone described as ace is extremely good at something. He is an **ace** soccer player.

agency [ā'jən-sē]   If you work at an agency, your job is to help others to get something done. My neighbor works for a health **agency**.

amount [ə-mount']   An amount is how much there is of something. I would like a small **amount** of juice.

argue [är'gyoō]   When you argue, you speak in an angry way that shows you do not agree. Do not **argue** with your brother.

B

battleground [băt'l-ground']   A battleground is where a fight takes place. I visited the **battleground** where the war was won many years ago.

bellowed [běl'ōd]   If you bellowed, you shouted in a loud, deep voice. "Get away from there!" she **bellowed**.

blamed [blāmd]   When you are blamed, someone thinks you did something wrong. The kids **blamed** each other for the mess.

booming [boōm'ĭng]   Something that is booming is loud like thunder. The **booming** sounds let us know that the fireworks show had started.

bounce [bouns]   When you bounce, you move up and down. I like to **bounce** my ball outside.

business [bĭz'nĭs]   A place open for business is ready to work, buy, or sell something. The coffee shop is now open for **business**.

C

cautiously [kô'shəs-lē]   If you do something cautiously, you do it very carefully to avoid danger. I walked **cautiously** on the icy sidewalk.

citizen [sĭt'ĭ-zən]   A citizen is a member of a community, state, or country. I am a **citizen** of the United States.

compliment [kŏm'plə-mənt]   A compliment is a nice thing to say about someone. My teacher gave me a **compliment** about my work at school today.

compromise [kŏm'prə-mīz']   A compromise is when people agree to something by each giving up a little of what they want. The team agreed on a **compromise**.

confidently [kŏn'fĭ-dənt-lē]   When you do something confidently, you are sure you will do it well. She spoke **confidently** to the crowd.

cool [kōōl]   To cool how you feel means to calm down. Taking deep breaths helps me to **cool** down.

D

decision [dĭ-sĭzh'ən]   When you make a decision, you make up your mind about something. I will make a **decision** about what to have for a snack.

difference [dĭf'ər-əns, dĭf'rəns]   When people make a difference, they do something that helps others. Picking up litter helps us make a **difference** in the community.

disagreement [dĭs'ə-grē'mənt]   In a disagreement, people have different ideas about things. They had a **disagreement** about what game to play.

disaster [dĭ-zăs'tər, dĭ-săs'tər]   A disaster is an event that goes horribly wrong. Leaving our dog alone with the new couch was a **disaster**, but we still love her.

dragged [drăgd]   If you dragged something, you worked hard to pull it along the ground. The boy **dragged** the heavy suitcase across the floor.

E

eagerly [ē′gər-lē]   When you do something eagerly, you really want to do it. The student **eagerly** accepted her award.

easily [ē′zə-lē]   Something that is done easily is not hard to do. You can win the race **easily**.

elected [ĭ-lĕkt′ĭd]   Someone who is elected has been chosen for a job. My friend was **elected** to be class president.

examine [ĭg-zăm′ĭn]   When you examine something, you look at it carefully. We went outside to **examine** the footprints in the yard.

example [ĭg-zăm′pəl]   An example is a part of a larger group of things that are alike. This beautiful painting is one **example** of my favorite artist's work.

excuses [ĭk-skyo͞os′ĭz]   Excuses are reasons why you cannot do something. He tried to make **excuses** for breaking the pitcher, but then he just apologized.

F

feud [fyo͞od]   A feud is a long fight. My brother and I had a **feud** about sharing our toys.

fiddled [fĭd′ld]   If you fiddled with something, you kept touching it or playing with it. The girl **fiddled** with the zipper on her jacket.

forms [fôrmz]   Something with many forms has different shapes or ways of being. We are learning about the different **forms** of water in school today.

frenzy [frĕn′zē]   A frenzy is a time of great excitement and wild behavior. The big sale caused a shopping **frenzy**.

frown [froun]   A frown is a sad or angry look. The boy had a **frown** on his face.

G

gasped [găspt]   If people gasped, they took a sharp breath in a surprised way. We **gasped** with surprise at the most exciting part.

greedy [grē′dē]   Someone who is greedy wants more than what is fair. Todd was being **greedy** with the popcorn.

grinned [grĭnd]   If you grinned, you smiled a wide smile. I **grinned** when I heard the happy news.

H

hamper [hăm′pər]   A hamper is a basket with a lid, used to hold dirty clothes. Please put your dirty clothes in the **hamper**.

handle [hăn′dl]   When you cannot handle something, you are not able to deal with it. I can **handle** doing more chores if I have some help.

hesitant [hĕz′ĭ-tənt]   If you are hesitant, you do something slowly because you are not sure about it. At first, Dan was **hesitant** to try the salad.

I

identify [ī-dĕn′tə-fī′]   When you identify something, you say what it is. I want to **identify** the type of insect we found.

invited [ĭn-vīt′ĭd]   When you are invited to a party, you have been asked to come. My big brother **invited** me to go to the talent show with him and his friends.

K

kind [kīnd]   Someone who is kind is nice, caring, or gentle. Helping others is one way to be **kind**.

L

local [lō′kəl]   Something that is local belongs to the area where you live. My mother works for the **local** newspaper.

located [lō′kāt′ĭd, lō-kāt′ĭd]   Where something is located is where it is. The map shows where the ponds are **located**.

M

material [mə-tîr′ē-əl]   Material is what something is made from. What **material** is that shirt made out of?

might [mīt]   Doing something with all your might is using all your power. He threw the ball with all his **might**.

mock [mŏk]   A mock version of something is not real. We set up a **mock** doctor's office for toys.

mood [mo͞od]   Your mood is the way you are feeling. I am in a great **mood** when I hear my favorite song.

mumbled [mŭm′bəld]   If you mumbled, you spoke quietly and not very clearly. She **mumbled** something that I did not understand.

munch [mŭnch]   When you munch food, you chew it loudly and completely. My friend likes to **munch** on carrots.

musical [myo͞o′zĭ-kəl]   Something that is musical has a tune. A trumpet is a **musical** instrument.

mystery [mĭs′tə-rē]   A mystery is something that is hard to understand or is not known about. The clues helped the detectives solve the **mystery**.

N

nearby [nîr′bī′]   Someone who is nearby is close to where you are. My friend lives in a **nearby** house.

P

panicked [păn′ĭkt]   If you panicked, you suddenly felt afraid. I **panicked** when I thought I'd lost my library book.

perfect [pûr′fĭkt]   When something is perfect, it is the best it can be. I felt proud of my **perfect** score on the quiz.

persuade [pər-swād′]   When you persuade, you try to get others to feel or think as you do. Please **persuade** her to join the fun.

planet [plăn′ĭt]   A planet is a large object in space that moves around a star. Earth is the third **planet** from the sun.

planned [plănd]   If you planned, you decided ahead of time how you would do something. She **planned** to do her homework tomorrow.

plead [plēd]   When you plead, you ask someone in a strong, hopeful way. We **plead** with our mother to let us go to the party.

plumes [plōōmz]   Plumes are long, thin shapes that look like feathers. He saw **plumes** of smoke in the air.

practice [prăk′tĭs]   Practice is when you do something over and over to get better at it. I try to **practice** piano every day.

prohibited [prō-hĭb′ĭt-əd]   If something is prohibited, it is not allowed. Playing ball is **prohibited** in the house, so we went to the park.

Q

queasy [kwē′zē]   If you are queasy, your stomach hurts and you feel sick. She knew she would feel **queasy** if she ate too much popcorn, so she just had a little bit.

301

R

record [rĭ-kôrd′]   When you record notes, you write them down. I like to **record** my story ideas in a notebook.

respectful [rĭ-spĕkt′fəl]   Respectful words are words that are polite and kind. The players are **respectful** of each other.

ridiculous [rĭ-dĭk′yə-ləs]   If something is ridiculous, it is hard to believe how silly it is. We all laughed at how **ridiculous** the giant dog looked in a ladybug costume.

rough [rŭf]   When you do something in a rough way, you are not being gentle. Some sports can be too **rough** for children.

S

scoots [sko͞ots]   When someone scoots, he or she moves very quickly. He **scoots** out the door so he won't miss the bus.

scowl [skoul]   A scowl is an angry frown. She had a **scowl** on her face after she heard the game was canceled.

screams [skrēmz]   When someone screams, he or she yells loudly. She **screams** with excitement on her favorite ride in the amusement park.

scurries [skûr′ēz, skŭr′ēz]   When someone scurries, he or she moves with short, fast steps. The chipmunk **scurries** across the yard.

seeps [sēps]   When something seeps, it passes slowly through a small opening. Honey **seeps** through a crack in the jar.

shove [shŭv]   When you shove something, you push it hard. Ian will **shove** the wagon for his sister.

skill [skĭl]   If you have great skill at something, you do that thing really well. Ethel can bake with great **skill**, and she loves to share with her friends.

space [spās]   Space is an open area or place. The pool takes up a large **space** in the yard.

strokes [strōks]   When something strokes something else, it moves gently over that thing. My dog likes when my friend **strokes** her fur.

T

tasty [tā'stē]   Something that is tasty is good to eat. This salad dressing is so **tasty**.

threatening [thrĕt'n-ĭng]   People who are threatening to do something are warning they will do it. The group is **threatening** to quit if they don't get their own way.

tumbling [tŭm'blĭng]   Something that is tumbling is rolling over and over. We had fun **tumbling** across the lawn.

W

wisps [wĭsps]   Wisps are thin streaks of something. I saw **wisps** of clouds in the sky.

wrinkled [rĭng'kəld]   You wrinkled up your face if you tightened muscles to make folds and lines in your skin. The baby **wrinkled** his little forehead.

Y

yanked [yăngkd]   If you yanked something, you pulled it hard and fast. The whole team **yanked** on the rope during the game of tug of war.

Index of Titles and Authors

Acknowledgments

Excerpt from *Being a Good Citizen* (retitled from *Being a Good Citizen: A Kids' Guide to Community Involvement*) by Rachelle Kreisman, illustrated by Tim Haggerty. Copyright © 2016 by Red Chair Press LLC. Reprinted with the permission of Red Chair Press LLC.

Big Red Lollipop by Rukhsana Khan. Illustrated by Sophie Blackall. Text copyright © 2010 by Rukhsana Khan. Illustrations copyright © 2010 by Sophie Blackall. Reprinted by permission of Viking Children's Books, an imprint of Penguin Young Readers Group, a division of Penguin Random House LLC and Charlotte Sheedy Literary Agency.

Clark the Shark by Bruce Hale, illustrated by Guy Francis. Text copyright © 2013 by Bruce Hale. Illustrations copyright © 2013 by Guy Francis. Reprinted by permission of HarperCollins Publishers.

Gingerbread for Liberty! (retitled from *Gingerbread for Liberty!: How a German Baker Helped Win the American Revolution*) by Mara Rockliff, illustrated by Vincent X. Kirsch. Text copyright © 2015 by Mara Rockliff. Illustrations copyright © 2015 by Vincent X. Kirsch. Reprinted by permission of Houghton Mifflin Harcourt Publishing Company and the Andrea Brown Literary Agency.

The Great Fuzz Frenzy by Janet Stevens and Susan Stevens Crummel. Text copyright © 2005 by Janet Stevens and Susan Stevens Crummel. Illustrations copyright © 2005 by Janet Stevens. Reprinted by permission of Houghton Mifflin Harcourt Publishing Company.

The Great Puppy Invasion by Alastair Heim, illustrated by Kim Smith. Text copyright © 2017 by Alastair Heim. Illustrations copyright © 2017 by Kim Smith. Reprinted by permission of Houghton Mifflin Harcourt Publishing Company.

Excerpt from *Many Kinds of Matter* (retitled from *Many Kinds of Matter: A Look at Solids, Liquids, and Gases*) by Jennifer Boothroyd. Text copyright © 2011 by Lerner Publishing Group, Inc. Reprinted with the permission of Lerner Publishing Company, a division of Lerner Publishing Group, Inc.

Pepita and the Bully/Pepita y la peleonera by Ofelia Dumas Lachtman, illustrated by Alex Pardo DeLange. Spanish translation by Gabriela Baeza Ventura. Text copyright © 2011 by Ofelia Dumas Lachtman. Illustrations copyright © 2011 by Alex Pardo DeLange. Reprinted by permission of Arte Público Press - University of Houston.

Picture Day Perfection by Deborah Diesen, illustrated by Dan Santat. Text copyright © 2013 by Deborah Diesen. Illustrations copyright © 2013 by Dan Santat. Reprinted by permission of Express Permissions on behalf of Abrams Books for Young Readers, an imprint of Harry N. Abrams, Inc., New York and Trident Media Group, LLC.

Excerpt by Christopher Reeve from http://www.spinalcordinjury-paralysis.org/blogs/16/1784. Text copyright © by Christopher Reeve. Reprinted by permission of the Estate of Christopher Reeve.

Water Rolls, Water Rises/El agua rueda, el agua sube by Pat Mora, illustrated by Meilo So. Text copyright © 2014 by Pat Mora. Illustrations copyright © 2014 by Meilo So. Reprinted by permission of Children's Book Press, an imprint of Lee & Low Books Inc.

Excerpt from *Working with Others* by Robin Nelson. Text copyright © 2006 by Lerner Publishing Group, Inc. Reprinted with the permission of Lerner Publications Company, a division of Lerner Publishing Group, Inc.

Credits